EATING AROUND THE WORLD

in

YOUR NEIGHBORHOOD

FRANCINE HALVORSEN

John Wiley & Sons, Inc.

New York • Chichester • Weinheim • Brisbane • Singapore • Toronto

This text is printed on acid-free paper.

Copyright © 1998 by Francine Halvorsen
Published by John Wiley & Sons, Inc.

All rights reserved. Published simultaneously in Canada.

Library of Congress Cataloging-in-Publication Data

Halvorsen, Francine.
    Eating around the world in your neighborhood / Francine Halvorsen.
        p.   cm.
    Includes index.
    ISBN 0–471–11892–3 (pbk. : alk. paper)
    1. Cookery, International.   2. Cookery, American.   I. Title.
TX725.A1H275 1997
641.59—dc21

                                                            97–21769

Printed in the United States of America

10 9 8 7 6 5 4 3 2 1

For my sons Jesse Halvorsen and Lionel Halvorsen,
who have gracefully and steadfastly shared meals
without number in neighborhoods without borders
and given me the gift of motherhood without end

CONTENTS

PREFACE

This book is written as a celebration of the global food bounty we enjoy wherever we live. In the neighborhoods of cities, suburbs, towns, and villages throughout the United States, at four-star restaurants, neighborhood bistros, fast-food joints, street vendors' carts, malls, and markets, food once thought exotic is rapidly becoming an accepted presence. People are not only eating it out, but are having it delivered or cooking it from scratch. Thanks to a remarkably large number of food-distribution networks, produce and packaged goods from all over the world are available not only at ethnic markets and gourmet shops but in local supermarkets. Those who want to take a food lover's journey will find culinary adventure without leaving home. The countries of origin read like a Hammond Atlas index, stunning in number and variety.

People are discovering that when they say "the food of my country," they are talking about the same ingredients someone from a country thousands of miles away is talking about when they say "the food of *my* country." So why all the fuss? Because the passion with which the palate's memories are expressed is remarkable. People speak in the same voice they use to share any intimate story. Often their faces light up as if the dishes they are discussing are something to be looked forward to as well as remembered. It is no mystery that in our stressful society we long for the simple comfort of cooking and eating.

If you ask someone to "tell me your favorite dish," many will extol fish and vegetables, noodles and sauces, chicken and rice. Trying to tease them to my point, I ask someone whose English is interspersed with Spanish, "Oh, so you are from Korea?" The person will laugh and say, "No, no, from Mexico." "So tell me then," I continue, "how do you know the chicken and rice you are so fond of is a Mexican dish and not a Korean one?" "That is easy," is always the reply. "It is the smell, the flavor, the look of the food, and the feel of it in my mouth." Chicken, rice, vegetables, and seasonings taste quite different in India than they do in France, Russia, or Mexico. A Moroccan Bestya is a chicken pie, but not the chicken pie served in the British Isles. Noodles and sauce in China, Italy, and Germany are distant cousins. Fried dough, sweet or savory, is enjoyed everywhere around the globe—from honey-soaked *buñuelos* to cinnamon donuts, to *zeppole*, to *dampfnuden*. Pancakes and flatbreads are eaten universally—from crepes to mu shu, tortillas to crispele.

As our neighborhoods become increasingly redolent with these aromatic mysteries, I think it is helpful and informative to open a few doors. The chapters of this book are a medley of food information. There are interviews with restaurateurs, chefs, and other food specialists, who add voices besides my own. During our conversations, each was as enthusiastic about the food of other countries as about his or her own. We spoke frequently about the simple goodness of fresh food. Everyone explained that he or she found the flavor of a potato cooked in a certain manner as delicious as the most elaborate delicacy, and would rhapsodize about truly vine-ripened fruit. I spent one evening talking with a famous chef and restaurateur about the best way to make oatmeal as we ate an elaborate, exotic dinner.

The food in this book is exciting to eat and to cook. It is by and large traditional, rather than *nuevo* or fusion anything. The dishes and ingredients from each part of the world are explained, and there are recipes and a list of sources for ingredients and supplies, though you will find most of them surprisingly easy to come by. And if you use some of the words in the glossaries in restaurants and markets, you will be rewarded with smiles and good will.

Some people go to new kinds of restaurants boldly, and will sooner or later try everything and eat their way through the menu. Others will stick to one or two dishes with as much trepidation as the sailors who thought the world was flat. People are always asking me about food that, like a newcomer to the neighborhood, has become recognizable, but has not yet been properly introduced.

It is no longer enough to say "Chinese food" or "Japanese food." Are we talking the spicy dishes of Sichuan, the milder menus of

Guangdong, or elaborate arrays of dim sum? Will it be a dinner of sushi or sashimi, or soba noodles with subtle sauces? Everyone has eaten Mexican food but many are still not certain about the difference between a tortilla and a taco, an enchilada and a quesadilla. Even French food, once exclusively a three- or four-star experience, has brought the dishes of bistros and charcuteries from Provence to Bordeaux to this country. Today, international gourmets will talk to you about jerk, salsa, coulis, mustard, and Fukien soy sauce the way they used to compare homemade mayonnaise to store-bought.

I have travelled a great deal and lived in various countries and I am a world-class eater. I was born in New York, an only child. From earliest memory, I have washed my hands and face, put on a clean dress, and left the house to pull up a chair at a table in new surroundings, to be surprised and entertained by dinner. I hope that this book surprises and entertains you and, more important, that it will encourage you to travel the world, first without tickets and passports, through the cuisines of many countries, and then with them, to sample the food in its original settings.

Acknowledgments

The most fun about writing this book was talking to the neighbors. Douglas Rodriguez at Patria, Josefina Howard at Rosa Mexicano, Alfredo Pedro at Ipanema, Dominick Cerrone at Solera, Hakan Swahn at Aquavit, Ilgar Pekar and Sedat Dakan at the Turkish Kitchen, Prem Nath Motiram at Bombay Palace, Autar Walla at Dawat, Romy Dorotan at Cendrillon, and Charles Huh at Zuttos all shared stories and delicious dishes. Many thanks.

At John Wiley, Claire Thompson Zuckerman quite simply could not have been better through good times and less than good times. Maria Colletti needs a special thank you for her seemingly endless patience and good humor. Thank you, Donna Conte for staying on top of the text and bringing it to order.

Linda Lee and Jesse Halvorsen, Peggy Hoban and Lionel Halvorsen tasted and tested beyond the call of duty. Between us we haven't met a cuisine we didn't like. I couldn't have done it without them.

××○○♡ for Robert Feldman in whose neighborhood this book was written.

Francine Halvorsen

INTRODUCTION

If you do not have a particular ethnic cuisine in your neighborhood, get ready: It will soon be appearing at a location near you. This book will help put you at ease as you explore new restaurants and try different dishes. *Eating Around the World in Your Neighborhood* gives more than a nod to the global bounty we enjoy. As you can see in the table of contents, every culture has delicious food that makes people happy and nourishes them—we have covered as many as possible here.

Though dishes may originally have been created with local resources to fit local customs, there have always been travelers who brought food and food ideas with them. Religious and social rituals formalized many recipes and menus, so that a lot of dishes have remained unchanged since time immemorial.

This book started out as simply a description of various ethnic restaurants and their menus. As I became more involved in what I was doing, my need to understand a little bit more about the history, geography, and culture of each food tradition grew more compelling. My experience has been that people are curious about odd bits of information.

Indonesia is the fourth largest country in the world, with thousands of miles of islands and a population of 150 million. Now what does that have to do with the food in your neighborhood? On the ships that passed through the Indonesian archipelago were peanuts from Africa, chili from Dominica, papayas and sweet potatoes from South America, anise and cinnamon from China. The world has been borrowing a cup of sugar and a cup of rice from neighbors for centuries.

In the United States of America, the first restaurants with menus that were clearly from other countries often took root along with the first wave of immigration from those countries. These places were generally opened to serve the needs of recent arrivals who were often not comfortable, and sometimes not welcome, in the mainstream restaurants already established. When people talk about "the cooking of my country," they do not mean only the ingredients but a special aroma or presentation. The look and smell of a dish, the manner in which the food is served, the sequence of the dishes, and the spirit of the conversation while eating and drinking all contribute to the identity of a cuisine.

As people have grown bolder in exploring the world's kitchens, the distinct tastes of individual cooking pots have replaced the undistinguished mingling in the melting pot. Each new group of immigrants has brought new cuisines. Many have been incorporated and others remain unique. Most people have eaten Chinese food and Mexican food, but some have yet to venture into an Indonesian or Thai restaurant. Ethnicity does not always dictate either price or quality. Most establishments are moderately priced, though quite a few are amazingly inexpensive, and some are exorbitant. Some, it goes without saying, have better chefs than others. Trust your taste. Almost all countries have recipes for chicken soup, vegetable soup, and pasta with various sauces. We see countless variations on many similar themes: tacos, *roti*, egg rolls, spring rolls, blintzes, manicotti, and *dosai* all consist of a light pastry folded over tasty fillings. *Arroz con pollo*, chicken *biryani*, Sichuan chicken, chicken *pilau*, and *paella Valenciana* all describe chicken and rice at its best. We satisfy our need to nibble with *piroghi, piroshki, wonton, siu mai, kreplach, ravioli, aushak,* and *samosas,* all of which are little, soft dough pockets filled with minced meat or an alternative. Pitas, tortillas, mu shu pancakes, *crêpes, chapatis,* rice-paper circles, and egg-roll wrappers are all quick-cooking flatbreads. *Saumon fumé,* Scotch or Norwegian smoked salmon, lox, *lachs,* or just plain nova will all be fine on our bagels. Whether we eat *crème caramel, flan, crème Anglaise, crema Catalana,* Thai *sang kaya,* or Vietnamese coconut *che,* all custards or puddings, our sweet tooth is served.

In addition to restaurants, there is the tradition of street vendors. Walking downtown, near Wall Street in New York City, you can visit a culinary United Nations. Among the assembled are: Italian sausage, shish kebab, gyros, "Jamaica on Wheels," jerk chicken, Sam's Falafel, Gloria's Mexican, curries, chilies, egg rolls, gazpacho, gelati, tacos, Ratner's soups, Hebrew National products. . . and more every day.

In the following chapters you will learn not only the names of dishes from many countries, but what goes into them. The glossaries will help, too. The recipes in the book are user friendly. Try making them and experience some wonderful new flavors and aromas in your own kitchen. You will be surprised at how many of the ingredients are available at your large supermarket or specialty grocery store. Substitutions for some hard-to-find ingredients are given, though usually if a local restaurant chef can purchase them, you will have access to them, too. At the end of the book there is also a list of purveyors of mail-order foods from all over the world. I have set out to explore the cuisines that can be found in most of our neighborhoods. Occasionally, this has led me down small side streets. I hope you enjoy these detours. When this book wanders a bit, please wander with it and have fun.

1

LATIN AMERICA AND THE CARIBBEAN

Mexico

When I was a child, I visited family in Los Angeles. The things I remember the best from my first visit to Olivera Street are the shops and fountains, the music, and the food. I don't remember what I ate, but I do remember that it was spicy and delicious, and that I had never eaten anything that smelled so good. I have since visited Mexico many times. My most recent trip was a few years ago with my son, Lionel, who made me promise to pack only what I could carry. I was glad I complied, because we were free to wander and take buses through Quintana Roo, where riding through the long stretches of tall grasses gave the illusion of sailing a green sea. At each stop, food vendors boarded the bus and, as when I was a child, I was again rewarded with delicious, aromatic dishes from an unlikely source.

The rest of us in North America benefit from the variety of Mexican food offered in establishments from *taquerias* to four-star restaurants; we can have such culinary adventures without taking a week off.

From the Caribbean along the Gulf of Mexico, to the Pacific Ocean, from the Rio Grande to the border of Guatemala, Mexico has brought together different heritages. The Spanish colonists arrived at the beginning of the sixteenth century and dominated for three-hundred years, but Mexico has a strong national and regional identity. It is wrong to think of Mexican cuisine as "Spanish" just because that is the prevailing language. Thousands of miles of seacoasts, tropical forests, and deserts have produced a wide range of agricultural conditions. In the central and southern plains are a variety of fruit, vegetables, grains, and pulses. Pre-Columbian records show that centuries ago maize, chilies, beans, avocado, papaya, vanilla, and cacao were domesticated and used with genius. The Aztecs thought chocolate a royal beverage; Montezuma served Cortez hot chocolate from a gold cup. Wheat, rice, bananas, and citrus fruit from Asia were added early on, by way of European adventurers. Indigenous fish and shellfish, small deer, rabbits, turkeys, and other fowl round out the Mexican diet.

The 32 states of Mexico have several thousand authentic dishes— a rich and expansive cuisine that comes from pre-Columbian roots and has developed unique culinary traditions in each state, and even in small communities. For example, the Mexico City area and *District Federale* are famous for *mole poblano*. Certain flavors, however, are virtually nationwide. These include corn, citrus, peppers, fish, and fowl; some type of *salsa cruda*, usually based on a chopped combination of tomatoes, onions, chilies, and coriander; *enchiladas* (spicy with chilies); *tacos* (usually made without hot chilies); *crepas de huitlacoche*, during the rainy season; *budin de huitlacoche* with layers of tortilla, tomato, cream, and chili. Papayas are everywhere. From Veracruz, fresh fish sautéed with tomatoes and onions are prepared *veracruzana*. The United States has adapted many Tex-Mex, Mexi-Cal, and New-Mex dishes that have popularized tamales, tortillas, refried beans, and guacamole, with varying degrees of authenticity. Some are excellent and these familiar *meriendas* (snacks) or *antojitos* (appetizers) are tasty tidbits, but they are a small selection. Limiting our view of Mexican food to them would be a little like thinking of Italian food as only pizza or spaghetti.

From Chihuahua, Durango, Jalisco, Tabasco, Tampico, Sonora, and the Yucatán, there is *pollo pibil*, chicken that is steamed in a pit and spiced with *annato* (or *achiote*), the crushed seeds of the annato tree, which gives reddish color to food, as well as a slightly smoky flavor.

A *papatzul* is a filled tortilla in spicy pumpkin-seed sauce. *Sopa de lima* is a chicken soup flavored with fresh limes and thickened with shredded fried tortillas. Another favorite is *mukbil polleo*, a dish like shepherd's pie, made with aromatic chicken under a cornmeal crust.

Rosa Mexicano Restaurant

Chef Josefina Howard

I knew I was going to meet someone special when Josefina Howard invited me to join her for dinner at eight, the most coveted seating, and usually the busiest in a restaurant. Rosa Mexicano is painted the warm rose of its name. As soon as we were settled, the waiter brought us frozen Rosa Margaritas, made with the addition of pomegranate juice. Mrs. Howard (the name she prefers) grew up in Spain, wintering in Madrid and summering in Asturias on the northern coast. One of the *famous dishes* of Asturias is *Fabadz*, spicy stew made with *fabes*, a white bean. Hard cider flavors many of the sauces made there. Food was eloquent and varied in her household. Though the family employed cooks, both her grandmother and father loved to cook, all of which led to her educated and sophisticated palate. After living in New York awhile, she moved to Mexico City with her then-husband and their sons. It turned into a sojourn of more than thirty years that nurtured a passion for the regional cuisine.

Josefina Howard started bringing Mexican food to New York—first by opening a real *taqueria* in the Wall Street area, and then as head chef at the restaurant Cinco de Mayo—before opening Rosa Mexicano. Her kitchen produces food with such resonance that professionals from Mexico regard her as a model, and many Mexican food journalists regard Rosa Mexicano as one of the best Mexican restaurants in the world. Mrs. Howard can't believe how unfamiliar Mexican cuisine is to people who are otherwise very knowledgeable about food. Her passion for Mexico is evident both in her food and in her personal style, which is warm and generous. This is not a manner reserved only for clients— her staff is treated the same way. It is contagious, too, because they

From the menu of

Rosa Mexicano

1063 First Avenue
New York, NY 10022

Appetizers

Guacamole en Molcajete
Prepared fresh at the table

Jalapenos Rellenos
Roasted and pickled green chiles filled with sardines

Ostiones Enchilados de Sinaloa
Oysters sautéed and served chilled in a marinade of chiles
and spices

Taquitos de Moranga
Small tortillas filled with blood pudding, fresh coriander and
sliced onions

Taquitos de Tinga Poblana
Small tortillas filled with sautéed shredded pork, smoked chile
chipotle, onions and tomato

Salpicon de Jaiba

Jumbo lump crabmeat sautéed with onions, celery, fresh coriander
and chiles served chilled

Ceviche

Fresh fish marinated in lemon juice with chopped onions,
tomatoes, green chiles and fresh coriander

Main dishes

Sweetwater Prawns

Sautéed with garlic and parsley and served with black squid rice

Crepas Camarones

Crepes filled with shrimp, covered with a chile pasilla sauce and
sprinkled with cheese, served with rice

Mixiote de Pollo de Tiaxcala

Pieces of chicken coated with chile sauce, wrapped in parchment
paper and steamed in beer

Budin Azteca

Multi-layered tortilla pie with shredded chicken, cheese and a chile
poblano sauce

Enchiladas de Mole Poblano

Two tortilla pie with shredded chicken, topped with mole sauce,
sliced onions and crumbled cheese, served with rice

From the menu of Rosa Mexicano *(continued)*

Enchiladas de Pato

Two tortillas, dipped in green mole sauce, filled with shredded duck, topped with more sauce, cheese and cream, served with rice

Chiles Rellenos

Chiles poblanos filled with cheese, coated in a light batter, fried and served with a tomato broth and rice

Pescado en Cilantro

Baked filet of fish with fresh coriander, tomato and onion, served with rice

Menudo Norteno

A stew of tripe served with an array of garnishes

Pozole

A stew with various cuts of pork, chicken, and hominy, served with an assortment of condiments

Tamal en Cazuel

Corn meal with chicken breast dipped in mole poblano sauce

are also outgoing and enthusiastic with customers, explaining dishes, preparing some, and finishing others right at the table.

Josefina Howard's philosophy is stated simply, right on the menu: "Because Rosa Mexicano presents classic Mexican cuisine, some of the popular Americanized dishes often associated with Mexican food are not included on our menu."

Our dinner started with a small cupful of *esquites*—corn kernels, chilies, the aromatic green herb *epazote*, and milk. A wonderful *guacamole*❋ was freshly made at the table in a three-legged mortar made of volcanic rock, called a *molcajete*. It was served with delicate tortillas, presented in a napkin to keep them soft and warm. *Hongos en Tamal en Cazuela,*❋ cornmeal grits cooked with bits of tomato and onion, were served with woodsy wild mushrooms sautéed with *epazote*, garlic, and chilies.

Ostiones Enchilados de Sinaloa, oysters from the western coast of Mexico, were lightly sautéed and served chilled and marinated. Even if you prefer your oysters raw, as I do, this dish is a lovely way to start a meal.

Then came crêpes filled with *huitlacoche* or *cuitlacoche*—a fungus that grows on the cobs of sweet corn. Baby corn kernels are embedded in the blue-black fungus, like tiny pearls on velvet. This fungus is the black truffle of Mexico. The taste is smoky-sweet, fabulous when pared from the cob and cooked with a bit of garlic, onion, and *poblano* pepper, seasoned with *epazote*, as a filling for crêpes with a sauce or with *crema, manchego* cheese, and *epazote*. Red snapper was served with a cooked-down sauce of black olives, capers, onions, and tomatoes. The homey *menudo* (tripe stew) and *pozole* (hominy stew with chicken and pigs' ears) may not be to every taste, but were great discoveries.

A surprising dessert was one that resembled *flan*, the familiar sweet egg custard, but was so subtle and rich I had to keep eating it to discover its secret. It is made by sautéing 1 cup of *huitlacoche* in 2 tablespoons of butter. One cup of cream is brought almost to a boil with 1/2 cup of sugar. Then the sautéed *huitlacoche* is added and set aside to cool. The mixture is processed or blended till smooth, then 1/4 cup of sherry is added. Refrigerated, it will keep for two days. It is served over ice cream, chocolate mousse, or even plain cake.

❋This symbol indicates that the recipe appears at the end of the section.

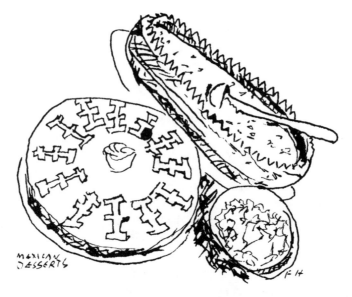

Mexican Desserts

Guacamole

Courtesy Josefina Howard—Rosa Mexicano

1 tablespoon chopped onion
1/2 teaspoon *serrano* chili, chopped
salt to taste
1 ripe avocado
1 ripe tomato, peeled, seeded, and diced
1 tablespoon minced, fresh coriander leaves

In a ceramic bowl, using a wooden spoon, mash the onion, chili, and salt. Remove the pit from the avocado and carefully score each half in the skin. Spoon the avocado into a bowl and mix with the onion and chili mixture. Add the diced tomato. Blend in the coriander. Do not overmix, but leave chunky. Serve with warm soft tortillas.

Yield: about 1 pint

Grilled Chicken with Adobo Marinade

Courtesy Josefina Howard—Rosa Mexicano

6 *pasilla* chilies
9 *ancho* chilies
1/2 cup white vinegar
5 cloves garlic
1/2 teaspoon dried oregano
1/2 teaspoon dried thyme
1/4 teaspoon black pepper
4 cups chicken stock
12 large boneless chicken thighs, skinned

Place the chilies on a hot griddle until they are pliable. Test and turn with tongs. Don't burn them. Remove from the heat and discard veins and seeds. Soak the chilies in a bowl of hot water for at least an hour or overnight. Drain the chilies and place in a food processor with the vinegar, garlic, herbs, and pepper. Add 1/2 cup of chicken stock, if needed, to make a smooth paste. Rub the chicken pieces with the chili paste and place them in a nonreactive dish. Pour the remaining chicken stock over all and marinate for 2 hours. Grill or broil the chicken.

Yield: 6 servings

Potted Wild Mushrooms and Cornmeal (Hongos en Tamal en Cazuela)

Courtesy Josefina Howard—Rosa Mexicano

Mushrooms:

3 tablespoons safflower oil
1 *serrano* chili, seeded, deveined, and minced
2 cloves garlic, minced
1 pound seasonal wild mushrooms, sliced
salt and pepper to taste
1 tablespoon fresh *epazote*, minced

Avocados and Tortillas

Corn grits:

> 2 tablespoons safflower oil
> 1 medium onion, minced
> 3 medium tomatoes, peeled, seeded, and diced
> 6 cups chicken stock (water may be used)
> salt and pepper to taste
> 3/4 pound Quaker brand quick grits
> 1 tablespoon *epazote*, minced

In 3 tablespoons of oil, sauté the chili and garlic until softened. Add the mushrooms, salt, pepper, and *epazote*. Sauté until the mushrooms are cooked, then keep warm on low heat.

Heat 2 tablespoons of oil in a pan large enough to cook the grits. Sauté the onion until it is transparent, add the tomatoes, and stir. Cook for 5 minutes. Add the chicken stock, salt, and pepper. Bring to a boil, and add the grits slowly (or according to package directions), stir, and cook for 10 minutes. Place a cup of the grit mixture in each individual bowl, top with mushrooms, and garnish with *epazote*.

Yield: 6 servings

Aztec Pudding with Huitlacoche
(Budin Azteca con Huitlacoche)

Courtesy Josefina Howard—Rosa Mexicano

1 tablespoon sweet butter for greasing pan
3 tablespoons safflower oil
1 medium onion, diced
2 cloves garlic, minced
2 *poblano* chilies, roasted, seeded, julienned
2 pounds (2–2½ cups) *huitlacoche*, chopped
salt and pepper to taste

18 corn tortillas

Chicken mixture:

2 tablespoons safflower oil
2 cups cooked chicken
1 small onion, diced
1 clove garlic, minced
3 tomatoes, peeled, seeded, and diced
1/2 teaspoon dried thyme
2 bay leaves
salt and pepper to taste

3/4 cup *béchamel* sauce
3/4 cup *manchego* cheese (or white cheddar), shredded

Garnish:

18 strips of sweet green pepper
18 strips of sweet red pepper

Preheat oven to 350°. Butter a 10″ springform pan.

Heat 3 tablespoons of the oil in a skillet and sauté the onion, garlic, chilies, and chopped *huitlacoche*. Season and lower the heat, cook for 20 minutes, to eliminate a good deal of the moisture.

For the chicken mixture, heat 2 tablespoons of the oil in a second pan. Shred the chicken and gently sauté it with onion, garlic, tomato, and seasonings for 10 minutes.

Line the pan with about half the soft tortillas, so that they go up the sides of the pan, as well as covering the bottom. First, layer half the *huitlacoche* mixture, then half the chicken mixture, topped with one half of the béchamel and one half of the cheese. Top with the remaining tortillas. Next add the remaining *huitlacoche*, then the chicken, and top it with the béchamel and cheese. Cover lightly with aluminum foil and bake for 15 minutes.

Remove the pan from the oven and let it cool for 10 minutes. Remove the sides of the pan and decorate the *budin* with 12 alternating red and green pepper strips, arranged like the spokes of a wheel. Cut the remaining strips and make cross hatch designs over the long strips. Cut into wedges to serve.

Yield: 6 servings

Garlic Soup (Sopa de Ajo)

18 slices of crusty French or Italian bread
9 cloves garlic
1/2 cup safflower oil
8 cups hot chicken stock
salt and pepper to taste
1/2 cup crumbled *queso fresco* (if unavailable, use white cheddar)

Slice the bread about 1/4-inch thick, and set on cake racks to dry a bit. Peel the garlic cloves and crush them slightly with the side of a knife. Heat the oil in a large skillet. Add the garlic and press it into the oil with the back of a wooden spoon. When the garlic is gold and aromatic, remove, and discard. Fry the bread on both sides, and put it into a warm soup tureen or casserole with a cover. Add the chicken stock to the skillet and bring it to a boil. Pour it immediately over the bread, top with the cheese, and serve.

Yield: 6 servings

Easy Fish Tostados

1/2 cup safflower oil
6 8-inch corn tortillas
2 teaspoons chopped pickled *jalapeño* peppers
2 teaspoons liquid from the *jalapeños*
1 pound cooked red snapper
1 medium onion, minced
1 large tomato, peeled, seeded, and diced
2 tablespoons fresh lemon or lime juice
2 tablespoons fresh coriander, chopped
salt and pepper to taste
1/3 cup crema or crème fraîche
1/2 head romaine lettuce, shredded
1 ripe avocado, diced

For garnish, one or all of the following:

1 tablespoon fresh cilantro leaves, chopped
1 tablespoon red onion, minced
2 tablespoons *queso blanco*, shredded, or *mascarpone* cheese, mashed

Heat oil in a heavy skillet large enough to hold one tortilla, flat. Fry the tortillas one by one, turning them with tongs to make sure they are crisp, but not burned. Set on paper towels to drain.

Mash the *jalapeños* with their liquid until they are pasty. In a large bowl, gently flake the fish and mix with onion, tomato, lemon or lime juice, jalapeño paste, and coriander until well blended but still coarse. Season to taste with salt and pepper. Top each crisp tortilla with a teaspoon of crema and some of the shredded lettuce. Place the fish on the lettuce and garnish. Serve as a first course or lunch salad.

Yield: 6 servings

Hot Sauce (Aji Molido con Aceite)

1 cup dried *pequin* or comparable chilies
1/2 cup olive oil
4 cloves peeled garlic, minced
1/2 teaspoon coarse salt
1 cup boiling water

Split the dried chilies. Remove the seeds and discard. Place the chilies in a small bowl and cover with 2 cups of boiling water. Soak for 2 hours or overnight. Drain. Combine the chilies with the oil, garlic, salt, and boiling water in a blender or processor and work to a paste. Store in a covered nonreactive container and refrigerate.

Yield: 1 *pint*

Ecuador and Peru

Ecuador and Peru have been Inca domains for millennia. As early as 2100 B.C.E. there were established fishing and trading communities in the area. Today both Spanish and *Quechua*, the Inca dialect, are spoken. Like the Chinese, who also developed food preservation techniques, the Inca used systems of air drying, sun drying, and salting meat and fish. Meat dried this way is called *charqui*, or "jerky." Unique to them was the freeze-drying of root vegetables, primarily potatoes, by bringing them high up in the mountains. After the food was frozen, the Inca crumbled it and stored it in sacks that let the air circulate.

Fish and seafood from oceans and rivers have remained abundant to this day. In Lake Titicaca are found fresh-water trout, smelt, and frogs for frog legs. The major staple is the potato, of which there are about one-hundred strains. Corn and other starches have been introduced and integrated into the cuisine over time, but the potato reigns.

Indigenous dishes include *papas a la Huancaina*, potatoes with spicy cheese sauce, and *Yacu-chupe*, a fantastic green soup made of potatoes, cheese, onions, garlic, eggs, coriander, chilies, and mint. *Causa* is a potato stew made with white and sweet potatoes, corn, hard-cooked eggs, and cheese, served on shredded lettuce and topped with onion sauce. Another soup is *parihuela*, made of seafood and flavored with *yuyo de mar*, a seaweed. *Caucau* is made with tripe and potatoes, chilies, and parsley, sometimes served with rice. *Sancochado*, a variation of the *sancocho* served throughout Latin-American countries, is a potato, meat, and vegetable stew flavored with garlic. *Empanadas*, filled pastries, are varied and flavorful. Dessert, in addition to fruit, often includes *picarones*, fried cassava fritters served with honey, or *paselillos*, made with yucca, sweet potato, and anise. More elaborate is the *mazamorra morada*, a concoction of sweetened purple maize, sweet potato, dried fruit, lemon, cinnamon, cloves, and aromatic pepper. Along the coast, as in most of the Americas, *ceviche* is everywhere in great assortments and combinations.

In Ecuador, street fare varies with the elevation and is usually served with hot seasoning on the side in the form of *aji*, a red chili paste. *Llapingachos* are snacks of fried mashed potatoes and cheese. *Humitas* are sweet-corn tamales, and the more standard *tamales* and *empanadas* have mixed fillings that often include chicken, pork, olives, and spices. *Cuy* is guinea pig, and is prepared in savory stews in the Andes, where little fish or livestock is available.

Colombia

Until the sixteenth century, Colombia was an area where small independent communities lived in isolation. So little was known about it that it is there that the famed *El Dorado*, the Golden City, was thought to be hidden in the badlands. This was said to be the reason the population was hidden and secretive, and the mountain passes arduous and dangerous. Bogotá is the capital city, at an elevation of almost 9,000 feet, but the mountains soar up from there, with the main roads leading down to the plains and coastal area. Half of the economy of Colombia is coffee based. The busy activities of growing, processing, packaging, and shipping coffee give it an international status.

Locros de choclos is a potato and corn soup that is surprisingly tasty. The local *sancocho* is made of well-seasoned varieties of potatoes, cassava pumpkin, lemon, tomato, and fish. *Mazorcas* are freshly picked corn, roasted on the cob, and served with assorted condiments. In big cities, Colombian *tamales*, called *hallacas*, are made of seasoned cornmeal dough wrapped around a rich assortment of beef, pork, potatoes, peas, eggs, olives, raisins, and onions, seasoned with cloves, garlic, and cumin. The whole mixture is wrapped in a banana leaf and steamed.

Fruit, pastries, and preserves are served for dessert along with an assortment of fresh fruit. Often fruit is made into juice or *sorbete*.

El Salvador

Though El Salvador has had more than its share of political and social turmoil, its traditional rough fare is both tasty and readily available.

In El Salvador, beans and corn are staple food items. *Pupusas* are savory, fried bean cakes. They are sold in the street and served in restaurants. *Gallo en chicha*, a chicken stew, is cooked and served in a variety of ways.

Sopa de frijoles☙ (bean soup), thickened with bread, is a popular mainstay.

Bean Soup (Sopa de Frijoles)

3 tablespoons cooking oil
1 large onion, diced
6 day-old tortillas, shredded with a knife or torn by hand
2 cups red beans, cooked
6 cups water
1/2 teaspoon cinnamon
1/4 teaspoon cloves
1 teaspoon thyme
1 cup corn kernels, optional
salt and pepper
lemon slices
2 tablespoons chopped, fresh coriander leaves

Heat the oil in a skillet and sauté the onions until they are slightly browned. Remove the onions and set aside. Brown the tortillas and set aside. (Add more oil to the pan, if necessary.) Mash 1 cup of the beans. Place 6 cups of water in a large stockpot along with the sautéed onions, mashed beans, whole beans, cinnamon, cloves, and thyme. Bring to a boil and simmer for 10 minutes. Add the corn (if using) and salt and pepper to taste, and cook another 4 minutes. Place the fried tortillas in a tureen or in individual bowls, and ladle the soup over them. Serve immediately, and garnish with lemon slices and coriander.

Yield: 6 servings

Brazil

In 1500, Cabral, a Portuguese explorer, established a settlement he named Salvador de Bahia, in what has become the fifth largest country in the world. Few people in North America realize that São Paulo, Brazil is the largest city in the Western hemisphere.

Brazil's first inhabitants—the Tupi-Guarani people—satisfied food needs by fishing and small game hunting. They also cultivated *manioc*, and processed it into *farinha de mandioca*, which is still a staple part of Brazilian cooking and baking. It is similar to tapioca, which is the Tupi-Guarani name. *Acaju*, cashew, is from the same language.

Europeans engaged in the slave trade quickly brought Africans to establish large communities and plantations. Africans also did a great deal of the cooking, and combined food crops that they brought with them with native crops. Corn, sweet potatoes, and peanuts were prevalent and okra, coconuts, and yams were added.

Candomblé, the ceremony of offering food to the gods, has its roots in the religion of the African settlers, and is still present in the religion of Bahia. Food sacrifice has been part of that tradition; since food for the gods has to be excellent, the food of Bahia became a standard for the rest of the country.

Portuguese is the official language of Brazil and, among the Portuguese, African, and Mestizo population, it is the dominant language. In large cities, a great deal of Spanish is spoken. There is a large Japanese population, which has had some cross-cultural language effects. *Please* is *por favor*, and *thank you* is *obrigado*.

In the eighteenth century, gold and diamonds were discovered in abundance, and vast coffee and sugar cane plantations proliferated. Coffee, cacao, and corn become major domesticated crops.

Strong African traditions extended into the culinary culture. A Bahian dish is *vatapá*, a spicy, peppery fish stew. It is made with fish, rice, cashews, ginger, mint, and parsley, garnished with a palm oil called *dendê*, which is used in the same way that Asian sesame oil is used to perfume food and tie the flavors together.

Among street food one finds are bean cakes, *acarajés*, served with hot sauce. These are fine on their own or served stuffed with *vatapá*. *Mugueca*, a spicy shellfish stew, and *xin-xin*, which is a combination of chicken and fish or shrimp cooked with onions, squash, and spices, are

From the menu of

Riodizio

471 Lafayette Street
New York, NY 10003

Little Dishes

Pao de Queijo
House-baked Brazilian cheese bread

Rio Wraps
Peruvian chicken, sundried tomatoes, and roasted potato
in a Brazil nut pesto

Lula Com Limao
Grilled baby squid with lemon and achiote olive oil

Camarao com Coco
Sauteed shrimp in a light coconut broth with chick peas, leeks,
tomatoes, and lime juice

Costela de Leitao
Spicy ribs marinated in cumin, oranges, and garlic

Coxinha
Three crispy potato teardrops stuffed with roasted chicken

Taro Frita
Fried taro chips with a sweet potato salsa

Panquecas de Batata
Sweet potato cakes with a cabrales cheese and
dried fruit dipping sauce

Salads

Choice of lime-mango or pomegranate vinaigrette dressing

Salada de Riodizio

Chopped house greens with hearts of palm, carrots, cucumbers, chick peas, red onion, tomato, and roasted beets

Salada de Legumes Assados

Roasted market fresh marinated vegetables, house greens, mango, papaya, polenta, cabrales, and reggianito cheese

Entrees

Frango de Peruana

Roasted chicken in Peruvian spices with mashed sweet potatoes and a mango-mustard seed slaw

Prato de Riodizio

A combination of black beans, steamed greens, rice, fried plantains, polenta, and market fresh marinated roasted vegetables

Moqueca de Camarao y Mejillones

A classical Northern Brazilian dish of shrimp and mussels in a light coconut and lime sauce. Served with Riodizio grains and daily greens

Porco com Frango

A combination of our spicy "Brazilian style" ribs and rotisserie Peruvian chicken served with mashed sweet potato

Salada de Legumes Assados Grande

A heaping bowl of roasted market fresh marinated vegetables, house greens, papaya, mango, polenta, cabrales and reggianito cheese topped with your choice of chicken breast, marinated shrimp, or sliced sirloin steak

Salada de Riodizio Grande

A dinner-sized version of our famous chopped "South American Cobb Salad" served with your choice of chicken, shrimp, or sliced sirloin steak

Sides

Ratata Palito

Sweet potato fries

Banana

Fried plantains

Feijao Preto

Black beans

Arrios de Riodizio

Steamed Riodizio grains

other specialties from Bahia. *Sop de peixe* is the general name for any local seafood chowder. *Caruru de camarão* is a shrimp dish with okra and peanuts. Another dish, *bife (ou frango) com arroz e feijao*, is beef (or chicken) with rice and black beans. *Cuscus de Galinha* is chicken, cornmeal, and vegetables with citrus, spices, chilies, and olives. *Empadinhas de camarão* are shrimp cakes with olives and hearts of palm. *Churrasco* is a mixed grill (served in most of South America) made with *farofa* and *couve* (collard greens) and served at all-you-can-eat *rodízios*.

Street fare consists of *salgados coxina*, spicy manioc fritters filled with meat or fish; *bolinhos de bacalahau*, which are fish balls made from dried salt cod; and *empadão, empadas*, and *empadinhas*, which are varieties of *empanadas*. These *tìra-gosto* or "just a taste" are eaten throughout the day. Two popular sweets are *bigadeiro*, similar to a chocolate truffle, and *cariocas*, coconut candy named after the natives of Rio de Janeiro. Vendors also sell *vitaminas*, vegetable juices; *caldo de cana*, a sugar-cane juice drink; and *Guarana*, a carbonated drink made from a small rainforest apple. *Guarana* is bottled by Antarctica, the same company that makes a very popular beer. *Cachaça*, a Brazilian sugar cane rum, is used for many drinks. In addition to the famous *caipirinha* are *batidas*, punches made with *maracujá*, passion fruit; *coco*, coconut; and *limão*, lemon and sugar. All these are becoming available in the United States.

Fruit sounds especially exotic in Portuguese. Papaya is common, and is called *mamão*; *abacaxi* is pineapple; *mora* are large raspberries and quite delicious, as are *manga* and *goiaba*, mango and guava; all of which are eaten or turned into juice. Throughout the day countless demitasse cups of *cafezinho*, strong, hot Brazilian coffee, are consumed. Although it has no official standing, *feijoada completa,*❦ may be the Brazilian national dish, and every Wednesday and Saturday it is featured in homes and restaurants. It is not unlike a *cassoulet*. It is made of beans, jerked beef, sausage, smoked tongue, bacon, ham, spices, herbs, and vegetables, stewed with *farofa*, manioc flour, and couve (collard greens), and served with orange slices and savories. This dish is said to have originated in the *senzala* or slave quarters of plantations, where it was made with the lesser parts of the pig, in addition to rice and beans and dried and preserved meats. That tradition has lasted, and both expensive cuts and giveaways are combined, cooked together, and served buffet-style with dishes of *farofa,*❦ various hot sauces, and tangy orange slices.

IPANEMA BRAZILIAN RESTAURANT

In New York City, West 46th Street between Fifth and Sixth Avenues is designated the *Street of Brazil* on official street signs. In addition to being a center for Brazilian products, it has several restaurants.

Ipanema is owned by Alfredo Pedro, who is a restaurateur committed to authenticity and excellence. His former place, the Brazilian Coffee House, was a popular landmark restaurant, ahead of the curve. When I ask what the defining tastes of Brazilian food are, he talks not only about the rich layers of tastes and textures that have grown together from three roots, Tupi-Guarani, Portuguese, and African, but about the unmistakable flavor of *dendê* and other coconut essences.

Dinner starts with *salgadinhos*, which are bite-sized *bolinhos de bacalhau*●; deep-fried portions of *bacalhau*; or *empadinhas*. An *aperitivo Brasileiro* is made of garlicky spiced, grilled shrimp in their shells, served on a salad of hearts of palm, greens, avocado, and tomato slices. *Caldo verde* is a hearty soup with collard greens, *linguiça* (a Portuguese sausage), and potatoes. *Filete de pargo grehaldo* is broiled red-snapper filet seasoned with *farofa* (a toasted mix of crumbled cassava flour and butter). Dessert is *qindão*, a cross between a coconut custard and a rich moist cake. Most desserts tend to be very sweet and moist, whether coconut- or chocolate-based.

Codfish Cakes (Bolinhos de Bacalhau)

Courtesy Ipanema Restaurant

1/2 pound dried codfish, rinsed and soaked for 2 hours
1/2 pound mashed white potatoes
1 medium onion, chopped
2 tablespoon, fresh, chopped parsley leaves
pepper to taste
2 large eggs
3 cups cooking oil

In a meat grinder or using appropriate blade on a food processor, grind the codfish. It may be necessary to grind it twice in a manual machine.

Mix well with potatoes, onion, parsley, and pepper. Blend eggs in well and form into 18 small balls. Heat oil in fryer and cook until golden brown, about 5 minutes, or follow instructions on electric fryer.

Yield: 18 *cakes*

Feijoada Completa (*Meats, Black Beans, Farofa, Rice, Collard Greens, Chili Sauces*)

Courtesy Ipanema Restaurant

Serving design: Meats are removed and carved into small portions, the beans are served in a separate bowl topped with the cooking liquid. Rice and *farofa* have their own bowls, as do the medium and hot chili sauces. A platter of freshly sliced oranges is set out on the buffet. Each diner takes a large rimmed plate and spoons first the rice, then beans on one side of his or her plate. This is topped with the *farofa*. Meats are placed on the other side and topped with orange slices. The chili sauces are used as desired.

Beans and meat:

4 cups black beans
2 large onions, sliced
8 cloves of garlic, sliced
4 bay leaves
1/2 teaspoon black pepper
2 pig's feet, split, optional
2 pounds pork
2 pounds beef or fresh boneless chuck
2 pounds ribs
1/2 pound slab bacon
1 pound *linguiça* (Portuguese sausage) or *chorizo*
1 pound jerked beef, optional

Additional seasoning:

2 tablespoons lard or oil
1 large onion, chopped
3 garlic cloves, minced
salt and pepper to taste

The night before cooking, pick over the beans, rinse them, and soak them in cold water to cover. If using jerked beef, soak it overnight in a separate bowl. Early in the day, place beans in a pot large enough to hold all the ingredients. Cover with water and add onion, garlic, bay leaves, and black pepper. Bring to a boil and simmer, uncovered, for 45 minutes.

If using pig's feet, rinse them and place them in a separate pot. Cover with cold water and boil for 30 minutes, then drain, and set aside. When the beans are cooked add the meats, layering them through the beans. Bring to a boil, lower heat, and simmer, partially covered, for 1 hour. Check for seasoning and make sure there is enough liquid. Cook for another hour. At this time prepare the *farofa,*◈ rice, and collard greens.◈

Additional seasoning is prepared by heating the lard or oil and sautéing the onions and garlic. Add enough salt and pepper to heighten taste.

Remove the meat from the pot, carve, and place on a warm platter. Mix the beans with additional seasoning in a large warm bowl.

Yield: 12 servings

Farofa
_____

3 tablespoons sweet butter
1½ cups cassava flour (available at Latin food specialty shops)
salt to taste

Melt the butter in a wide skillet and stir in the cassava flour. Stir the mixture briefly over medium heat until it resembles bread crumbs. Salt to taste. Serve at room temperature.

Yield: 1½ cups farofa

Rice Brazilian Style
_____

3 tablespoons cooking oil
1 medium onion, chopped
1 garlic clove, minced
1½ cups long-grain rice
3 cups boiling water

Heat the oil in a heavy saucepan in which the rice will be cooked. Add the onion and garlic and cook until transparent. Stir in the rice and, stirring constantly, cook for 5 minutes. Add boiling water and cook until the water is absorbed. Stir rice lightly with a fork. Cover tightly, lower heat as far as possible. After 5 minutes, turn off heat and let rice sit, covered, until ready to serve, between 15 minutes and 1 hour. Fluff with a fork and place in bowl.

Yield: 3 *cups*

Collard Greens (Couve)

3 pounds collards or 2 packages frozen chopped collards
3 tablespoons bacon fat, lard, or cooking oil

Strip the leaves from the collards and discard the coarsest stems. Shred the leaves and boil 15 to 20 minutes, until tender, being careful not to overcook them. Drain and reserve. For frozen collards follow package instructions. Before serving time, heat oil in a large skillet, add the collards, stir, and heat without browning. Transfer to a warm bowl.

Yield: 12 *or more servings*

Quindão

1 tablespoon sweet butter to grease pan
1 tablespoon sugar to sprinkle on pan
1 pound grated unsweetened coconut, fresh or packaged
3 whole eggs
9 egg yolks
4 cups sugar
boiling water

Preheat the oven to 350°. Butter and sprinkle with sugar a 2-quart ring mold. Set out a pan, such as a roasting pan, in which the ring mold can be placed.

Fluff the coconut with a fork. Beat the whole eggs and egg yolks, sugar, and coconut and incorporate. Pour into prepared ring mold. Place in large pan and pour boiling water half way up the sides of the *Quindão*, being careful not to splash it on the custard. Bake for 1 hour, or until a wooden skewer comes out clean. Check a few times to be sure there is water in the larger pan. Note: A variety of this dish called *quindim* is made in tiny individual molds and served as a *tira-gosto*.

Yield: 12 servings

Argentina

Most Argentinean restaurants in North America specialize in steak and other beef dishes. Argentina has the highest beef consumption per capita in the world, and a weekend without a mixed *asado*, or assorted barbecue, is considered to be like one with no food at all. It must be said, though, that the cattle are a little leaner and lower in cholesterol than other nations', because they are grass fed. Because beef export is a large part of the Argentinean economy, a great deal of research on cholesterol is being done there.

Chile

Chile has a 2,600-hundred-mile coastline, so the popularity of fish and shellfish is hardly surprising. Tons of Chilean shrimp are imported each month to North American markets. A more unique flavor is that of the sea urchin, called *erizo*. Up and down the coast, *chupe de mariscos*, seafood chowder, is served with different combinations.

The central valley is laden with fruit. Apple, citrus, peach, pear, and plum trees are abundant. Chilean strawberries are the precursors of those cultivated throughout the world. Grapes are grown both for eating and winemaking. Chilean wines are excellent and well worth pursuing.

The Caribbean

The very thought of warm island breezes, gentle surf, and pristine beaches evokes a tranquil respite. The spicy food and island bands that play reggae, salsa, calypso, and steel-band music awaken the senses.

The Caribbean Archipelago casts its spell in an arc almost 3,000 miles long from Florida to Venezuela. It was from the Caribbean that Columbus brought chocolate and great varieties of chilies. Originally occupied by the Arawaks and Caribs, the islands have over centuries become a multicultural population of African, Danish, Dutch, English, French, Native American, Portuguese, Spanish, and Scandinavian descent.

Cuba, Jamaica, Haiti, the Dominican Republic, the Caymans, the Bahamas, Puerto Rico, and the Virgin Islands are names that capture our imagination.

Cuba, which navigators long regarded as the key to the new world, is a surprising 750 miles long. Many Cuban dishes feature black or turtle beans—there are a hundred ways to prepare black-bean soup and rice and beans. Cuban restaurants serve a great range of dishes, often accompanied by soft Cuban bread. A favorite take-out Cuban dish is a Cubano sandwich made with hot roast pork, ham, pickles, cheese, mustard, and mayonnaise. *Pastelles* are another popular street food— cornmeal dumplings filled with spicy ground meat, wrapped in plantain leaves, and steamed.

The Island of Hispaniola where Columbus's ships landed in 1492 is now comprised of 2 countries: the Dominican Republic and Haiti.

Watercress Soup

2 tablespoons canola oil
1 large onion, diced
1/2 pound watercress, washed, drained, and shredded
1 small fresh or dried chili pepper
2 cups coconut milk
3 tablespoons flour, dissolved in 1/2 cup chicken or vegetable stock
2 cups chicken or vegetable stock
3/4 teaspoon grated nutmeg
salt and pepper to taste

Heat the oil in a heavy-bottomed 2-quart pan. Sauté onion until lightly browned. Stir in watercress until it becomes quite limp. Add chili pepper and coconut milk and bring to a boil. Add flour dissolved in stock and simmer for a few minutes, slowly adding the remaining stock. Season with nutmeg, salt, and pepper to taste.

Yield: 4 servings

Another soup served throughout the area is *callaloo.* This rich dish is made with callaloo greens, which have their origin in Africa, and also contains okra as well as pork and crab.

Callaloo

1 pound callaloo leaves (spinach may be substituted)
20 okra, the size of a little finger
3 cloves garlic, minced
1 onion, minced
1 *jalapeño* pepper, minced
1/4 pound salt pork, diced
3 quarts boiling water
4 crabs (1 pound crabmeat may be substituted)
1½ cups freshly cooked hot white rice
2 limes, cut into wedges

Wash the callaloo leaves and shred them. Slice the okra into 3/4″ slices.
    Add the callaloo, okra, garlic, onion, jalapeño, and salt pork to the water over medium heat. Return to a boil and simmer for 2 hours. Clean and remove crabmeat from carapace and add crabmeat to soup. Simmer for 20 minutes. Serve in shallow soup bowls with rice and lime sections.

Yield: 6 servings

Cassava, a form of yucca or manioc, is used throughout the Americas, as is coconut. The following cake combines them both.

Cassava Cake

1 cup shredded cassava
1 cup shredded coconut, fresh or packaged
2 tablespoons cooking oil
3/4 cup sugar
1/4 cup flour
1 teaspoon baking powder
1/2 teaspoon allspice

1/2 teaspoon cinnamon
1 teaspoon vanilla
1 cup milk
1/2 cup water

Preheat oven to 375°. Grease and flour an 8-inch square cake pan.

Mix together cassava and coconut and stir in oil. Blend sugar, flour, baking powder, allspice, and cinnamon and stir into cassava mixture. Pour together the vanilla, milk, and water and stir into other ingredients until well mixed. Let stand 15 minutes. Place in prepared pan and bake for 1 hour until it is brown and a tester comes out clean. Serve immediately or let cool in refrigerator.

Yield: 16 2-inch squares

Xamayca was named by the Arawak Indians, and then by the sixteenth century there were Spanish colonies. Sugar, rum, molasses, and ginger are very plentiful and are major exports. One of the most popular cooking styles from Jamaica is *jerk*, a form of barbecuing or smoking meat, fish, or poultry with a dry spicy rub. It is especially delicious because of the combination of sweet and savory spices used. Plantain chips and fragrant salads and salsas made with tropical fruits are served with jerk. Both beef patties and codfish patties are popular handheld foods. *Platanos fritos* and *platanos rellenos*, one a dish of fried plantains, the other plantains stuffed with spicy ground beef and fried, are wonderful dishes. They can be found at Rositas Comidas Latinas on upper Broadway in New York City.

Jamaica Ginger Cake

1/2 cup raisins
1/4 cup dark rum
1½ teaspoons ground ginger
1½ cups flour
6 tablespoons sweet butter
1/2 cup brown sugar
1/3 cup molasses
1/4 cup milk at room temperature
1 teaspoon baking soda
1 large egg, slightly beaten

Preheat the oven to 325°. Line an 8-inch square cake pan with waxed paper.

Soak the raisins in the rum for 10 minutes. Mix ginger into flour in bowl large enough to hold all ingredients. In small pan, heat butter, brown sugar, and molasses, stirring until sugar is dissolved. Remove from heat and add the raisins in rum. Beat the milk, baking soda, and egg together. Add alternately to the flour mixture. Pour into prepared pan and bake for 1 hour, or until tester comes out clean.

Yield: 1 8-inch cake

Classic Black Beans (Frijoles Negros)

2 cups dried black beans
3 bay leaves
1/3 cup Spanish olive oil
1 teaspoon salt
3 tablespoons Spanish olive oil
1 large Spanish onion, diced
2 sweet peppers, seeded and diced
1 tablespoon fresh oregano minced, or 1/2 teaspoon dried
1 tablespoon sugar
1/2 teaspoon (approximately) freshly ground black pepper

Place the beans in a container with water to cover, adding the bay leaves, 1/3 cup olive oil, and 1/2 teaspoon salt. Let soak in the refrigerator for 6 hours or overnight. Drain beans, rinse them, and place in large pot with water to cover the beans by 4 inches. Bring the beans to a boil over high heat for 20 minutes, then lower heat to medium low and simmer for 1½ hours, stirring occasionally, and making sure that there is always enough water to cover the beans.

While the beans are cooking prepare a *sofrito*. Heat 3 tablespoons olive oil in a frying pan over high heat; add the onion, peppers, oregano, 1/2 teaspoon salt, pepper, and sugar. Reduce heat to medium low, and sauté for about 10 minutes. Add to beans about 1/2 hour before they are fully cooked. Stir well. Serve with rice and hot chili condiments (optional).

Yield: 6 to 8 servings

PATRIA

Chef Douglas Rodriguez

When I asked Douglas Rodriguez what he regarded as the source of Latin-American cooking, he said, "Anywhere south of here." He has traveled in Peru, Ecuador, and Colombia, eating not only in fine restaurants but in street stalls and private homes. The taste of white corn on the cob, skewered and roasted over a fire to bring out the sweetness, served from a cart with pasilla peppers, chopped onions, and cilantro is described with the same enthusiasm he brings to his recipes for *arepas*, which originate in Colombia and Venezuela. These golden corn cakes are made with yellow cornmeal, fresh corn kernels, cheese, and butter. They are slightly sweet and are served with an aromatic *bacalao* and *foie gras*. There is also the homier white cornmeal *arepa*, made with hominy with the addition of water and salt and often stuffed with spicy beans or meat and fried or stewed like a dumpling.

We are always advised not to eat anything raw or almost raw when we travel, but those of us who are adventurous can't resist. Rodriguez says there were at least twenty-two different kinds of ceviche on one menu in Ecuador: black clam, razor clam, lobster, crab, shrimp, fish roe; with citrus, cilantro, and other herbs in inventive combinations, each one more delicious than the last.

Rodriguez makes a fried oyster dish with *huacatay* sauce, which is mainly black mint with a bit of cheese and spicy pepper.

Homey foods like *Yuca con Mojo* are texture-rich and flavorful. Rodriguez treats the ubiquitous tuber with care. First it is cut into 1-inch by 3-inch pieces, steamed, then fried, so that it is creamy yet grainy when bitten into. *Mojo* is the name of a four-part sauce used in Latin cooking. One element is citrus, used individually or in combination, including tangerine, orange, grapefruit, as well as the more common lemon and lime. The second component is one of the pungent lilies—shallots, onions, leeks, garlic, or even scallions; the third, an herb or herbs, such as rosemary, coriander, or bay laurel. The selections are blended with fine olive oil. The combinations are infinite. A favorite is tangerine, shallots, rosemary, and oil.

From the menu of

Patria

250 Park Avenue South
New York, NY 10036

Appetizers

Ecuadorian Ceviche
Shrimp, tomato, avocado and crunchy corn nuts

Cured Beef Roll
Plantain filled with tasajo, white bean salad, chipolte ketchup

Chicharonn de Ostra
Crispy oysters with fufu, spinach and Huacatay sauce

Empanada Cabrales
Spanish blue cheese with mixed greens and walnut pear
vinaigrette

Peruvian Ceviche
Spicy seafood in black marinade, potatoes à la Huancaina and
Mama Juana

Open Face Arepa
Colombian sweet corn cake with foie gras and stewed bacalao

Honduran Fire and Ice
Ceviche of tuna, chilies, ginger and coconut milk

Ropa Vieja Empanada
Stewed shredded beef, wild mushroom ceviche and
shaved manchego cheese

Venezuelan Empanada

White arepa dough filled with black beans, roasted corn and tomato salsa

Clam Tamal

With sauteed greens, chorizo and garlic tomato broth

Eggplant Empanada

Roasted eggplant and goat cheese filled pastry with asparagus and smoked morel sauce

Sides

Plantain Chips with Salsa

Black Beans with Rice

Arepas/Corncakes

Patacones and Roasted Pepper Cheese Salsa

Entrees

The Original

Plantain coated striped bass with fufu and grilled lily salad

Puerto Rican Pastel

Vegetarian tamal with roasted spinach and vegetable mushroom escabeche

Sugar Cane Tuna

Coconut glazed loin with malanga puree, chayote and dried shrimp salsa

From the menu of Patria (continued)

Patria Pork

Boniato puree, black bean broth and jalapeño vinegar

Enchilado Camarones

Cuban style shrimp in a chili tomato sauce with garbanzo rice and pickled cabbage

Churrasco Lacayo

Nicaraguan style beef tenderloin with chimichurri, moros and beet relish

Guatemalan Chicken

In mole sauce with green rice, avocado salad and patacones

Red Snapper

Crispy whole fish, coconut conch rice and Dominican style cole slaw

Duck Combo

Roasted leg and escabeche breast with orange scented sweet potato

Swordfish

Grilled, with banana lentil salad, horseradish cream and oyster croquettas

Boneless Ribs

Braised short ribs with Paraguayan chipa guasu and garlic wilted greens

Serrano Rabbit

Loin wrapped in serrano style ham with dried cherry vinaigrette, wilted greens and stuffed yuca

Chef Rodriguez also makes an empanada with a reduced oxtail broth that is clarified to a jelly, then put into a savory cornmeal empanada pastry and fried. A chicken dish from Paraguay features *Olla Porrida* (rotten pot), a stew of cabbage, carrots, potatoes, and chicken. The ingredients are served separately from the broth and accompanied by aromatic mustard. The chef also makes braised beef in a similar manner, served with *chipa guasu*, which is another Paraguayan dish that is a cross between a corn soufflé and a flan.

CauCau Mondongo, Inca tripe stew, is a classic. To prepare the tripe, it must be boiled a total of four hours, draining the tripe and changing the water every half hour. Limestone is used in the water for the first two hours to help draw out any impurities. Yukon Gold potatoes, onions, carrots, garlic, and turmeric are simmered in veal and chicken stock. A bit of *aji mojido* (red-chili paste) is added. The soup is served with side dishes of cilantro and *aji mojido* salsa, diced tomatoes and chives, and a dish of marinated red onions and cilantro.

A turkey empanada is savory with a touch of sweetness. Turkey, walnuts, queso blanco, and air-dried cherries are flavored with cinnamon, allspice, cumin, and anise, then served on a slice of Serrano ham on a bed of greens.

An innovation is a goat-cheese-and-eggplant empanada in a dough flavored with chili pepper, served with asparagus and mushrooms and a sauce of smoked morels and sherry.

In Colombia there are street vendors making waffles as thin as communion wafers. *Araquepa*, a syrupy caramelized milk, is sandwiched between two wafers. At Patria, the dessert menu offers *Torta de Higos*, made from roasted figs in a hazelnut shell, and a vanilla passion-fruit flan, served with caramel sauce and fruit, as well as Banana Tres Leches, plated with chocolate mousse and vanilla meringue. Sorbets and ice creams from fruit in season are made on premises.

There is a wonderful and varied wine list at Patria. The steward has carefully selected a Spanish Val Sotillo Ribera del Duero Riserva 1990, which is a Bordeaux-like red with overtones of berry and some vanilla from the American oak in which it is aged. A wonderful dinner wine, it complements the meal from beginning to end. A choice of interesting beers is also available.

The Port Royal from Honduras is vaguely sweet, and *Cuzco* from Peru and *Cerveza Aquila* from Venezuela are both light and refreshing.

Chef Rodriguez is a member of the recently formed Chef's Conclave that is advising American Airlines on both regional food and Latin microbreweries for in-flight service.

Croquettes with Banana Lentil Salad and Horseradish Cream

Courtesy Douglas Rodriguez—Patria

1/4 cup olive oil
1/2 cup white onion, chopped
1/2 cup sweet red pepper, chopped
5 cloves garlic, minced
1 pound fresh oysters
1 cup heavy cream
1½ cups flour
1 teaspoon nutmeg

For breading:

2 cups unbleached all-purpose flour
2 cups cracker meal
6 eggs
salt and pepper to taste
oil for frying, 1-inch deep in heavy pan, about 1 cup

In a heavy pan, heat the olive oil and sauté the onion and pepper for 2 minutes; add the garlic, lower flame, and continue cooking while you drain the oysters, reserving the liquid for another use.

Add oysters and cook for about 10 minutes or until mixture is dry. Add the cream, and stir while cooking for 3 minutes. Slowly add flour, stirring with a wooden spoon until mixture forms a ball. Remove from heat and cool in the refrigerator for 2 hours. This is a good time to make the Banana Lentil Salad● and Horseradish Cream.●

Place flour and cracker meal in two separate shallow bowls. Whisk the eggs with salt and pepper in a third bowl.

With the oyster mixture, form 20 cigar-shaped croquettes and place them back in the refrigerator for 20 minutes.

Dip the croquettes first in flour, then in the beaten eggs, and then roll them in cracker meal. (They may be frozen at this point.)

In a heavy-bottomed pan, heat 1 inch of oil until 325° and fry the croquettes 2–3 minutes on each side until golden brown. Drain and serve immediately.

Yield: 20 *croquettes*

Horseradish Cream

3 tablespoons prepared white horseradish
1 tablespoon *wasabi* powder (Japanese product found in specialty stores)
1 tablespoon grated fresh ginger
1/4 cup sour cream
1 ounce heavy cream

Place all ingredients in a blender and blend well. Serve chilled.

Yield: 3/4 *cup*

Banana Lentil Salad

1 cup brown lentils
1 cup yellow or red lentils
3 tablespoons olive oil
1 large red onion, diced
1 sweet red pepper, diced
6 cloves chopped garlic
3 firm yellow bananas, peeled, and cut in large dice
2 tablespoons chopped fresh parsley
3 tablespoons chopped fresh cilantro
1/4 cup balsamic vinegar
salt and pepper to taste

Soak the lentils overnight. Strain and bring to a boil in 6 cups of water. Simmer until tender, about 15 minutes. While lentils are simmering, heat the olive oil and sauté the onion, red pepper, and then garlic, until tender. Set aside. Drain the lentils, if necessary, and cool. Blend in sautéed mixture, and then gently stir in the other ingredients until well blended. Chill for at least 1 hour before serving with the horseradish cream.

Yield: 6 *servings*

Fried Plantains (Patacones)

Courtesy Douglas Rodriguez—Patria

6 large green plantains
oil for frying

Peel the plantains.* Fry plantains whole (if they don't fit, cut them in half crosswise). Remove from the oil and drain on paper towels. Cover them loosely with paper towels and let them cool. Place the cool plantains, one at a time, on a clean, damp tea towel. Fold the towel in half, and roll the plantains flat with a rolling pin, as you would a pie crust. Once the plantains are rolled thin, sandwich them between layers of plastic wrap and roll them quite thin. With a sharp knife, cut flattened plantains into any shape desired. Heat about 1/2 inch of the oil in a heavy pan, and fry until crisp.

Yield: 8 servings

Pompano Cooked in a Banana Leaf with Crab Topping

Courtesy Douglas Rodriguez—Patria

4 tablespoons *achiote* oil (olive oil may be substituted)
2 medium onions, julienned
1 large red sweet pepper, julienned
3 cloves minced garlic
6 sprigs parsley, leaves only, chopped
6 pompano filets
2 teaspoons paprika
salt and pepper to taste
2 large banana leaves cut into 6 18-inch by 18-inch squares
cooking oil spray
1/2 cup white wine

---

*Hint: An easy way to peel green plantains is to fill the sink with very warm water. Cut tip ends from the plantains and make 3 or 4 lengthwise cuts through the plantain skin to the fruit. Soak in water for 10 minutes. The skin will come off easily.

For crab topping:

1/2 pound cooked lump jumbo crab meat, picked for cartilage.
2 small tomatoes, peeled, seeded, and diced small
1 small red onion, diced small
2 green onions, sliced thin
2 tablespoons fresh, chopped cilantro leaves
2 tablespoons fresh lime juice
1 tablespoon olive oil
salt and pepper to taste

Mix the ingredients together and let rest for 20 minutes. Set aside until needed.

Preheat the oven to 500°.

Heat a skillet over high heat, add the oil, and sauté onions, pepper, garlic, and parsley leaves. Cook 3 minutes. Remove from the heat and let cool. Sprinkle filets with paprika, salt, and pepper. Place 1 tablespoon of onion mixture on each banana leaf, top with the fish, and fold banana leaf to form a square-cornered packet. Coat with cooking oil a pan large enough to hold the fish in a single layer. Arrange fish and pour the wine over all. Bake for 25 minutes. Remove from the oven and place on serving platter or individual plates, slit open packets, and top with room-temperature crab topping.

Yield: 6 large servings

Guava Cream-Cheese Turnovers

Courtesy Douglas Rodriguez—Patria

2 sticks margarine, softened
8 ounces cream cheese, softened
pinch of salt
2 cups unbleached all-purpose flour
1 12-ounce box guava paste (available in Latin markets or specialty shops)

Preheat the oven to 375°.

With a hand mixer, cream the margarine and cheese, then add salt. Add the flour all at once and mix by hand until well blended. Wrap the dough in plastic wrap and chill for 15 minutes.

Divide the dough in half. Leave half in refrigerator; roll other half to 1/8-inch thickness. Cut into 10 3-inch squares. Repeat with remaining dough. Place a 1/4-inch slice of guava paste on each square. Bring diagonal points together to form a sealed triangle. Pinch edges by hand or with the tines of a fork. Place on ungreased baking sheets, and bake in preheated oven for 15 minutes, or until golden brown. Rich orange marmalade is sometimes substituted for the guava paste.

Yield: 20 turnovers

Beverages

Throughout the Americas, coffee and chocolate are drunk at all hours. A really thick Mexican hot chocolate made with milk and just a hint of cinnamon is available in most Mexican restaurants if you ask for chocolate *caldo*. *Café con leche, café au lait,* and various forms of coffee and hot milk are also popular. Strong espressolike drip coffee is also served.

Coffee is often made in an *olla*, an earthenware pot, in the following way:

Coffee (Cafe)

1 small earthenware pot
1 liter of water
4 tablespoons dark-roasted, coarsely ground coffee
2 cinnamon sticks
turbinado sugar to taste

Bring the water to boil in the pot, add ingredients, bring to boil again, and serve.

Yield: 4 cups

Coffee originated in Africa and came to South America through the Arab trade. Colombia and Brazil are the largest producers, though it grows in many regions. Surprisingly, instant coffee is very popular, simply because it is such a treat for many people to have a cup in a hurry. Often the *café con leche* drunk in the morning is a cup of hot milk with some coffee granules and brown sugar stirred in. *Cafecito* is the equivalent of demitasse and is served at street cafes and restaurants, sometimes with the addition of cinnamon or liqueur.

Té negro (black tea) is popular, and there are many herbal teas, like *té de cabello de elote* (corn-silk tea), *manzanilla* (chamomile), *hierbabuena* (mint), *anis estrella* (star anise), and *té de hojas de naranja* (orange-leaf tea). *Yerba maté*, an herb that contains a lot of caffeine and has long been the brew of choice, hot or cold, throughout Argentina, Chile, Brazil, Paraguay, and Uruguay. Though it is now going out of fashion, it is part of a long tradition.

Fruit juices and fruit sodas are popular, and are served at street stalls as well as in restaurants. Many juice bars serve various tropical combinations. *Betides*, *liquios*, and *aguas frescas* are fruit-based shakes made in blenders. They are delicious and healthy thirst quenchers.

Piña coladas, planter's punches, and daiquiris are some of the better known fruit-based alcoholic drinks.

There are some good wines from the regions; both Chile and Mexico produce some exceptional ones. There are also world-class beers and some aficionados will drink no others.

Indigenous alcoholic beverages tend to be very strong. The *pulque* of Mexico is notorious. *Aguardiente* is a rough rum processed from sugar cane; the *cachaça* of Brazil is much smoother and is used to make a cocktail called *caipirinha*.◐

Kahlua, from Mexico, and Tia Maria, from Jamaica, are both smooth coffee-based liqueurs that are good after-dinner drinks. From Curaçao comes an orange liqueur called, unsurprisingly, *Curaçao*. Trinidad gives us the famous angostura bitters, which are used in a shandy. The shandy is a mixture of beer and ginger beer with angostura bitters.

Tequila has been refined and is generally served in a margarita◐ or the less well-known sangrita,◐ a recipe that I have adapted for the home bar.

Peru produces a brandy called *Pisco*, after the port from which it is shipped. Every so often Pisco sours◐ come into fashion in the U.S.

Caipirinha

8 ice cubes
1 ripe lime
1 tablespoon superfine sugar
1 ounce *cachaça*

Place the ice cubes in a covered cocktail shaker or jar. Cut the lime into quarters, squeeze thoroughly over the ice, and add the rinds. Add sugar and *cachaça*, cover, and shake energetically. Pour into a glass, with or without the ice.

Yield: 1 *serving*

Margarita

1/4 fresh lime
a saucer of coarse salt
6 ice cubes
2 ounces tequila
1 ounce Triple Sec
1 ounce lime juice

Rub the rim of a large-stemmed glass with the lime, and twirl the rim of the glass in the saucer of salt. Place the remaining ingredients in a covered shaker and shake a few times. Pour into the prepared glass, with or without ice, as desired. To make a frozen margarita, place the ice cubes and remaining ingredients in a blender and blend to a slushy consistency. Serve immediately.

Yield: 1 *serving*

Pisco Sour

1 tablespoon water
1 tablespoon superfine sugar
3 ounces Pisco
2 teaspoons fresh lemon juice

In a mixer, combine the water and sugar till dissolved. Add remaining ingredients and shake till well mixed. Strain into glass.

Yield: 1 *serving*

Sangrita (Home Version)

2 cups tomato juice
juice of 1 ripe lime
1 tablespoon frozen orange juice concentrate
1 tablespoon grenadine syrup
4 splashes Tabasco, or to taste
salt and pepper to taste
4 ounces tequila
8 ice cubes

Garnish:

2 slices of orange
2 slices of lime

Place all the ingredients except the garnishes in mixer and shake, making sure frozen orange concentrate is dissolved. Pour into chilled glasses and serve with slices of orange and lime for garnish.

Yield: 2 servings

Hot Chili Peppers on a Scale of Zero to Ten

Chili peppers are an ancient crop in Latin America and the Caribbean, dating back to about 6000 B.C.E. They have been cultivated in what is now New Mexico for at least 500 years.

In 1912, Wilbur Scoville, a chemist at Parke-Davis pharmaceutical company, designed a test to find the intensity of the capsaicin, or "burning property," of chili peppers, by extracting the element and mixing it with sugar water, in parts per million. He had a panel of tasters report their reactions, and as a result the Scoville Scale became a popular rating system. A sweet (or bell) pepper is at zero Scoville units, and a habañero is at 300,000 units. It works with exactitude in a laboratory, but it indicates the relative heat of peppers in the marketplace. There are other variables. If you remove the seeds and/or the white membranes, you cut the severity of the heat dramatically. Capsaicin is distributed unevenly through single peppers and groups of them. The 0 to 10 scale here is merely comparative.

There are no health risks to eating chili peppers. That being said, the capsaicin can cause blisters if eaten indiscriminately. Science has shown that they do not produce either ulcers or hemorrhoids and, in fact, are beneficial. Hot or sweet peppers have a high vitamin C content and some beta carotene. Used in generous amounts in chicken soup, the capsaicin enhances the soup as a cold reliever. It is a decongestant as well, and is an ingredient in "Fisherman's Friend," an old-time throat lozenge. Capsaicin is also an anticoagulant, and studies are being done to see if it has any place in controlling hypertension. Some people take cayenne tablets under supervision. Capsaicin is also used to desensitize sore mouths, and it will relieve certain types of headaches. Often, eating chili peppers will stimulate the appetite—the reason generally given is that they release endorphins that create a slightly euphoric feeling. Should you eat a hot pepper that is too hot for you, bread, rice, yogurt, or milk are the best coolers, as they will absorb and neutralize the oil somewhat.

Experiment not only with heat factors but essential flavors. If you blend various peppers, you will get a resonance that may be hot at first and then quickly dissipate. It is popular now to prepare chili peppers while wearing rubber gloves. Most chefs do not, because they wash their hands frequently and would not think of rubbing their eyes or other sensitive areas after handling chilies. If you want to take this extra precaution use disposable gloves and discard them after you have finished handling the hot chilies.

aji Though there are hundreds of varieties, the most common is *aji amarillo.* So named because it is yellow at some point in its growth. It is orange or red when ripe and three to five inches long. It is originally from Peru and is one of the oldest known chilies to flavor Andean dishes. Pictures of it appear in ancient jewelry and pottery. (9)*

ancho-poblano This green, broad, heart-shaped chili looks like a miniature bell pepper. Fresh, it is often used to make *chile rellenos* (stuffed chilies). It comes from Puebla in Mexico. The dried form is called *ancho* and is sold dried, whole, or powdered. (3)

cascabel or cherry pepper A small, round pepper, often pickled or dried. (3)

cayenne A straight to slightly curved, pinkie-shaped pepper, about three

---

*Numbers in parentheses indicate heat level—zero being the mildest.

inches long. It is wrinkled and red. Today, most *cayenne* is grown in Africa and Asia, but it is also cultivated in Louisiana. Commonly sold in powdered form to heat up sauces, it is also available pickled. (8)

chilaca/pasilla A dark, black-red chili pepper from Latin America, it is about seven inches long and usually sold dried and whole. Generally it is called *chilaca* when fresh and *pasilla* when dried, though over time the names have come to be used interchangeably. It is most often used in *mole* dishes, and to blend with other hotter chilies to give a subtle flavor. (2)

chimayo This is a North-American chili, named for a town in New Mexico. Picked when it is green and fresh, it is used extensively for salsas. Dried, it is very popular for chili-powder mixes. Because of their six to eight inch size, they are used to make the beautiful *ristras* (dried chili pepper wreaths) seen in the Southwest. (4)

guero Sometimes called the California green pepper because it grows there in abundance. It can be as large as three inches in diameter and four inches long. It is tapered, and the color is a variegated yellow-yellow green. A mild chili, it is mainly used fresh. (2)

habañero This is a small, round pepper about two-and-one-half inches in diameter. It is brightly colored yellow, orange, or vermilion and grows mainly in the Yucatan and the Caribbean. It has a slightly fruity taste. (10)

hontaka A small, red chili developed in Japan and used in Japanese dishes. Usually sold whole and dried. (5)

Hungarian yellow wax pepper A long, narrow pepper, it often grows to five inches although it is less than one inch in diameter. It is orange-red when ripe and is usually used fresh. (2–6)

jalapeño/chipotle A smooth green chili, it is often minced fresh and used as a condiment. They are also sold pickled or preserved in cans. In this form, they are used to flavor and garnish everything from tacos to pizza. (5) When *jalapeños* are dried and smoked they are called *chipotle*. It is a dark, puckered-looking chili that is tapered and twisted. It is usually sold whole in Latin-American markets, and it is used most often whole to flavor sauces and long-cooking dishes, and is removed before eating. (7)

mulato A dark, smoky-tasting chili grown in Latin America. It is about four inches long and only used dried. (4)

pequin/tepin A shiny-red, oval chili, about one-half inch long and quite thin. The smallest of the commercially available chilies, they are often bottled in vinegar and used as a condiment. Dried, they are used in very hot dishes. Because of their small size, these are often grown in small pots in home kitchens. (8.5)

rocotillo Shaped like a miniature inch-diameter pattipan squash, it is pale green or red with brown to black seeds. It originated in the Andes and was a staple, but now it is grown throughout Central America. (5)

Scotch bonnet Similar to the habañero, it looks like a crushed beret. It grows in the Caribbean. (8)

serrano A savory, small, bright-green chili that is not only hot, but has a distinctive savory taste. It grows in Mexico and the American Southwest. (6)

sweet green, red, or yellow peppers Sometimes called *bell peppers* and, in some regions mango peppers, these have no heat at all, and will impart a slightly citrusy taste to foods when cooked. Raw, they taste anywhere from actually sweet to tart. Usually, the yellow are the sweetest and the darkest green the tartest. (0)

Thai chili pepper A small, green or red chili that is a little thicker than a toothpick. Grown in Southeast Asia and California, it is often set on the table as a condiment. (2)

tabasco A small, red pod (one to one-and-one-half inches long), it is famous for being the chili that John McIlhenny brought from Mexico to his salt-rich island. It was there that he started making the tabasco infusion that bears his name, and bottling it in his wife's discarded perfume bottles. (9)

Latin America—Glossary

(*Please note*: Some of these are general terms and will vary in different localities. The vocabulary for Brazil is primarily Portuguese and is included in that section, as well as in the description of the food of Brazil.)

Polite Phrases and Useful Terms

¿Que recomienda hoy?   What do you recommend today?

Es muy bueno.   It's very good.

Saludos al cucinero.   Compliments to the chef.

Por favor.   Please.

Gracias.   Thank you.

Dining Phrases and Terms

restaurante restaurant

picanteria restaurant (Peru)

comida meal

desayuno breakfast

almuerzo lunch

antojito appetizer (a "little whim")

merienda snack

cena supper

cocina kitchen

la carte menu

cuchillo knife

tenedor fork

cuchera spoon

cucharita coffee spoon

servilleta napkin

platillo plate

la cuenta the bill

propina tip

The Food

aceitunas olives

adobo, adobado sauce of chilies, herbs, and vinegar

agrio sour

agua water

aguacate avocado

agua mineral mineral water

ajo garlic

ajonjoli sesame seeds

albóndigas meatballs

alcachofas artichokes

almejas clams

almendras almonds

annato (or *achiote*) crushed seeds of the annato tree

arroz rice

asado grilled

bacalao dried cod

berenjena eggplant

budin pudding

buñuelo fritter

calabacita zucchini

calabaza pumpkin

caldo broth

camarones shrimp

camote sweet potato, yam

carne meat

carnero lamb

cazuela earthenware casserole

cebolla onion

cebiche fish marinated in citrus juice

chayote bland pearlike squash

chiles en nogada stuffed peppers with fruit, nuts, walnut sauce, and pomegranate seeds

chimayo custard apple

chorizo spicy sausage

cilantro fresh coriander

clavos cloves

coco coconut

col cabbage

cumino cumin

dulce sweet

durazno peach

elote fresh corn on the cob

enchilada filled tortilla with sauce

ensalada salad

epazote aromatic herb (goosefoot)

escabeche pickle

estofado stew

flan caramel custard

frambuesas raspberries

fresas   strawberries

frito   fried

garbanzo   chick-pea

granada   pomegranate

higado   liver

higos   figs

hongos   mushrooms

huachinango   red snapper

huevos   eggs

huevos rancheros   ranch-style eggs, served on tortillas with spicy sauce and various toppings

huitlacoche   corn fungus, similar in use to black truffles

jicama   crisp root, used in salads, tastes similar to a water chestnut

langosta   lobster

leche   milk

lenguado   flounder

manzana   apple

membrillo   quince (usually the pulp is sweetened and sold in squares)

menudo   tripe soup or stew

molé poblano   turkey (usually) in a spicy sauce made with chocolate

naranjo   orange

nogada   walnut sauce

nopal   padded leaf of the opuntia cactus, used in sweet or savory dishes

ostiones   oysters

pan   bread

panela   blocks of brown sugar

papa   potato

pastel   cake

pato   duck

pavo   turkey

pechuga   chicken breast

pepita   pumpkin seed

pescado   fish

pimientas   peppercorns

pimiento   sweet pepper

piña   pineapple

piñones   pine nuts

plátano   banana

plátano macho   plantain

plátano relleno   stuffed plantain

poblana   green chili

pozole   a special form of hominy

puerco, cerdo   pork

quesadilla   rolled tortilla

queso   cheese

relleno   stuffing or stuffed

salsa   sauce

sandia   watermelon

sopa   soup

sorbete   sorbet

taco   soft hot or fried tortilla rolled around a filling, usually served with sauce

tamal   cornmeal mush

tamales   cornmeal dumpling, plain or with a sweet or savory filling, wrapped in a corn or plantain leaf and steamed

tortilla   flat, unleavened bread made of ground corn flour (sometimes wheat flour is used)

tostada   tortilla fried flat and topped with refried beans, chicken, lettuce, tomato, cheese, chilies, and sour cream

uva   grape

yucca   a small, sweet cassava or manioc

2

EUROPE

France

Most of us have grown up thinking of French food as Parisian *haute cuisine*. On my first trip to France, I was amazed to find out that the French ate what we think of as normal food. It might be comforting to know that the word restaurant is derived from the word *restauratif*—a restorer or refresher. After the 1939 World's Fair in New York closed, many of the working-class French bistros and cafes that had opened near the Hudson River docks on the west side of Manhattan stayed open. As more and more people found their way to them, the word got back to France and several chefs and restaurateurs opened Parisian-style French restaurants in New York, and the rest is history. Places like Le Cirque and Lutece became icons.

The cooking of France has been the benchmark for culinary excellence for so long that people tend to measure other cuisines by the French model. Though the haute cuisine of Paris has been developing for centuries, the regional food is now acknowledged as microcuisines that are rich in flavor and history.

The *crêpes* of Brittany are well known, but this region, on the Atlantic Ocean, is a source of many seafood and shellfish dishes. One of the most interesting is *cotriade*, an eel stew. Strawberries are abundant and often served with the local Muscadet wine.

From the menu of

Provence

38 MacDougal Street
New York, NY 10002

Pissaladière
Provencal onion and anchovy tart

Moules Gratinee Catalane
Gratin of mussel with almonds and garlic

Petits Farcis de Provence
Stuffed and baked baby vegetables

Brandade de Morue
Salt cod, potato, garlic, olive oil gratinee

Pate du Chef
Homemade pate with cured vinegar fruits

Ravioles d'Escargots
Ravioli stuffed with snails, herbs, garlic, olive oil sauce

Soupe de Poissons
Provencal fish soup garnished with gruyere and rouille

Rougets St. Tropez
Broiled filet of red mullet with ratatouille sauce

Morue en Tapenade
Olive crusted cod fish

Bourride Setoise
Poached fish in a aioli thickened broth

Aioli Arlésien
Steamed vegetables garnished with cod, mussels and garlic mayonnaise

Assiette Vegetarienne
Roasted and grilled vegetables with aioli or herb emulsion

Tian d'agneau Ratatouille
Pan roasted lamb and ratatouille

Poussin Rôti aux gousses d'ail en chemise
Roasted baby chicken with whole garlic cloves

Civet Capin
Red wine braised rabbit stew with soft polenta

Steak Frites
Grilled steak with french fries

Desserts

Tarte Maison
Fruit tart of the day

Marquise au chocolat
Chocolate terrine with coffee cream anglaise

Creme Brulee Catalane
Light custard under burnt sugar crust

Sorbets arrosees
Different fruit sorbets with its corresponding eau de vie

Bordeaux is found on the menu primarily for its exquisite wines. The Medocs, St. Émilions, Margaux, and Pomerols are unequaled. For dessert wines, the Château d'Yquem Sauternes are a treat. The sauce Bordelaise is a specialty, often served over small *entrecôte* grilled over vine twigs. The forest *cêpes* are eaten fresh and sold dried, in which form they maintain their woodsy scent.

The wine-infused dishes of Burgundy are familiar to us, and all home cooks have a recipe for *boeuf bourguignonne*● in their repertory. The classic platter of *escargot* roasted in garlic butter is a traditional first course throughout the region. The Dijon mustard of Burgundy is on a shelf in every supermarket and *cassis*, the fragrant black currant liqueur, in every cabinet.

Dishes served Lyonnaise are found on many menus and generally indicate the presence of onions and/or vinegar, served with hearty fare such as sausage and potatoes. *Beaujolais* and *Gamay* are the wines of Lyon.

The Germanic influence in the cooking of Alsace-Lorraine produced the famous *pâté de foie gras*, and the original *quiche lorraine*,● a savory, creamy melt-in-your-mouth custard tart with bits of bacon or ham. *Faisan* (pheasant) *à la choucroute* is the best of both worlds, as are both the cherry soup and the beer soup.

Normandy is an apple-growing region and produces Calvados, a rich apple brandy, drunk after dinner and used in many dishes, most notably *tripes à la mode de Caen*. The sweet butter of Normandy is valued everywhere.

The aromatic herb-and-olive-oil-based food of Provence is a blend of Mediterranean and French at its best. *Bouillabaisse* is probably the most celebrated dish of Provence. This saffron-infused fish-and-shellfish extravaganza is much prized and takes careful preparation so that each morsel is cooked to tenderness. *Ratatouille* is a baked, aromatic, vegetable dish that incorporates the produce of the area. There are various *tapenades*, savory spreads and purees that include olives and garlic and *aioli*,● a garlic mayonnaise. The blend of herbs known as *herbes de* Provence is the best combination of dried herbs available to the home cook. Herb teas, now so much in favor, reach aromatic heights in the tisanes of Provence. Camomile, elderflower, lemon balm, lime, mint, raspberry leaf, sage, verbena, and wild thyme from hills and field are used to make infusions that are world famous. *Chateauneuf du Pape* is the regional wine.

The Pyrenees and Gascony border on Spain and share some similar dishes with that country. The *piperade Basquaise* is closer to what we think of as a Spanish omelet than the Spanish one, which is traditionally made of potatoes and eggs. The honey of the Pyrenees is varied and much valued for baking.

Savoy, in the northeast, borders Switzerland and Germany, and favors some heavy Alpine dishes cooked with cabbage, either as an accompaniment or stuffed into the rolled leaves or hollowed head. There are also fondues, both sweet and savory, and desserts and candies made from the honey of Alpine bees.

Tournedos

Tournedos with Béarnaise Sauce

Sauce:

1/4 cup white-wine vinegar
1/4 cup white wine
2 tablespoons chopped, fresh tarragon or 2 teaspoons dried
1 tablespoon minced shallots
3 egg yolks
1/2 cup sweet butter

Toast:

3 tablespoons unsalted butter, cut into small pieces
6 slices of fresh white bread, crusts trimmed

Tournedos:

2½ pounds fine-quality beef filet, 6 slices 3/4- to 1-inch thick
salt and pepper to taste
watercress for garnish

In a small, heavy-bottomed saucepan, combine the vinegar, wine, and half the tarragon. Bring just to boiling point, lower heat, and cook to reduce by half, about 10 minutes. Pour into the top of a double boiler set over barely simmering—not boiling—water and whisk in the egg yolks one at a time. Add the butter bit by bit, whisking continuously. Add the remaining tarragon and cover the pan. Add cold water to the bottom pan of the double boiler to bring it to lukewarm. Set aside.

Trim the bread to match the round shape of the steaks. In a skillet large enough to hold the bread in one layer, melt the butter, and brown the toast on both sides. Add the remaining butter and sear the tournedos. Cook them 4 to 5 minutes per side. Salt and pepper to taste. Place each on a toast round and serve on a warm platter or individual plates, garnished with watercress. Pass with warm *béarnaise* sauce.

Yield: 6 servings

Beef Burgundy (Boeuf Bourguignonne)

3 pounds boneless beef chuck cut in 1½-inch cubes
2 tablespoons olive oil
4 tablespoons cognac
6 slices bacon cut into 1-inch pieces
1 medium onion, diced
1 carrot, thinly sliced
2 cloves garlic, crushed
4 tablespoons olive oil
1 pound pearl onions, peeled
1 pound white mushrooms
3 cups Burgundy (other red wine may be substituted)
1 tablespoon bouquet garni (thyme, bayleaf, parsley)
1/2 teaspoon freshly ground black pepper
salt to taste
2 tablespoons chopped fresh parsley leaves

In a skillet, over a medium-high flame, brown the beef in the oil. Turn off the flame, pour the cognac over the beef, and ignite. Let it burn out and remove the meat to a heavy, covered, flameproof casserole or dutch oven large enough to hold all the ingredients, and set aside. Brown the bacon in the skillet and add the sliced onion, carrot, and garlic. Brown the vegetables and add to the meat. In the skillet, add the remaining oil and brown the mushrooms and pearl onions. Add them to the meat in the casserole, then add the wine, herbs, and seasonings. Cover securely and bring to a boil. Lower heat and simmer slowly for 2 or more hours. This is best done the day before serving. Refrigerate overnight. Heat in a covered casserole at 375° for 1 hour before serving and garnish with fresh chopped parsley.

Yield: 8 servings

Garlic Mayonnaise (Aioli)

16 cloves garlic, minced
2 egg yolks*
salt and pepper to taste
2 cups olive oil
juice of 2 medium lemons
up to 1 tablespoon water

Though this is traditionally made with a mortar and pestle, it can be done successfully in a food processor. Start with the garlic, egg yolks, salt, and pepper and pulse till smooth. With the motor running, add the oil in a thin stream. Do this very slowly to start, and, as it begins to thicken, it can be poured a bit more steadily. Add the lemon juice and water if necessary. Taste the mixture and adjust it to your liking.

Yield: 8 servings

Quiche Lorraine

1/2 pound bacon, best quality
1 baked savory 9-inch pie or tart shell
3 ounces shredded Gruyère cheese
3 eggs, lightly beaten
1½ cups cream
salt and white pepper to taste
1 whole nutmeg

Preheat oven to 375°.

Cook the bacon in a skillet until cooked but not overly crisp. Drain the bacon and crumble it over the pie shell. Add the shredded cheese. Whisk the eggs and cream together with the salt and pepper, and pour over the bacon and cheese. Grate the nutmeg over all. Bake for 30 minutes or until cake tester comes out clean. Serve warm or at room temperature.

Yield: one 9-inch quiche

Please note: The use of uncooked egg yolks has come under question. Make sure the eggs are fresh and from a reliable source. When in doubt, don't use them.

Strawberry Tart

France—Glossary

Some Polite Words and Phrases

Je voudrais.   I'd like.

Pouvons nous avoir?   Could we have?

S'il vous plait.   Please.

Merci.   Thank you.

Merci beaucoup.   Thank you very much.

Oui, s'il vous plait.   Yes, please.

Non, merci.   No, thank you.

De rien.   You're welcome.

Il n'y a pas de quoi.   It's nothing.

Bien.   Fine.

Je comprends.   I understand.

Je ne comprends pas.   I don't understand.

At the Table

une serviette   a napkin

une assiette   a plate

une cuiller   a spoon

un verre   a glass

un couteau   a knife

une entrée   an appetizer

soupe   soup

legumes   vegetables

crudités   raw vegetables

hors d'oeuvre varies   assorted appetizers

pâté   liver purée

salade   mixed green salad

salade Niçoise   composed salad that includes, tuna, potatoes, capers, olives, and anchovies

bisque   smooth cream soup

bouillon   clear broth

crème d'   cream of

potage   a hearty soup

crevettes   shrimp

homard   lobster

huitres   oysters

alourdes   clams

saumon   salmon

thon   tuna

truite   trout

coquilles St. Jacques   gratin of scallops served baked in a scallop shell

bourride   fish chowder

charcuterie   assorted sausages and cold cuts

boeuf   beef

agneau   lamb

porc   pork

veau   veal

steak frites   beefsteak and french-fried potatoes

chateaubriand   filet of porterhouse

entrecôte   filet of rib steak

tournedos   filet of T-bone

boeuf bourguignonne   pan-roasted beef in Burgundy wine

cassoulet   casserole made with, goose, beans, and salt pork *ragout*   stew

ratatouille   fragrant vegetable stew served warm or cold

coq au vin   chicken stewed in red wine

oie   goose

poulet   chicken

suprême   chicken breast

poussin   spring chicken

canard   duck

croque-monsieur   batter-dipped, toasted, ham-and-cheese sandwich

fondue   hot cheese melted with wine and seasoning, served with fresh bread that is dipped into the mixture with a long fork

quenelles   small, light, poached dumplings often made from fish

artichaut   artichoke

asperges   asparagus

aubergine   eggplant

cepes   variety of mushroom

champignons   mushrooms

chou   cabbage

choucrout   sauerkraut

chou-fleur   cauliflower

courgette   zucchini

cresson   watercress

epinard   spinach

haricots verts   small string beans

laitue   lettuce

mais   corn

navets   turnips

oignons   onions

petits pois   small green peas

pommes   potatoes

potiron   pumpkin

radis   radish

tomates   tomatoes

cornichons   tiny pickles

nouilles   noodles

riz   rice

Cooking Methods

bouilli   boiled

braisé   braised

cuit au four   baked

en chemise   baked in parchment or foil

a l'etouffèe   stewed

frit   fried

grillé   grilled

mariné   marinated

poché   poached

rôti   roasted

sauté   sautéed

fumé   smoked

cuit a la vapeur   steamed

Sauces

aioli   garlic mayonnaise

amandine   with almonds

américaine   sauce for shellfish made from shells and tomatoes

au jus   with pan juices

aurora   tomato cream sauce

ballottine   boneless meat or poultry, stuffed and rolled, then sliced

béarnaise   a classic sauce of butter, wine, shallots, and tarragon

bechamel   standard white sauce

beurre blanc   butter, shallots, vinegar, wine

bordelaise   sauce with mushrooms, Burgundy wine, and beef marrow

bourguignonne   made with Burgundy wine and herbs

breton   with white beans

champenoise   made with champagne

diable   spicy sauce with cayenne

en papiotte   portion of food baked in parchment or foil

farci   stuffed

financiere   Madeira wine, truffles, olives, mushrooms

fines herbes   delicate aromatic mix of fresh or dried herbs

florentine   with spinach

gratin   baked dish with a crisp cheese or crumb crust

hollandaise   butter-and-egg sauce with fresh lemon

indienne   using curry

jardiniere   a dish garnished with fresh slivers of vegetables

lyonnaise   sauce with onions and vinegar

meuniére   brown butter, parsley, lemon juice

milannaise   a scallop of meat or chicken coated in bread crumbs and cheese, and sautéed

mornay   a white sauce with cheese added

mousseline   a puree incorporating beaten egg white or cream, or both

moutarde   mustard sauce

normande   sweet or savory dish cooked with apples

perigourdine   with *foie gras* and/or truffles

poivre   peppercorns, generally black

provençale   Mediterranean, often with olive oil and garlic

remoulade   mayonnaise with mustard and herbs

tartare   mayonnaise with gherkins, capers, olives

veronique   with grapes

verte   mayonnaise with pureed greens such as spinach or watercress

vinaigrette   vinegar dressing usually made with olive oil

Spain

By the late sixteenth century, under Philip II, the Iberian nations had developed outposts in the Caribbean, South America, Mexico, southern Italy, India, and Malaysia, through the exploration of Spanish and Portuguese navigators. As a result, port cities and the new capital, Madrid, became filled with small restaurants to accommodate travellers. There were more places to eat out than in any other Western city, and dining out became the thing to do. Food was touched with international elements that combined vegetables and fruit from the New World and the rice and spices of the old. Spanish cuisine may be the most underrated in all of Europe. I lived there for a year and didn't come close to sampling all the varieties. Luckily, there are so many Spanish restaurants in North America that it is possible to explore the rich and varied possibilities.

Spanish flavorings utilize the green herbs of each region, such as rosemary, thyme, oregano, and cilantro, as well as chilies, fennel, and cloves; but the distinctive taste is that of saffron and *pimenton*, a sweet or savory paprika. Garlic, pine nuts, and parsley are used as they are throughout the Mediterranean.

First-time visitors to Galicia are surprised to find reminders of the Celts' passage through the area in the occasional dressup of kilts and knee socks, the playing of bagpipes, and the making and eating of oniony meat and fish pies called *empanadas gallegas*, which are similar to pasties. Cornbread is popular here as well as in Asturias.

The Basque country specializes in rustic, flavorful fish and seafood. *Bacalao pil-pil* is the famous salt-cod dish that is the model for all others. Lamb is also popular. Dishes are often served *con salsa piparrada*, an herbed mixture of tomatoes, onions, and peppers, cooked with Spanish olive oil and vinegar. A spring specialty is *minestra de legumbres*, a stew of baby vegetables with bits of smoked ham.

Cataluña, the region in which Catalan is spoken, includes Barcelona, which has arguably the most fabulous *tapas*.❦ *Zarzuela de mariscos* is a seafood stew made with white wine. *Olla podrida* is the regional pork stew, and from La Mancha comes *pisto manchego*, a vegetable dish served with smoked ham and poached eggs.

From the southeast the most famous dish is *paella*; each town and village makes a variety of combinations. It is called *Paella a la Valenciana* on most American menus, because that is where rice, a major component of the dish, grows abundantly. In Barcelona, *arroz con pollo* with saffron rice, chorizo, and clams, and *zarzuelas*, mixed seafood soups in vegetable broth accented with sherry, are popular.

The eastern part of Spain, which most retains the Moorish influence, is rich in citrus fruit with which many dishes are cooked.

From Andalucia come the most famous of the red-tomato-and-pepper gazpachos, as well as the simple white ones made of Spanish olive oil and vinegar, garlic, and almonds. Sometimes bread and peeled grapes are added. Castile is the region of the capital, Madrid. As with most capitals, it has not only national but international flavors. The *cocido madrileño* is a chick-pea stew made with meat and vegetables but, by and large, meat and fish are served roasted or grilled and served with quickly cooked vegetables, salads, and 50 kinds of potato dishes. Dessert is often fruit or flan, and an occasional sweet.

For the most part, pastries are reserved for lunch, *la comida*, or a late-afternoon *merienda*, snack. Generally an early coffee or hot chocolate is accompanied by bread and honey or marmalade, or the ubiquitous *churros*, fried sweet batons. The *almuerzo*, brunch, is the time for a true Spanish omelet, which consists of delicately fried potato slices over which lightly beaten eggs are cooked, like a *tortilla*. Cooked in fine Spanish olive oil with thin slices of earthy potatoes, this simple dish is memorable. *Tapas*, though they can be served at any time, are available almost everywhere between 6 and 10 in the evening.

People drink what they please, and hard and soft drinks are abundant, but the traditional accompaniment for these little dishes is dry sherry. Grapes from Jerez are used for sherry; they are fermented and blended by an old method called *solera*. The dry finos, of which *manzanilla* is a favorite, are usually served with savories. The medium sweet *oloroso* is served with dessert.

Amontillado, which has a higher alcohol content, is frequently served as either an aperitif or after-dinner drink. The Riojas are the best-known wines, and there are excellent ones both red and white. There are many outstanding regional wines that are becoming more available in the United States; many restaurants and liquor stores are developing fine Spanish cellars. Sangria, a punch, is going out of favor, but when made with fresh citrus juice, fresh fruit, good-quality wine, mineral water, and a touch of brandy or liqueur, it is a pleasant summer drink.

In New York, at Solera, a restaurant in the East 50's, Chef Dominick Cerrone has created both a *tapas* and regular service menu that reflects the best in Spanish cooking. One of the nice things about a *tapas* bar is that even though the time to eat them in Spain is a couple of hours before a late lunch or dinner, they are served from noon to midnight so that one can have them as lunch or dinner at any time.

The thirty or so *tapas* plates that are available at Solera represent only a small portion of the several hundred that are in the chef's repertory. Only in the largest of bars in big Spanish cities will one find available one hundred varieties at a time. The small dishes range from almonds and olives, cold Spanish *tortillas* (potato omelet), garlic shrimp or *calamares*, oysters and ham, or *escalivada*, aromatic roasted vegetables potted in a terrine, or wild mushrooms and snails. There might be a *cazuela* with *chorizo* sausage and beans, *calamari gabardina* (in

From the menu of

Solera

216 East 53rd Street
New York, NY 10022

Cold Appetizers

Organic Greens & Herbs
Serrano style ham and grilled country bread with tomato

Warm Scallop Slices
With saffron oil, celeriac-fennel salad

House Smoked Salmon Tart
With creamed leeks, roe, chive and couscous dressing

Fishers Island Oysters on the Half Shell

Country Style Terrine
With game meats

Hot Appetizers

Spicy Fried Calamares
With chili ali-oli

Garlic Shrimp
With lemon, ginger and parsley

Red Peppers Stuffed
With eggplant and goat cheese, parsley-toasted cumin sauce

Manila Clams Stewed
With albarino wine and fresh cranberry beans

Casserole of Braised Duck, Mushrooms and Chorizo
Topped with potato-foie gras puree

Roasted Seasonal Vegetables
With hazelnut oil and orange

Crab Brandada Layered
With avocado and tomato, fennel-mint vinagreta

Entrees

Grilled Salmon
With vegetables and condiments in a lemon-horseradish dressing

Steamed Cod
With mushrooms, spicy chickpeas and turnip greens
in a light ginger-soy bouillon

Poached Trout Stuffed
With Serrano ham, port wine bouillon with root vegetables

Red Snapper in a Saffron Burrida on a Compote of Scallion
With squid ink potato

Prime Lamb Chops
Over lentil piperade, braised stuffed cabbage

New Zealand Venison Loin in a Pepper-Juniper Reduction
Autumn fruit and vegetable preparations

Roasted Breast of Organic Duckling
With foie gras and a red wine pear sauce

From the menu of Solera (continued)

Paella Menu

Saffron Rice
With lobster, shrimp, scallop, squid, clams and mussels

Chicken-Chorizo-Vegetable Paella
With wild and brown rice

Desserts

Warm Apricot Mousse
With cranberries

Orange Flan
With candied squashes and pine nuts

Fondant of Green and Golden Apples
Spiced cider sauce

Macerated Melon and Pineapple
With a raspberry sauce

a shirt, with a spicy *ajo hervido*), or *brandada*, a mousse of salt cod and mushrooms. Small flavorful fried *croquetas* with different fillings; *boquerones*, which are marinated anchovies; or tiny fried eels in garlic, the favorite of gourmands who are willing to order in advance and pay a great deal for them, are well worth a try.

In addition to fabulous paellas, made either with a rich selection of seafood or vegetables in the traditional Valencian manner with imported solana or grana rice flavored with saffron, there are unique specialties such as *fabada*, a lamb-and-bean casserole or lamb served with *cabrales polenta* (*cabrales* is a fine Spanish blue cheese); or Basque-style lamb chops with lentil piperade. Chef Cerrone, whose roots are Italian, and who has also been a chef of French cuisine, understands the blending of Provençal and Italian food with the Spanish. In a from-scratch kitchen, he approaches the food with authenticity, experience, and enthusiasm. For dessert, there are flans such as the *crema Catalana* served with saffron-infused pineapple; or *majarete*, a Dominican-influenced corn-and-coconut custard with candied, diced red pepper and caramelized walnuts. There are always various fruit dishes that reflect the seasons.

In addition to the more than a dozen sherries available by the glass each day, there are fine ports and brandies, to be tasted individually or in a tasting offering.

The Balearic Islands, where I lived for a while in Ibiza, have the freshest fish, fruit, and vegetables anyone can hope for. Even our small garden was overgrown with artichokes, lemons, and pomegranates. Tomatoes, eggplants, and peppers grow like wildflowers. The *Ensaimada*❋ recipe that follows is an approximation of the ones served early in the morning across from the post office in Santa Eulalia on Ibiza.

Sweet Snail Rolls (Ensaimadas)

Courtesy Dominick Cerrone—Solera

Dough base:

   1 package dry yeast
   1 teaspoon sugar
   1/2 cup unbleached flour
   oil for greasing the bowl

Rolls:

   1 egg, slightly beaten
   pinch of salt
   1/4 cup sugar
   1½ cups unbleached flour
   2 tablespoons Spanish olive oil
   4 tablespoons melted, sweet butter
   powdered sugar for dusting

Dissolve the yeast in 1/4 cup warm water, add the sugar, and stir. Add the flour and knead until the flour is incorporated and forms a small ball. Slit the top with a sharp knife and place in a lightly oiled bowl. Cover and set aside. In a medium bowl mix 1/3 cup warm water with the slightly beaten egg, a pinch of salt, and the sugar. Add the flour and incorporate it. On a floured board, turn out both the yeasted-flour mixture and the flour-egg mixture. Knead the 2 together, gradually adding the oil. Knead until smooth. Let rest for 15 minutes.

Divide the dough into 10 equal pieces. Roll each piece into a rope 1/2" wide. On an unfloured surface, using a rolling pin, roll each piece into a 3-inch length about 2-inches wide. Brush with melted butter and roll tightly. Cut each rope in half to make 20 pieces. Take each piece and curl into a flat spiral. Pinch the outer edge under the "snail" to seal it. Set them on a tray and cover with a large tea towel or pillowcase and let rise for 2½ hours or until more or less doubled. Brush the rolls with water and dust them with powdered sugar. Place them in a preheated 350° oven and bake for about 12 minutes. They should be cooked through but just lightly browned. Serve warm with additional powdered sugar.

Yield: 20 snails

Tapas (*Assorted Small Savory Dishes*)

Most *tapas* are served at room temperature. They may be served hot from the oven or grill but rarely are they cold. One of the favorite *tapas* is a dish of *angulas*, baby eels sautéed in Spanish olive oil, seasoned with garlic and red hot pepper flakes. They are difficult to find here and large eels, though eaten, are not a substitute.

Pork Meatballs (Albondigas)

Courtesy Dominick Cerrone—Solera

1/2 pound ground pork
6 tablespoons minced parsley
4 cloves garlic, minced
2 tablespoons minced onion
3 tablespoons fine bread crumbs
2 eggs, slightly beaten
salt and pepper to taste
flour for dusting
Spanish olive oil for frying

Combine the pork, parsley, garlic, onion, bread crumbs, 1/2 the beaten egg, salt, and pepper. Form into 20 to 24 small meatballs. Dip in beaten egg and roll in flour. In a skillet that will hold all the meatballs in a single layer, pour the oil to a depth of about 1/4 inch and heat until slightly smoking. Add the meatballs, turning constantly, so that they are brown on the outside and cooked thoroughly.

Yield: 20 small meatballs

Chorizo Sausage Cooked in Cider (Chorizo con Sidra)

3 tablespoons Spanish olive oil
1 small Spanish onion, diced
1/2 pound chorizo sausage in 1/2″ slices
2 Golden Delicious apples, cored and cut in 1″ cubes
1 cup hard apple cider (or 1 cup cider and 3 tablespoons cognac, optional)

Heat the oil in a skillet and sauté the onions until lightly browned. Add the chorizo and apples and sauté until the apples are browned on all sides.

Yield: 6 tapas servings

Cold Vegetable Soup (Gazpacho)

2 pounds ripe tomatoes, peeled and seeded
1 sweet green pepper, charred, peeled, and seeded
1 sweet red pepper, charred, peeled, and seeded
1/2 large Spanish onion, cut into small dice
2 small cucumbers, peeled and seeded
4 cloves garlic, crushed
1/3 cup Spanish sherry vinegar
1 teaspoon sugar
salt and pepper to taste
up to 1 ½ cups water
2 tablespoons parsley leaves, minced

Croutons:

3 tablespoons Spanish olive oil
1 garlic clove, crushed
4 slices rustic bread cut into 3/4-inch dice

Chop the tomatoes, peppers, onion, and cucumber, preferably with an old-fashioned single-bladed chopper and wooden bowl. In a smaller bowl add the crushed garlic, removing any fibrous parts. Mix with vinegar and sugar. Add to the tomato mixture salt and pepper to taste. Stir in the water (if necessary add up to 1 ½ cups water). Mix in the parsley.

   To make the croutons, heat the oil in a skillet. Add the garlic and fry the bread cubes on all sides. Drain and add to the gazpacho.

Yield: 6 servings

Squid in Sherry (Calamare al Jerez)

2 pounds squid, cleaned and sliced
3 tablespoons Spanish olive oil
1 medium onion, diced
3 cloves garlic, minced
1/2 cup blanched almonds
pinch of saffron
1/2 cup dry sherry
2 tablespoons minced parsley leaves
salt and pepper to taste

Dry the squid and reserve. Heat the oil in a nonreactive pan with a cover, large enough to hold all ingredients. Lightly brown the onion, garlic, and almonds. Remove from the heat and place in a blender or processor with the saffron and sherry. Rewarm the oil in the pan and add the squid, stirring constantly. When the squid is coated with the oil add the blended ingredients and stir. Add the parsley, salt, and pepper to taste. Cover and cook over medium heat for 30 minutes.

Yield: 6 servings

Chicken in Garlic Sauce (Pollo al Ajillo)

1 3-pound chicken, cut into 8 parts
5 tablespoons Spanish olive oil
2 heads garlic, peeled and separated into cloves
salt and pepper to taste
1/3 cup Spanish brandy

Dry chicken thoroughly. Heat the oil in a skillet large enough to hold the chicken in one layer. Add the chicken and brown, turning occasionally. Cook over medium high heat for about 15 minutes. Add the garlic, salt, and pepper and cook for another 15 minutes over medium heat. Carefully add the brandy and, even more carefully, ignite it and let it burn itself out. Make sure there are no towels, curtains, or potholders anywhere in or near the area. Cover and cook another 10 minutes. Place on warm platter or plates and serve immediately.

Yield: 6 servings

Pork Chops with Prunes (Chuletas de Cerdo con Ciruela Pasa)

3/4 cup red wine
3/4 cup water
1 teaspoon cinnamon
1/4 teaspoon cloves
1 tablespoon sugar
1/2 pound pitted prunes
4 medium-large lean pork chops
salt and pepper to taste
3 tablespoons Spanish olive oil
2 cloves garlic, minced

Heat the wine and water with the cinnamon, cloves, and sugar. Add the prunes and bring to a gentle boil. Lower heat and simmer for 10 minutes. Trim the chops of any fatty edges and season with salt and pepper. Heat the oil in a skillet and add the minced garlic. Stir to disperse the garlic evenly. Add the pork chops and brown, lower the flame, and cook the chops until well done, about 25 minutes. Test for doneness by slicing into one and making sure it is cooked through. With a slotted spoon, add the prunes to the skillet. Cook the prune/wine liquid down to half its volume, and pour over all. Serve immediately.

Yield: 4 servings

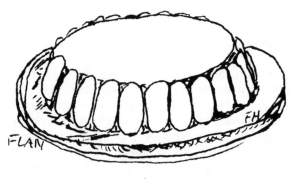

Flan

Caramel Custard (Flan)

Caramel:

10 tablespoons sugar
5 teaspoons water

Custard:

3 whole eggs
3 egg yolks
6 tablespoons sugar
2 cups milk
1/2 cup cream

Preheat oven to 350°.

Heat water and sugar in small skillet. When it is golden brown pour it into 6 individual custard cups.

Beat eggs and egg yolks together; add sugar, milk, and cream. Pour over the caramel mixture and place in metal baking dish or lasagna pan filled to half the height of the custard cups with hot water. Bake for 1 hour, or until knife or cake tester comes out clean. Remove, cool, and refrigerate. Invert onto dessert dishes to serve. It may be necessary to loosen the custard around the edges with a knife before inverting.

Yield: 6 servings

Germany

Though modern Germany was not established until 1871, the general region was a loosely held area of kingdoms, cities, villages, and towns. A Roman writer described the food as bread, wild game, berries, milk, and cheese. The Renaissance brought an influx of Italian and French manners and cuisine that became incorporated into the German culinary vocabulary.

Bordering the North Sea and the Baltic, the northern plains have developed fish dishes based on halibut, flounder, sole, and turbot.

Smoked eel and pickled herring are another mainstay. Ducks and geese are plentiful and are cooked and preserved in a variety of ways. This is also the region of barley, oats, rye, and hops. Beets, cabbages, cucumbers, and potatoes are farmed. There are also pig farms and many dishes include ham and bacon.

The most famous ham comes from Westphalia in central Germany. The capital of Westphalia is Dortmund, which produces the Dortmunder beer so praised everywhere.

The central district is primarily devoted to mining, industry, and farming. The hearty fare of this region reflects the needs of its citizens. *Pfefferpothast* is an aromatic thick stew of short ribs cooked with lots of chopped onions, celery, and carrots, seasoned with lemon, capers, cloves, bay laurel, and as much freshly ground black pepper as the cook determines. Usually served with potatoes and salad, beer accompanies it. The area is not big on sauce but the one Goethe favored is *Grüne Sosse*. This green sauce is made of a large medley of leaves in almost any combination. Borage, chervil, dill, parsley, savory, sorrel, and tarragon are minced or processed with oil and vinegar and a bit of salt, pepper, and sugar. The American hot dog derives from the *Frankfurter Würstchen*, which is made of beef and has a spicy tang. Dresdner stollen and streusel are local pastry favorites.

The southern part of Germany, through which flow the Danube, the Rhine, the Rhone, and the Mosel rivers, is a wine-growing area.

In Bavaria, the forests offer many kinds of wild mushrooms and berries that enhance dishes both fresh and air-dried, as well as fowl and game. Wursts are made in literally hundreds of combinations. The most well known here are *Knackwurst*, which is made of pork flavored with garlic; *Leberwurst*, a mild liver sausage; and the heavier *Bratwurst*, made of pork and veal and usually roasted with potatoes and onions. *Spätzle*, a type of noodle in various flavors, is a regional favorite, often used in place of potatoes. Tortillalike *pfannkuchen* are pan-sized flat omelets with bits of savories beaten in with the eggs.

Bavarian desserts are familiar to us: *Spekulatius*, spicy butter cookies especially popular at Christmas, and *Schwarzwälder Kirschtorte*, Black Forest chocolate cake filled with whipped cream and cherries, are from this area and are available not only at German *Konditorie*. Strudel is, of course, the best-known of all and comes with a great range of fillings and flavorings.

By and large, the German restaurants in America emphasize traditional German food. The *Vorspeisen*, appetizers in the form of smoked meat and fish and spicy salads, are recognizable in many delicatessens, as are the thick, rich soups and dark bread. *Bratens*, roasts, are best-known through sauerbraten, made sweet and sour. *Schnitzel* is a way of sautéing chops, usually veal.

Frühstück, breakfast; *Mittagessen*, lunch; *Kaffee*, a late afternoon break; and *Abendbrot*, dinner or, literally, evening bread, are the traditional meals. Contemporarily, the tradition of the large midday meal and a small evening one is being reversed and, now, in most places, it is more usual to have a light lunch and a fuller dinner. *Schnellküche* or fast-cooking is as popular in Germany as it is elsewhere, though the *Schön decken*, a nice table, is still appreciated.

Haussner's restaurant in Baltimore has an elaborate menu in an even more elaborate setting. The art collection alone is worth the trip. The extensive menu includes not only the various *wursts* and *schnitzels* but *Hasenpfeffer*, a marinated rabbit dish served with *spaetzle*, and *Kasseler Rippchen*, a smoked loin of pork served with sauerkraut.

Desserts are *Pflaumenkuchen*, *Apfelkuchen*, *Streuselkuchen*, or an assortment of torten. *Lebkuchen* are spiced honey cakes that are very popular. *Marzipan*, a ground almond paste, is made into decorative sculptured shapes that are tinted and given as gifts; the most famous ones come from Lübeck. Sweet or savory pretzels are another small treat.

Coffee is drunk far more than tea, and beer is certainly a favorite. The dark dunkels such as the bocks and the light *helles pilsners* are the most popular. *Berliner Weisse* is a local specialty, served with a splash of raspberry syrup. It is available in many German restaurants. The flowery white German Rhine wines and Mosels have gained popularity. *Schnapps* is not drunk very much in this country, but the aromatic *Kirschwasser* is used to flavor many desserts.

The Berghoff Restaurant in Chicago, which started as the Berghoff Beer Brewery in 1887 in Fort Wayne, Indiana, has been in business since 1898. Still using family recipes, the restaurant is thriving.

From the menu of

Berghoff

17 West Adams Street
Chicago, IL 60603

Classic Berghoff Favorites

Sauerbraten

With potato pancake or spaetzels and creamed spinach

Wiener Schnitzel

Breaded veal cutlet, German fried potatoes and
creamed spinach

Smoked Thuringer Sausage

With sauerkraut and boiled new potatoes

Geschnetzeltes

Veal with sauteed mushrooms in wine sauce.
Served with mashed potatoes

Boiled Brisket of Corned Beef

With new cabbage and boiled new potatoes

Bratwurst

With sauteed onions, sauerkraut and German fried potatoes

Boiled Pork Shank

With boiled new potatoes and sauerkraut

Roast Top Round of Beef au Jus

With mashed potatoes and tossed salad

Broiled Chopped Steak (8 oz.)

With french fried onion rings, choice of potato.
Served with tossed salad

German Pot Roast

Sirloin of beef. Served with mashed potatoes and
creamed spinach

Fried Calf's Liver

With sauteed onions and choice of potato and vegetable

Schlacht-Platte

Combination of Bratwurst, "Kasseler Rippchen"
(tender smoked pork loin), smoked thuringer
with sauerkraut and tossed salad

Rahm Schnitzel

Breaded pork cutlet with sauteed mushrooms in a wine sauce.
Served with spaetzels and fresh fruit compote

Roasted Young Tom Turkey

With dressing, cranberry sauce, mashed potatoes and
tossed salad

Sweet-and-Sour Beef Pot Roast (Sauerbraten)

4 tablespoons lard or vegetable oil
4 pounds boneless round roast
2 cups red wine
2 cups cider vinegar
2 tablespoons brown sugar
1 large onion, sliced paper thin
1 teaspoon crushed black pepper
4 bay leaves
1/2 cup raisins
1/2 cup gingersnap crumbs

Preheat oven to 350°.

On the top of the stove, in a casserole or Dutch oven large enough to hold all the ingredients, heat the lard or oil. Brown the roast on all sides. Remove the meat from the pan and set aside. Place all ingredients except the raisins and gingersnap crumbs into the casserole and bring to a boil. Return the meat to the pot, cover, and place in the oven for 2 hours. I prefer to do this part the day before serving and, at this point, let the sauerbraten cool and refrigerate it overnight. Either way, after removing the pot from the stove or refrigerator, remove the meat from the pan and set aside.

Discard bay leaves. Bring the sauce to a boil, lower heat, add raisins and gingersnaps, simmer for 1/2 hour. Slice the meat and return it to the pan until it is very hot. Serve on warm platter.

Yield: 8 servings

Potato Dumplings (Kartoffelklösse)

1/2 cup unbleached all-purpose flour
1/2 cup farina
1 tablespoon coarse salt
1/4 teaspoon nutmeg
1/4 teaspoon white pepper
3 eggs, slightly beaten
4 cups riced or mashed potatoes

Set a wide 5-quart pot of water to boil. Mix the flour, farina, and spices in a bowl. Alternately beat the eggs and flour mixture into the potatoes. Using about 2 tablespoons of the mixture, form about 20 dumplings. Drop into the boiling water, lower heat, and simmer for 15 minutes. Be careful that they don't stick together; gently separate them with a slotted spoon. When the dumplings rise to the top, remove them to a warm platter and serve with sauerbraten.

Yield: 20 *dumplings*

Red Cabbage with Apples (Rotkohl Mit Åpfeln)

3 tablespoons lard or vegetable oil
2 red onions, sliced
1 2-pound red cabbage cut as for slaw
2 Granny Smith or Golden Delicious apples, sliced thin
3/4 cup apple-cider vinegar
1/3 cup honey
1/2 cup raisins
1/8 teaspoon powdered cloves
salt and pepper to taste
1 cup boiling water

Heat the lard or oil in a skillet and stir in the onion. Sauté until it is transparent. Add the cabbage and cook until it is wilted. Stir in the apples and cook for 10 minutes. Add the remaining ingredients and mix well. Cook for another 10 minutes.

Yield: 8 *servings*

Potato Pancakes (Kartoffelpuffer)

6 medium baking potatoes
2 large eggs
1/4 cup finely grated onion
1/3 cup flour
1 teaspoon coarse salt
1/4 teaspoon ground white pepper
peanut oil for frying
2 cups applesauce

Preheat oven to 250°.

Peel uncut potatoes and place in large bowl of cold water. In a bowl large enough to hold all the ingredients, whisk the eggs and add the grated onion, flour, salt, and pepper. One at a time, dry the potatoes and grate them on the medium or coarse part of the grater. Dry them and squeeze out any extra moisture.

Incorporate the potatoes into the egg mixture. Heat 1/4 inch oil in a large skillet. Have an oven-proof platter or cookie sheet ready. Using about 1/2 cup of the potato mixture, drop it into the oil and immediately flatten gently with a spatula into a pancake. Fry for about 2 minutes and turn over. Fry another 2 or 3 minutes or until the pancake is dark brown. Remove to platter and place in warm oven as the rest are being cooked. Keep adding oil to the pan so that there is always a depth of 1/4 inch. Serve pancakes as hot as possible with applesauce.

Yield: 12 *pancakes*

Italy

It has been my pleasure to experience the widest possible array of Italian food. When I was a student at Columbia, I chose to live on Mulberry Street where every purveyor gave me recipes and history. I went on to live in Italy for a while, and never miss a chance to visit. Italian food, like the Italian language, is the most forgiving cuisine you can encounter. Substitutions are given a nod of approval.

There was a time in America when the cooking of Naples and Sicily was the Italian food available. Since early in this century, restaurants and groceries have sold Neapolitan-Companian food. Pizza, the best-known, biggest-selling fast-food item in America, is made with the ingredients of this region: tomatoes (brought to Italy in Columbus's time), onions, green peppers, anchovies, sausage, mushrooms, oregano, olive oil, and mozzarella. The cheese, made from water-buffalo milk, was once a homey staple, and is now a menu delicacy. Calzone are fried or baked turnovers, made from pizza dough, with a filling of mozzarella and other cheeses, sometimes with flecks of ham. Lasagna is made throughout Italy. In this region it is done with tomato and meat sauces and layers of soft cheese.

Antipasti vary, but usually include various cured sausages, roasted and pickled vegetables, fresh and smoked fish, olives, stuffed small peppers, and *caponata*, an eggplant salad.

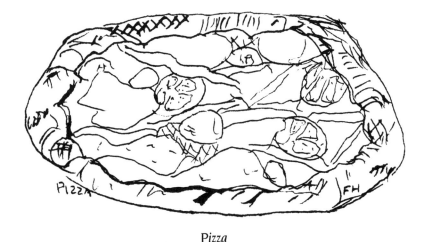

Pizza

The Arab influence in Sicily has produced the sweets Americans think of when they think of Italian pastry and dessert, such as cannoli, the crisp tubular pastry filled with sweetened cheese and dotted with candied fruit and pieces of chocolate. *Cassata siciliana* is an Italian version of a trifle: Sponge cake doused with liqueur is layered with ricotta mixed with candied fruit and chocolate bits and covered with chocolate icing.

Marsala wine is similar to sherry and can also be dry or sweet. It is used in cooking and can also serve as an aperitif or after-dinner drink.

The flavor palette is rich in basil, bay leaf, celery, cloves, fresh coriander, fennel, garlic, green pepper, lemon juice, marjoram, mint, oregano, parsley, peppercorns, rosemary, sage, tarragon, and thyme, with accents of olive oil, wine, and vinegar.

Everyday soups fall into two categories: *minestra*, thick soups dense with vegetables, legumes, and pasta; or *brodo*, clear soups with the addition of bits of meat or chicken and rice or pasta.

In Rome, the legacy of thousands of years continues in some rustic dishes. There are some specialty dishes that are served in the large Jewish community in Rome. *Carciofi alla guidea*, in which small artichokes are pressed flat to resemble flowers and fried, is a favorite and easy to make. These are served with lemon wedges and are a good change from the fried zucchini and calamari seen everywhere.

From the menu of

Botticelli Trattoria

7382 SW 56th Avenue
Miami, FL 33143

Antipasti/Appetizers

Antipasto Botticelli

Roasted peppers, fresh mozzarella, tomato, marinated
mushrooms, caponatina

Mozzarella Caprese

Vine-ripe tomatoes and bufala mozzarella drizzled with olive oil,
basil, balsamic vinegar

Caesar Salad

Romaine lettuce, homemade croutons, parmigiano, tossed with
our special caesar dressing

Carpaccio di Salmone

With fresh dill and a honey mustard sauce

Carpaccio di Manzo

Topped with virgin olive oil, shaved parmigiano and lemon

Insalata di Mare

Shrimp, calamari, mussels, bell peppers, red onion and celery over
watercress, in a lemon olive oil dressing

Mussels or Clams Posillipo

Plump mussels or clams steamed in a marinara sauce or white wine, garlic and herbs

Mozzarella in Carozza

Breaded mozzarella, lightly fried and topped with a red pepper cream sauce and a touch of anchovy

Calamari Fritti

Fresh, tender squid, lightly fried to a golden crisp, served with marinara sauce

Farinacci/Pasta

The following pastas, combined with your choice of sauce: spaghetti, linguini, fettuccini, capellini, penne, fusilli, tortellini, shells, gnocchi

Angelina

Fresh tomatoes, arugula, sundried tomatoes, garlic and olive oil

Apetitosa

Mild Italian sausage and mushrooms in a spicy marinara sauce

Bella Luana

Cream, porcini mushrooms and sundried tomatoes

Bolognese

Thick blend of marinated tomato sauce, ground beef, green peppers, garlic and onion

From the menu of Botticelli Trattoria (continued)

Pasta Ripiena/Stuffed Pasta

Meat Lasagna

This homemade version is lasagna noodles layered with meat
sauce, ricotta, mozzarella and herbs

The Vegetarian Lasagna

Lasagna noodles layered with vegetables, ricotta, mozzarella and
herbs in a light cream sauce

Risotto/Rice

Milanese

Grilled shrimp and a touch of saffron or marinara sauce

Porcini

Porcini mushrooms, parmigiano cheese and champagne sauce

Frutti di Mare

Calamari, shrimps and mussels in a marinara or white wine sauce

Nero

Risotto blended with squid ink and served with calamari or shrimp

Marjoram is abundant, but it is *basilico*, basil, that perfumes the hills of Liguria and is the main ingredient of pesto. That once local sauce is now an international favorite. The name *pesto*, comes from the wooden pestle used to crush the basil, olive oil, pecorino cheese, pine nuts, and garlic in a marble mortar. Spices from the East were only items of trade to merchant seafarers and not depleted for kitchen use, but the green herbs of the hills have been used forever to flavor the dishes of the region with rosemary and mountain thyme. Liguria, the Italian Riviera, is also alive with ancient olive trees, and olives and olive oil of excellence are produced there. A *panne alle olive*, olive bread, is delicious.

The fish and seafood of Genoa are second to none; lobsters, memorable mussels, eels, sea truffle (similar to a bumpy quahog), sardines, and anchovies are abundant. And of course, squid, sea bream, perch, mackerel, and mullet are all cooked simply or turned into soups and stews like *cioppa*, the model for San Francisco's cioppino.

Genoa's version of *fritto misto*, *bignè di pesci misti*, is mixed fish and seafood fried in a thick batter. *Cappon magro* (this is not capon) is a composed cold fish salad with lots of marinated vegetables and a green sauce, topped decoratively with seafood. Dried cod, used all over the world, is best prepared, in my opinion, in Genoa, where it is made with potatoes, tomatoes, olive oil, green olives, and pine nuts.

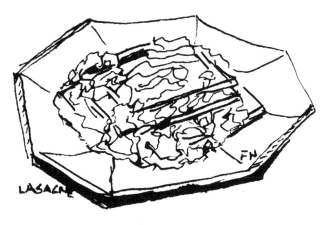

Lasagna

The unification of these diverse regions of Italy began in 1861 under King Victor Immanuel II, from Piedmont's house of Savoy. The Piedmontese say "Italy was born here." A favorite Piedmontese spice blend is bay laurel leaf, cinnamon, cloves, nutmeg, and white pepper, used in marinades with Barolo wine to flavor delicious beef stews. Local wine made of Nebbiolo grapes was praised by Julius Caesar while camping in the region during battles with the Gauls. It is now an expensive treat. The Nebbiolo grapes produce the fine red Barolos, as well as Barbaresco. Both Cinzano and Martini and Rossi are established here and use "secret" herbs to make vermouths used around the world. Turin is where the finest *grappa* is made from Barolo wine grapes.

Thomas Jefferson was so impressed with the region's wine that he brought grapestock to Virginia and hired a Piedmontese vintner. He also brought seeds for Piedmont rice, which he thought the best in Europe, to America. Both crops did well in Virginia.

When they are in season, white truffles are a regional favorite. Alba, in the Langhe Valley, is the most famous location for this delicacy. *Bollito misto*, mixed boiled meats, is a favorite and is served with *bagna cauda*, a hot sauce made from olive oil, garlic, anchovies, and butter.

In Tuscany, the pastas are delicate and the olives heavily aromatic. It is customary to find not only a bowl of olives, but a small saucer of rich, green olive oil on the table. It is expected that you will tear your bread into bite-sized pieces and dip them in the oil, perhaps add a sprinkle of salt, and nibble healthily and deliciously away. The Tuscan grapes produce not only world-class *Chiantis* but wonderful local wines that are appearing more and more on American shelves.

Cattle farming is an old tradition. Beef is cooked in many ways. In Florence, *Bistecca Fiorentina* and a local *Chianti* make for a simple dinner that can be found on the menus of many Italian restaurants in the United States.

Italian desserts have long been popular and are now found almost everywhere.

Tiramisu can now be found in American supermarkets. This lively dessert is based on sponge cake soaked in espress and layered with sweetened marscapone cheese and chocolate. *Pannettone* is no longer

RAVIOLI

Ravioli

relegated to Christmas, but is found all through the year. This light fruitcake makes delicious toast. *Gelato* is being sold everywhere as well: It most resembles American frozen custard and comes in a great variety of flavors. *Granitas* are coarse sorbets made with fresh fruit or espresso. A *cafe granita con panna*—a coffee ice served with fresh whipped cream—is a favorite summer evening snack.

I still have my stove top espresso maker from my year on Mulberry Street, though I use my Gaggia electric machine every morning. It is not without amusement that I have seen the proliferation of shops that sell *espresso, doppios, cappuccinos,* and madeup concoctions with Italian-sounding names. I think it's great. Espresso has less caffeine per cup and is easier to digest because of the steaming process than other kinds of coffee. Because it is so rich in flavor, one needn't drink tons of it.

Dessert liqueurs that are popular are *Sambucca,* an anise-flavored drink; *Amaretto,* almond-based; and the various *grappas,* from grape skins. The grappas are *aqua vitae;* the best are exquisite but astronomically expensive. *Vino Santo* is a light, sweet dessert wine from Tuscany.

From the Lombardy region come classic local dishes. *Risotto alla Milanese*⦾ is saffron-flavored arborio rice. *Osso buco* is an aromatic dish of veal shanks braised with onions, garlic, and mushrooms in wine, stock, shredded lemon peel, and a touch of tomato paste. It is served with rice and garnished with *gremolata*, a minced mixture of fresh parsley leaves, lemon zest, and a bit of garlic. The marrow of the veal shanks is regarded as a delicacy and is eaten with a marrow spoon or oyster fork. *Costoletta alla Milanese* is a veal chop that is similar to the *Schnitzel* of Austria but more delicate. *Zuppa pavese* is a clear broth served with an egg poached in it. Panettone is the delicious, light, yeasted fruitcake that is a Christmas favorite. *Bel Paese*, *Gorgonzola*, and *Taleggio* are the best-known cheeses of the region

Prosciutto, Parmesan cheese, and balsamic vinegar are the most famous food products of the Emilia-Romagna region. They are available now in all fifty states.

The chefs and home cooks of Bologna make endless varieties of risotto and gnocchi. It is possible to eat them in a different style every day of the month.

In Venice and the Veneto region, it is no surprise that fish is popular, but the ways in which it is cooked can be surprising. Venice is famous for *saor*, a somewhat sweet-and-sour flavor that is imparted to many dishes. A favorite dish is *Fegato ale Veneziana*, calves liver thinly sliced and sautéed with onions and sweet peppers in wine and vinegar, sometimes served with triangles of polenta.

Savory Grilled Tomato-Basil Bread (Bruschetta con Basilico Pomodoro)

1 pound ripe tomatoes, peeled, seeded, and cut in small dice
1/2 red onion, finely chopped
16 basil leaves, minced
1/3 cup red vermouth
2 tablespoons Italian olive oil
coarse salt and freshly ground pepper to taste
1 loaf Italian bread
2 cloves garlic, crushed, fibrous parts removed
1/3 cup Italian olive oil
basil leaves for garnish

Preheat broiler.

Combine the tomatoes, onion, basil, vermouth, and 2 tablespoons oil with the salt and pepper. Refrigerate for an hour or two. Slice bread into 16 thick slices. Grill bread under broiler, turning once so that both sides are crisp or grill on outdoor grill. Mash the crushed garlic and oil (there should be no visible pieces of garlic) and spread lightly on each piece of toast. Drain tomato mixture and place 2 tablespoons on each of the slices. Garnish with basil and serve immediately.

Yield: 8 servings

Tender T-Bone Steak, Florentine Style (Bistecca alla Fiorentina)

1½-inch-thick T-bone steak weighing 1¾ to 2 pounds, bone in
up to 1/4 cup olive oil
fresh sprigs of rosemary
1 lemon sliced paper thin
freshly ground black pepper

Preheat a grill or broiler to high.

Trim and dry the steak. Brush with olive oil and lay sprigs of rosemary on grill. Broil steak 4 minutes per side. Season with freshly ground pepper and serve immediately on a warm platter garnished with lemon slices.

Yield: 4 servings

Saffron Risotto (Risotto alla Milanese)

6 cups chicken stock
5 tablespoons Italian olive oil
1 cup minced shallots
2 cups arborio rice
1 cup dry white wine
1 teaspoon saffron
2 tablespoons sweet butter in fine dice
2/3 cup freshly grated Parmigiano-Reggiano cheese
coarse salt and freshly ground black pepper to taste

Heat the stock in a light pot and keep it warm as you use it to make the risotto.

In a heavy-bottomed 4-quart pot with a cover, heat the oil and sauté the shallots over medium-high heat until they are lightly colored and transparent. Stir in the rice, and continue to stir until each grain is coated with oil. Add the wine and keep stirring. Add 1 cup of warm stock. Keep stirring until the liquid is absorbed. Add the stock, approximately 1 cup every 7 or 8 minutes, as it gets absorbed. Dissolve the saffron in the last cup of stock and incorporate it into the rice. This dish must be stirred continuously. When the liquid is absorbed and the rice is creamy and fluffy, remove from heat and stir in butter and cheese. In season shaved truffles may be added.

Yield: 6 servings

Veal Scallops with Sage and Prosciutto (Saltimbocca alla Romana)

12 slices of veal scallops, 1½ pounds total
12 fresh sage leaves
12 slices prosciutto de Parma
flour shaker for dusting
3 tablespoons sweet butter
3 tablespoons olive oil
1 cup white wine
1½ pounds freshly cooked spinach seasoned with salt and pepper

Spread out veal scallops and lay one sage leaf and one slice of prosciutto on each. Roll tidily and secure with toothpicks. Dust each lightly with flour. Heat the butter and oil in a skillet large enough to hold all the rolls in one layer. Sauté the saltimbocca until brown. Lift the veal from the pan and set aside on a warm platter. Add the wine to the skillet, add salt and pepper to taste, and cook to reduce the volume by half. Arrange the hot spinach on a warm dish, place the veal on it, and cover with the wine sauce.

Yield: 6 servings

Cannoli

18 premade *cannoli* shells

Filling:

    2 pounds ricotta cheese, drained
    2 cups confectioner's sugar
    1 tablespoon orange-flower water
    1/4 cup candied orange and citron, in small dice
    2 ounces semisweet chocolate
    1/3 cup shelled pistachio nuts, chopped medium fine

Mix ricotta with confectioner's sugar until it is no longer grainy. Blend in orange-flower water, fruit, and chocolate. Whisk until very creamy. Place filling in a wide-nozzled pastry tube and fill the shells. Place the chopped nuts on a flat surface and lightly dip both ends of the cannoli into the nuts to decorate.

Yield: 18 *cannoli*

Great Britain and Ireland

England

The eating establishments of England outside the home have traditionally been clubs and pubs. The mainstay of British cooking is the home kitchen. Though it varies in quality and quantity, the food is pretty much the same "upstairs" and "downstairs." People are surprised to hear that I enjoy eating in England. Except for the fact that portions are generally too large, you can eat simply and well from a British menu. And teatime is something that is being emulated in many large cities across the United States.

The roast beef of England, served with Yorkshire pudding,✻ is really a London dish. Throughout England there are many regional versions, and though beef and lamb are eaten everywhere, the British have a few special ways of preparing them. Versions of shepherd's pie are popular everywhere.

Roast Beef and Yorkshire Pudding

6 pounds beef sirloin
freshly ground black pepper
sprigs of rosemary

Yorkshire pudding:

2 eggs, separated
1 cup Wondra or other "instant" flour
1 cup milk
3/4 cup pan juices
salt and pepper to taste

Preheat oven to 450°.

On a rack in a roasting pan, place the beef rubbed with the black pepper. Place the rosemary in the pan and roast for 1/2 hour. Lower heat to 350° and roast for 1 hour for rare, up to 1½ hours for well done. Baste from time to time with the pan juices. Remove about 3/4 cup of the pan juices and reserve for the pudding.

To make the pudding batter, whisk the egg yolks, incorporating the flour and the milk. Salt and pepper to taste. Just before baking whip the egg whites and incorporate them into the batter. Place the pan drippings in a 9-inch square cake pan. Pour the batter over the juices, and put in the oven with the roast 1/2 hour before it is done. Serve immediately.

Yield: 8 servings

Toad in the Hole

1 cup unbleached all-purpose flour
2 eggs
1 cup milk
1/2 teaspoon salt
2 tablespoons sweet butter or margarine
1/2 pound breakfast sausage links

Preheat oven to 425°.

In a bowl, mix the flour, eggs, milk, and salt and let rest. Place butter or margarine in an 8-inch baking dish with the sausage and bake for 10 minutes. Pour the batter over the sausage, lower heat to 375°, and bake for 30 minutes. Serve immediately.

Yield: 4 *servings*

Trifle

2 8-inch plain sponge cakes
24 almond macaroons
1/2 cup cognac
3/4 cup raspberry jam
2 cups soft, fresh custard✪
1 cup glacé fruit, in small dice
1 cup toasted nuts, coarsely chopped
1 cup heavy cream
3 tablespoons sugar
1/2 teaspoon vanilla
glacé fruit and nuts to garnish

Slice sponge cake into 1-inch pieces and line the bottom and sides of a deep bowl large enough to hold all the ingredients and attractive enough to serve in. Douse the cake with the brandy. Spread the jam over the cake and top with the macaroons. Layer the custard, the glacé fruit, the chopped nuts, and any cake and macaroons not used in lining the bowl. Whip the heavy cream with 3 tablespoons of sugar and 1/2 teaspoon of vanilla. Top the trifle with the whipped cream. There will be enough cream to serve in a small separate bowl to accompany the trifle as it is served. Top with the glacéed fruit and nuts.

Custard:

2 cups milk
1/4 cup sugar
4 egg yolks
1 teaspoon vanilla

Bring the milk to a boil in the top part of a double boiler over direct heat. Meanwhile, bring water in the bottom of the double boiler to a boil. Lower heat and keep simmering. Add sugar to the milk and when it is dissolved, turn the heat off. Whisk the eggs and vanilla in a bowl large enough to hold all the custard ingredients. Pour the milk over the beaten eggs and then pour the mixture back into the top part of the double boiler. Place over simmering water. Stir until the milk-egg mixture coats the back of a spoon. Remove from heat, set aside, and stir from time to time until it is used.

Yield: 12 *servings*

Christmas Pudding

1 cup unbleached all-purpose flour
1/2 teaspoon salt
2 teaspoons each: ground cinnamon, clove, and nutmeg
1/2 pound brown sugar
1/2 pound ground suet
1 pound fresh, coarse bread crumbs
6 eggs
1/2 pound each: black raisins, yellow raisins, currants, candied cherries
1/2 pound chopped candied citrus peel
2 oranges: juice, and grated rind
1 cup brandy
Unsalted butter to grease pudding bowls

In a very large bowl, incorporate all the pudding ingredients. Grease two 2-quart pudding basins with the butter and divide the batter. Tie buttered brown paper over the top of the bowl with heavy twine. Use the lip rim of the bowl as a guide. Be sure that no water gets inside. Set the bowl in a steamer or on a plate in a stockpot with water barely up to the string. Simmer for 4 hours. Remove from water and set in a cool, dark place for up to 6 weeks. Resteam for an hour or more just before serving. It is traditional to pour brandy or rum over the inverted pudding and set it aflame. Serve topped with hard sauce. ✿

Yield: 16 *servings*

Hard sauce or brandy butter:

1½ cups sweet butter
1½ cups powdered sugar
1/2 cup brandy or rum

Cream together all ingredients.

Scotland

This mysteriously beautiful country has a bad reputation in culinary circles, based on jokes about *haggis*. This dish is nothing more than an oatmeal sausage that uses a sheep's stomach as its casing—but enough said about that.

Caledonia's pantry is filled with fish and seafood, game, mushrooms, herbs, and surprisingly numerous fruits and berries. Aberdeen Angus beef and highland honey are available in the United States. Though there are not many restaurants that serve only the food of Scotland, Americans eat it regularly. Scotch broth,❀ cock-a-leekie soup, and finnan haddie are on many menus. Oatmeal porridge is one of the best foods in the world. Scones and orange marmalade, made from Seville oranges, which are too bitter for juice, are a common tea dish. Shortbread wafers in the familiar plaid packaging are imported in vast quantities, but the things Scotland seems best known for in this country are smoked salmon and Scotch malt liquor.

Scotch Broth

1½ pounds lean beef
3 quarts boiling water
1 carrot
1 turnip
1 medium onion
2 leeks
2 ounces pearl barley
salt and pepper to taste
2 tablespoons freshly minced parsley

Trim the beef and cut into bite-sized pieces. Add to the boiling water. Cook for 1/2 hour. Trim and dice the vegetables and add to the beef. Add the barley and stir to separate. Add the salt and pepper to taste and simmer for about 45 minutes. Serve hot, topped with parsley.

Yield: 6 servings

Currant Scones

1⅓ cup unbleached all-purpose flour
1 teaspoon cream of tartar
1/2 teaspoon baking soda
4 tablespoons sweet butter, softened
2 tablespoons sugar
1/2 cup currants
1/2 cup milk

Preheat oven to 450°.

Mix together the flour, cream of tartar, and baking soda. Blend in the butter and sugar. Incorporate the currants. The scones can be rolled and cut into rounds or, as I prefer to do, simply shape them by hand into six scones and place them on a buttered and floured baking sheet. Bake for 12 to 15 minutes. These are best made in small amounts and eaten fresh because they do not freeze well.

Yield: 6 scones

Wales

There are not, to the best of my knowledge, any Welsh restaurants in the United States, but that does not mean we do not enjoy some Welsh foods. Leek soup✷ is the precursor of vichyssoise and is often far superior. Welsh rarebit is a standby in many households. Salmon and Caerphilly cheese are imported in large quantities.

Leek Soup

---

5 Maine potatoes
4 large leeks
1 onion
4 tablespoons sweet butter
1/4 cup unbleached all-purpose flour
4 cups water
2 eggs, lightly beaten with
1/2 cup water
3/4 cup heavy cream
salt and pepper to taste

Peel the potatoes, dice, and boil. Drain, reserving the liquid. Sieve or mash the potatoes and set aside. Slice and clean the leeks. Peel and dice the onion. In a heavy-bottomed saucepan large enough to hold all the ingredients, heat the butter and lightly brown the leeks and onion. Stir in the flour forming a *roux*. Add 4 cups of water and the potatoes. Stir until well mixed. Add salt and pepper to taste. Slowly add the egg mixture and then the cream. Serve immediately.

Yield: 6 servings

Welsh Lamb with Honey Garlic and White Wine (Cig Oen Cymreig Gyda Mel, Garlleg a Gwin Gwyn)

---

3 pounds shoulder of lamb
1 head garlic
1/2 cup honey
2 cups dry white wine
salt and pepper to taste
3 sprigs of fresh rosemary or 1 tablespoon dried rosemary, crushed

Score any fat on the lamb surface. Peel and crush garlic and mix with honey, wine, salt, and pepper. If using fresh rosemary, reserve. If using dried, add it to the mixture. Rub the lamb with mixture and marinate for 1 hour in the refrigerator.

Preheat oven to 450°. Place lamb on rack in roasting pan. Pour marinade over the lamb. Place fresh rosemary in the pan and roast for 1 hour, basting occasionally. Serve with roasted potatoes and green peas.

Yield: 6 servings

Ireland

Sir Walter Raleigh brought the new world potato to Ireland in 1585 and planted a crop of them at his estate in County Cork. By the seventeenth century, the country was dependent on them as a food staple. They were often eaten simply boiled or mashed with chopped kale in a dish called *colcannon,*● or in a mixture of grated raw and cooked potatoes mixed with flour to make the pancakes called *boxty.*● Cooked with lamb, onions, herbs, potatoes, and water, the famous Irish stew is simmered for hours. The Irish culinary heritage may be rustic, but it is not fossilized. There are so many good things to eat that traditional food is served in the best restaurants, as well as farm cottages, with generous hospitality. Myrtle Allen, an Irish chef, followed Paul Bocuse as president of Eurotoques. Her cooking school, Ballymaloe House, which started as a bed and breakfast, is responsible for most of the world-class Irish chefs in this country. They exemplify not only quality cooking, but the art of using local food in season.

Both salt- and freshwater fish are abundant and salmon is eaten fresh or smoked. Irish salmon is smoked over peat and has a much smokier flavor than the oak-cured salmon of Scotland, which is more popular. If you are lucky enough to find them, Dublin prawns and Rossmore oysters are exceptional.

Irish whiskey is barley-based and has less of the kiln-smoked taste than do most of the Scotch blends. It is not surprising that Irish coffee is the drink that most Americans think of as Irish, but it originated in San Francisco.

Potato Soup

3 tablespoons sweet butter
2 pounds potatoes, peeled and sliced
3 leeks, split, washed, and cut into slices
1 quart milk
2 cups water
salt and pepper to taste
1 cup cream
6 slices well-cooked, crisp bacon, crumbled
1 tablespoon minced chives
1 tablespoon minced parsley leaves

Melt the butter in a heavy-bottomed saucepan large enough to hold all the ingredients. Over medium heat, cook the sliced potatoes and leeks for 10 to 12 minutes or until they are soft. Don't brown them. Add the milk and water; salt and pepper to taste. Cover and simmer for an hour. Many people purée the soup at this point, but I prefer to drain it, and fork-mash the potatoes and thinly slice the leeks and return them to the milk broth. Over medium-low heat, add the cream and bacon; top with chopped chives and parsley. Serve hot.

Yield: 8 servings

Boxty

1 pound raw potatoes
2 cups mashed potatoes
1 pound flour
salt and pepper to taste
1/3 cup melted sweet butter

Preheat oven to 300°.

Peel and grate the raw potatoes. Put them in a clean tea towel and wring them dry. Mix them with the mashed potatoes, flour, salt, and pepper. Knead the dough and roll it thick and flat. Divide into 4 parts, and cut a shallow cross into each of them so that they can be divided easily. Place them on a greased baking sheet and bake for 35 to 45 minutes.

Yield: 16 pieces

Leek-and-Oatmeal Soup (Brotchán Foltchep)

6 leeks, split and thoroughly washed
2 tablespoons sweet butter
1 quart milk or stock
2 tablespoons quick cooking oatmeal
salt and pepper to taste
1 tablespoon fresh parsley leaves, chopped

When the leeks are cleaned of all grit, cut them into 1-inch slices. Heat the butter and stir in the leeks until slightly coated and wilted. Add the milk or stock and when it is at a boil, add the oatmeal. Salt and pepper to taste and lower the heat, cover and simmer for 1 hour. Top with parsley and serve very hot.

Yield: 6 servings

Spiced Beef

Spiced beef is a holiday dish that is marinated for as long as a week, but two or three days should do the trick.

Marinade:

3 bay leaves
1 teaspoon ground cloves
1/4 teaspoon mace
1 teaspoon black peppercorns
2 cloves garlic
1 teaspoon allspice
2 tablespoons brown sugar
2 teaspoons saltpeter
1 cup coarse salt
1 5-pound boneless round roast

In a mortar and pestle, grind all the ingredients together. Rub the mixture over the roast and place in the refrigerator in a covered nonreactive pan. Turn two or three times a day. When ready to cook, rinse the roast and dry it.

Cooking preparation:

1 celery stick, chopped
1 medium onion, chopped
3 sliced carrots, chopped
2 cups Guinness stout
1 teaspoon ground cloves
1/2 teaspoon ground pepper
salt to taste

Place the chopped vegetables and Guinness stout in a covered casserole that can be used on top of the stove. Add spices and water to cover. Cover the pot and bring to a boil. Lower heat and simmer for 3 to 4 hours. Serve with colcannon. ❧

Yield: 8 servings

Colcannon

3 ounces sweet butter
1 medium/large onion, sliced
1½ pounds peeled potatoes, cooked and hot
1/2 pound shredded cabbage or kale, cooked and hot
salt and pepper to taste

Heat the butter in a pan large enough to whip all the ingredients in. Sauté the onions. Add the potatoes and start mashing them, adding the cabbage and cream. Salt and pepper to taste. Over low heat, whisk the potatoes with an electric mixer until they are smooth.

Yield: 8 servings

Irish Soda Bread

4 cups unbleached all-purpose flour
1 teaspoon baking soda
1 teaspoon salt
3/4 cup raisins
2 tablespoons caraway seeds
1 cup buttermilk

Preheat oven to 425°

Mix the flour, baking soda, and salt. Incorporate the raisins and caraway seeds. Add the buttermilk all at once and mix it in. Knead the dough on a lightly floured board. Immediately form into a round loaf on a nonstick baking sheet. With a razor blade, score a cross on the top from top to bottom and side to side. Lay a piece of tinfoil over it. Bake for five minutes in a hot oven. Lower heat to 250° and bake 30 minutes. Remove tinfoil and bake another 10 minutes.

Yield: 16 servings

Porter Cake

Irish soda bread, flavored with caraway seeds and raisins, is made with baking soda and buttermilk. Porter cake is a favorite sweet, even though it is made with Guinness stout.

1 pound cake flour
1/2 pound sweet butter
1 pound brown sugar
1/4 teaspoon cloves
2 teaspoons cinnamon
1/2 teaspoon nutmeg
1/2 pound seedless black raisins
1/2 pound seedless golden raisins
1/2 cup currants
1 cup glacé cherries
1 cup blanched, chopped almonds
1 cup chopped, candied citrus peel
1 teaspoon baking soda, dissolved in
1 cup warm Guinness stout
4 eggs, lightly beaten

Preheat oven to 250°.

Grease and line a 9-inch springform pan with parchment paper, and cut a 9-inch circle to cover the cake as it bakes. Cream the flour and butter. Incorporate the sugar and spices. Blend the raisins and currants into the mixture with your hands. Add the remaining fruit and nuts. Mix in the warm Guinness stout with the baking soda and the eggs. Work this thoroughly into the dry batter.

Put batter into prepared pan and cover with a circle of parchment paper. Bake for 2½ hours. Remove the paper and bake for another 1/2 hour or until a cake tester comes out clean.

Yield: one 9" cake

Yeasted Fruitcake (Barm Brack)

1 package dry yeast
1/4 cup warm water
1 teaspoon sugar
pinch of salt
1 pound unbleached all-purpose flour
1½ cups sugar
1/4 teaspoon ground cinnamon
1/4 teaspoon ground nutmeg
1/4 cup sweet butter at room temperature
1 cup warm milk
1 egg, lightly beaten
1/2 pound raisins
1 cup currants
1/2 cup candied citrus peel

Proof the yeast in the warm water, adding the teaspoon of sugar and a pinch of salt. Combine the flour, sugar, spices, and cream in the butter. Mix the milk and egg together and whisk into the yeast mixture. Pour the liquid into the flour and beat, incorporating the raisins, currants, and peel. Place the dough in a large bowl and cover with a clean tea towel. Let rise till double in bulk.

Butter two 8" cake pans. Divide dough in two and set into pans. Cover and let rise for 1/2 hour. Preheat oven to 400°.

Bake for 45 minutes or until tester comes out clean. Cool before serving.

Yield: two 8" cakes

Irish Coffee

1 cup fresh hot coffee
1 teaspoon sugar (optional)
2 ounces best-quality Irish whiskey
2 tablespoons heavy cream or 3 tablespoons whipped cream

Warm a glass. Pour in the coffee. If you are using sugar, put it in first so that it dissolves. Add the whiskey and then slowly pour the cream into the glass over the back of a spoon so that it floats on the surface of the coffee.

Yield: 1 serving

3

SCANDINAVIA

The seafarers who pushed the frontiers of the known world to all continents developed a stable food culture. The Vikings, when they were not warring or pirating, were farmers. To endure long, dark, cold winters, the arts of preserving food and storing ale were of utmost importance.

After a summer visit to Lapland, I took a train to Narvik, Norway. I arrived at midnight and the sun was shining. I was greeted at my small hotel with an array of salads and fish dishes, fresh bread, and butter. Sleepiness cast aside, I went exploring and was rewarded with historic rock carvings high on the cliffs facing the sea. After a day or so, I took a public bus south to Oslo. We boarded many ferries to cross the fjords and stopped to look at stave churches, old farms, and ancient boats. I don't remember a bad meal.

Norway shares an inland border with Sweden. Together, they jut out toward Denmark, which is composed of a peninsula that extends from Germany and many islands. Finland is separated from Sweden by the Gulf of Bothnia and borders Russia on the east. Scandinavian food is abundant in the United States. The classic Norwegian smoked salmon is found everywhere and almost everyone who likes fish knows what *gravlaks* is. Classic *smörgåsbord*, a panorama of salads and open sandwiches, has become as familiar here as it is throughout the Scandinavian countries.

There is an increasing number of Scandinavian restaurants in the United States. It is not surprising that fish is the centerpiece of most meals. Scandinavian chefs tend to serve it simply; the additions of potatoes, root vegetables, and a cucumber salad let the food speak for itself. Dill, chives, and parsley are prevalent herbs. One of the characteristic things about Scandinavian cooking is the use of sweet and sour. Even pickled herring will be made with a touch of sugar and, sometimes, apple. Meat and fish are often served with fruit or berries. Many boiled dishes are served with sweet-and-sour dill sauce

Breakfast is mostly muesli or hot porridge served with yogurt and dried fruit and nuts. Sometimes flatbread and cheese is served with coffee. There is not likely to be anything too heavy or too sweet to start the day. A fancy breakfast or brunch might be made from leftover roast meat in a dish much like hash, called *pytt i panna*, and topped with an egg or two.

Lunch is often an occasion for cold salmon, salads, and bread. In public places, *smörgåsbord* (bread-and-butter table) is frequently presented for lunch. When it is presented for dinner it is usually a first course. A Thursday night tradition that is exercised everywhere from fishing shack to royal palace is *årter med flåsk,*● yellow pea soup flavored with ham, ginger, and marjoram, and *plåtter*, pancakes, usually accompanied with *glögg*.

Dinner frequently begins with a herring dish, then soup, fish, and vegetables, followed by a cheese course, coffee, and dessert. As for meat, pork and ham served with prunes and/or apples are used extensively as well as regional game like deer or elk. For supé, a late night meal served after theater or other entertainment, *smörgåsbord* is again the favored presentation. The festive difference is that many of the dishes are hot. Soufflés, creamed dishes, and slices of freshly baked *limpa,*● an aromatic dark yeast bread, are served. Coffee is imported, but processed in Sweden, as it is preferred fresh and dark and is drunk in large amounts throughout the day.

The most important of the three major holidays is Christmas eve, which is celebrated with fish dishes like *lutefisk* in cream. *Lutefisk* is a type of cod that is cured and dried the way it was before salt was freely available—with lye (not dissimilar to the Mediterranean *bacalao*). Dessert is often a rice pudding made with the addition of a single almond. The superstition is that the one who eats it will be the next to be married.

In Sweden, Saint Lucia's Day, on the shortest day of December, is a major celebration. It has become a ritual to have the national representative of Saint Lucia be a beauty contestant winner—she often goes on to become Miss Sweden.

Midsömmar, at the summer solstice on June 24, is a holiday that lasts for at least two days. There is literally dancing in the streets, as work comes to a halt, and food, drink, and festivities take over. Aquavit, distilled from potatoes or grain (generally flavored with caraway), is drunk in shots and is often followed with a beer chaser. *Skål* is the usual toast.

Sweden

AQUAVIT, NEW YORK

Håkan Swahn, who has been a quiet presence at Aquavit, understands the range of dishes and flavors that translate from Sweden to New York. He was one of the original restaurant's partners, and was *gastronomique* council to the Royal House, and had five restaurants in Stockholm. Aquavit has two sections. The informal cafe, which nods to the home cooking of Sweden, is a hip-pocket restaurant where open-faced sandwiches, soups, stews, and simple fish dishes are served. The formal room, downstairs, has more elaborate versions of seafood, shellfish, and beef or game like venison, boar, and wild duck. Mushrooms and berries bring the woodsy flavors of the northern landscape to each dish.

Even at its fanciest, Swedish food has a feel for basics. Nothing is smothered with anything. Even the ingredients for stews are often cooked separately to bring out each individual flavor, then cooked together to mix them at their best. Sweden has benefited from long-time

From the menu of

Aquavit

13 West 54th Street
New York, NY 10019

First Course

Mixed Green Salad

Root vegetable julienne, toasted walnuts and roasted tomatoes

Lobster Bisque

Västerbotten cheese and pepper crackers

Gravlax

Dill flat bread, pickled fennel and espresso mustard sauce

Second Course

Sauteed Atlantic Salmon

Sweet potato pancake, swiss chard, orange fennel broth

Horseradish Crusted Bluefish

Mushroom truffle broth, stewed potatoes

Oven Roasted Chicken

Wild rice, sauteed greens, tomato caper concasse and
black olive oil

Pan Sauteed Loin of Beef

Potato cake, spinach and mushroom onion saute

Desserts

Hazelnut Pancakes
Blueberry ice cream and coulis

Swedish Cheesecake
Red gooseberry juice

Arctic Circle
Cloudberry Sauce

Warm Chocolate Cake
White chocolate sorbet and arctic berry compote

Ginger Bread "Lockelse"
Mascarpone ice cream and licorice sauce

An Assortment of Cheese
Black mission figs, port wine creme brulee,
roasted hazelnuts

foreign trade. From Germany are sausage and cabbage dishes cooked with pork. The Swedish royal family has French antecedents, and many cooking techniques have entered the cuisine through the court.

There are traditional daily foods in Sweden. Wednesday is brown beans❦ and pork; Thursday, pea soup❦ and pancakes; Friday, fish; Sunday, steak or roast with wild berries and potatoes. From farmhouses to manor houses people are comfortable with these menus. Aquavit always has these on the appropriate days.

Another treat at Aquavit is ice wine, a rare wine made from grapes that have been left on the vine past the frost. Pickers often harvest in an Arctic wind and, quickly, the vintners start the process. The water in the grape freezes and separates from the syrupy, sweet juice in the wine press.

Horseradish-Crusted Bluefish with Stewed Potatoes

Courtesy Aquavit, New York

2 tablespoons sweet butter
1½ pounds bluefish filets
2 tablespoons olive oil
salt and pepper to taste
1 medium-large horseradish root
6 medium potatoes, boiled and peeled

Preheat oven to 425°.

Butter a baking dish that will hold the bluefish in a single layer. Cut fish into 8 small pieces. Brush fish with olive oil and sear on skin side for two minutes. Season with salt and pepper. Grate the horseradish. Place fish skin-side down in buttered baking dish and place grated horseradish on top of the fish. Cut the potatoes in half lengthwise and set aside.

Sauce:

1 tablespoon sweet butter
1 clove garlic, minced
1 medium onion, chopped
1/2 sweet red pepper, diced
1/4 cup fresh lemon juice
2 cups fish stock
1 cup chicken stock
1½ tablespoons sour cream
1 teaspoon capers
1 cup white wine
2 tablespoons olive oil
salt and pepper

Place the butter in a heavy-bottomed pan that will hold all ingredients except the fish and horseradish. Sauté garlic, onion, and red pepper. Add the lemon juice, fish stock, and chicken stock and simmer for 20 minutes. Lower heat and stir in the sour cream, capers, white wine, and cooked potatoes. Add olive oil, and salt and pepper to taste. Bring to a gentle boil. Place bluefish in the oven and roast until horseradish is golden brown, about 3 minutes. Place potatoes and sauce in individual shallow bowls and top with crusted fish. Serve immediately.

Yield: 4 servings

Swedish Cheesecake

Courtesy Aquavit, New York

1/4 cup almonds, scalded and skinned
3 eggs
5 tablespoons sugar
1/4 cup flour
1/2 cup heavy cream
3/4 cup milk
1 pound cottage cheese
fresh or preserved lingonberries
(other berries may be substituted)
3/4 cup whipped cream, optional

Preheat oven to 350°.

Chop almonds coarsely and set them aside. Whisk together eggs and sugar until thick. Gradually and thoroughly mix in flour, cream, milk, cheese, and almonds. Pour the batter in a 1½-quart baking dish, and bake for 1 hour or until tester comes out clean. Serve warm or cold with berries and cream.

Yield: 6 servings

Ikea

I spoke with some of the staff at a cafe at Ikea, the Swedish company that has many stores located throughout the United States. It was a visit with aficionados of Scandinavian culture and cuisine. Since most of the large stores are not in malls, but located in freestanding areas, Ikea founders conceived the idea of having restaurants where people could not only take a break from the selling atmosphere, but share traditional Swedish dishes and peruse a selection of imported packaged food and beverages.

The cafes offer simple home-style cooking and swedish meatballs, pea soup with ham, and pancakes with lingonberries are presented with deserved pride. These are dishes that customers can duplicate in their own kitchen if they wish.

Swedish Christmas Rice Pudding
(Risgrynsgröt)

6 cups milk
1 cup long-grain rice
1/4 cup sugar
1/2 teaspoon salt
1 whole almond
1 cup berry sauce

Place milk, rice, sugar, and salt in the top of a double boiler over simmering water. Cover and cook for 2½ to 3 hours. If the mixture is not thickening, remove cover and let moisture evaporate after 2 hours. Place in bowl and bury the almond in it.

Raspberry Sauce (Bringebar Saft)

2 cups fresh raspberries (frozen may be substituted)
1/2 cup sugar
2 teaspoons cornstarch dissolved in 1 tablespoon cold water

In food mill or processor, puree berries. In nonreactive saucepan, place berry puree, sugar, and cornstarch paste. Bring to a boil over medium heat and stir. Simmer 3 to 4 minutes, remove from heat, and let cool.

Yield: 8 *servings*

Swedish Brown Beans (Bruna Bönor)

1 pound Swedish brown beans
3/4 cup dark corn syrup
1/3 cup apple-cider vinegar
1/4 cup brown sugar
2 teaspoons salt

Bring 2 quarts of water to a boil in a covered pan. Add beans gradually, so that the water does not stop boiling. Making sure the water is boiling, cover the pan and lower the heat. Let the beans simmer for 5 minutes. Turn off heat and let beans remain in covered pot for 1 hour. Bring back to a boil; make sure the beans are covered with water. Add up to 2 more cups of water. Cover and simmer for 1 hour. Stir in corn syrup, vinegar, sugar, and salt, then simmer for 1 hour more or until beans are tender.

Yield: 8 *servings*

Swedish Aromatic Rye Bread (Limpa)

1 package dry yeast
1/4 cup warm water
1 teaspoon sugar
pinch of salt
1/2 cup brown sugar
1/3 cup molasses
1 tablespoon shortening
2 teaspoons salt
1 tablespoon caraway seed
1 teaspoon anise
1½ cups hot water
1 cup unbleached all-purpose flour
2 cups rye flour
2½ to 3½ cups unbleached flour
2 tablespoons safflower oil to grease rising bowl

Preheat oven to 375°. Grease 2 baking sheets.

Mix yeast with water, sugar, and salt. Let proof for 10 minutes. In a large bowl, mix together brown sugar, molasses, shortening, salt, caraway, and anise. Pour the hot water over the mixture and beat in 1 cup of unbleached all-purpose flour. Add the proofed yeast and incorporate. Add rye flour and beat in, adding enough unbleached white flour to form a soft dough. Turn dough out onto a lightly floured surface. Allow the dough to rest for 10 minutes and then knead. Form a large ball of dough and place in greased deep bowl, turning the dough once to make sure it is coated with oil. Cover with a clean tea towel and set aside to rise until double in size. Punch dough down in bowl. Pull edges in toward the center and turn over in the bowl. Cover and let rise again until it has doubled again. Punch dough down and place on lightly floured surface. Divide into 2 loaves and place on greased baking sheets. Cover and let rise until almost doubled. Bake 25 minutes or until lightly browned. Cool thoroughly on racks before slicing.

Yield: 2 loaves

Yellow Pea Soup with Pork
(Årter Med Fläsk)

2 cups Swedish, dried, whole yellow peas (packaged yellow split peas may be substituted but will not need to be soaked)
2 quarts cold water
1 pound smoked pork shoulder or shank
3 quarts water
1 large white onion, diced
1 teaspoon salt
1/4 teaspoon white pepper
1 teaspoon sugar
1 teaspoon dried marjoram

Soak the whole dried peas in 2 quarts of water 6 hours or overnight.

Drain peas. In a large pot, place peas, pork, onion, and seasoning. Bring to a boil and simmer 1½ to 2 hours. Remove pork, trim, and dice. Return to soup, stir, and serve.

Yield: 6 servings

Denmark

In the Danish lowlands, there are beautiful farms and pastures and many cows that produce butter, cheese, cream, and milk. Many dishes, especially soup, are served creamed. Beef is eaten, but not in large amounts, and usually in combination with other ingredients. *Hakkebøf* are hacked beef patties with onions and gravy. *Frikadeller*, Danish meatballs, are simpler than others and are made of the finest beef and pork, ground together with onion, salt, and pepper and mixed with milk. Danish ham and bacon are world class, but *fläskkarre*, pork roasted with prunes and apples, which is enjoyed in the rest of Scandinavia is equally popular here. Served with *pressgurka*, cucumber salad, and *rödkål*, red cabbage, the Danish way with potatoes is to caramelize them in a dish called *brunede kartofler*. *Smørrebrød* is also called a *kolde bord*. Since early in the nineteenth century, this spread of open sandwiches and salads has been a custom. Artfully displayed, they are meant to entertain as well as nourish. Starting with thinly sliced rye bread spread with sweet butter and topped with shrimp, smoked salmon, or lobster garnished with dill, they are sometimes elaborately cut and decorated. Carlsberg and Tuborg are world-class beers with headquarters in Copenhagen, but breweries everywhere, including the USA.

Finland

Suomi is the Finns' name for their country. Finnish is part of the small Finno-ugrian language group, and has more in common with Estonian than Swedish, which is Finland's official second language. Finland was part of Sweden until 1815. *Kiitoksia* means "thank you," and *smörgåsbord* is *voileipäpoytä*, *voi* (butter), *leipä* (bread), *poytä* (table). It is literally a buttered bread table.

The ingredients of the *voileipäpoytä* are similar to those of the rest of Scandinavia—assorted buttered breads and as many as fifty different dishes. First the fish dishes: Baltic herrings, smoked, pickled, fried, in salad or spread; salmon in similar ways, as well as trout, whitefish, and other seafood. Then cold meats are served: roasted, smoked, dried, in slices or sausage. The third part consists of hot dishes: meatballs, stew, creamed potatoes, and cabbage. Cheese is usually served at that time, also.

Cheeses vary from the strong blue cheese, *aura*, to the mild *kartano*.

There are hundreds of edible mushrooms, and Arctic cloudberries and brambleberries are made into accompaniments. Beer often accompanies cheese. Sometimes the drink of choice is a shot of iced akvavit followed by a beer chaser.

Russian dishes have entered the cuisine and borscht and blini are served as frequently as vodka.

Salmon Soup (Lohikeitto)

3 tablespoons sweet butter
1 medium white onion, diced
2 medium leeks, julienned
2 tablespoons "instant" flour
3 cups water
2 tablespoons lemon juice
1 pound salmon filet, sliced (cooked salmon may be substituted)
1½ cups heavy cream
1/2 teaspoon mace
1/2 teaspoon ginger
salt and pepper to taste
1/2 cup heavy cream, whipped, optional garnish
1/3 cup fresh dill, minced, garnish
(dried dill, in a smaller amount, may be substituted)

Heat the butter in a saucepan large enough to hold all the ingredients. Sauté the onion and leeks over medium heat until transparent. Stir in the flour and add the water and lemon juice. Stir and simmer until somewhat thickened and add the salmon. Cook for 5 minutes. Lower heat and add cream and seasonings. Serve topped with a bit of whipped cream and dill.

Yield: 8 servings

Whole-Wheat Rusks

1 cup milk
1 package instant dry yeast
1 teaspoon coarse salt
1 teaspoon granulated sugar
1¼ cups unbleached all-purpose flour
4 tablespoons sweet butter, melted
1/4 cup brown sugar
1¼ cups whole-wheat bread flour
oil for greasing bowl

Scald the milk, then cool until tepid. Add yeast, salt, and granulated sugar. Let sit 10 minutes. Add the flour and mix until thick. Add the butter and brown sugar. Mix well. Add the whole-wheat flour and, when too thick to mix, turn out onto floured board and knead for 10 minutes. Place in clean, oiled mixing bowl. Turn once, so that surface of dough is slightly covered with oil. Cover and set to rise until doubled, about 2 hours.

Preheat oven to 425°.

Knead dough into a tube about 2″ in diameter. Cut into 12 slices and place cut-side down on floured baking sheet. Cover and let rise for 30 minutes. Bake 12 minutes, then remove from oven. Maintain oven heat. Cool the rusks for 20 minutes and split them in half. Return them to the oven, split-side up. After 5 minutes, lower oven temperature to 200° and bake for 45 minutes. Turn oven heat off. Make sure rusks are light and dry. If they are not, leave them in the oven with the heat off and the door closed for another 30 minutes. Serve immediately or store in an airtight container.

Yield: 24 rusks

Norway

Norwegian favorite home-cooked foods, as reported by a recent Oslo newspaper survey, are meat cakes, potato dumplings,❀ fresh cod, and lutefisk. It was surprising not to see salmon on the list. Norwegian salmon is delicious.

Traditionally, men and boys went to sea, while women and children farmed and raised cattle. Excellent dairy products are everywhere available, and *Gjetost*, a firm smoked cheese, is available in North-

American supermarkets, as are other fine Norwegian cheeses. Packaged baked goods such as flatbread or firm griddlecakes called *lefse* are also distributed in areas with a large Scandinavian population.

Norwegian Meatballs and Gravy (Kjötkaker)

Meatballs:

> 2 tablespoons sweet butter
> 1/2 cup chopped onion
> 1 pound ground beef
> 1/2 pound ground pork
> 1/2 cup coarse bread crumbs
> 1/2 cup milk
> 1 egg, slightly beaten
> 2 teaspoons sugar
> 1/2 teaspoon salt
> 1/2 teaspoon nutmeg
> 1/4 teaspoon cloves
> 2 tablespoons cooking oil

Gravy:

> 3 tablespoons unbleached all-purpose flour
> 1 teaspoon sugar
> 1/2 teaspoon salt
> 1/4 teaspoon pepper
> 1/2 cup water
> 1 cup heavy cream

Heat the butter in a skillet large enough to hold all ingredients. Sauté onions until golden brown. Place onions in a large mixing bowl and turn off heat under the skillet until ready to cook the meatballs. Mix onions, ground meats, bread crumbs, milk, egg, and seasoning. Form into approximately 36 small meatballs. Heat oil in skillet. Brown and cook meatballs. Remove to covered dish and stir flour into pan drippings. Add seasoning and keep stirring until flour is browned. Stir in water and cream. Cook for 2 to 3 minutes but do not boil. Pour over meatballs and serve.

Yield: 6 servings

Sweet-and-Sour Red Cabbage (Rödkål)

1 2-pound red cabbage
1/2 teaspoon salt
1/2 cup brown sugar
1 tablespoon caraway seeds
1/2 cup apple cider vinegar
3 tablespoons sweet butter

Remove any wilted leaves and core the cabbage. Shred and place in 3-quart saucepan. Cover with water, then add the salt, sugar, and caraway seeds and bring to a boil. Cook at a low boil for 10 minutes. Remove from heat and drain. Place the cabbage in a large bowl and immediately add the vinegar and butter. Serve hot.

Yield: 6 servings

Potato Dumplings

2 pounds Maine potatoes
1 egg, slightly beaten
1 cup barley meal (matzoh meal may be substituted)
1 cup unbleached all-purpose flour
1 teaspoon salt

Peel and grate the potatoes. Place the potatoes in a colander lined with paper towels. Press with a wooden spoon to release some of the moisture from the potatoes. Transfer to a bowl, stir together all the ingredients, and knead slightly. Bring 3 quarts of water and the salt to a boil. Lower heat, so that the water remains at a moderate boil. Shape mixture into 24 dumplings, and lower them into the boiling water 1 or 2 at a time, so that the water keeps boiling. Simmer 30 minutes. Serve immediately.

Yield: 24 dumplings

Pickled Herring

3 salted herrings
2/3 cup vinegar
1/3 cup sugar
1 cup water
1 large onion, peeled and sliced paper thin
8 black peppercorns, crushed
2 tablespoons chopped, fresh dill

Soak, clean, and fillet the herring. Cut crosswise into 1½" slices. Bring the vinegar, sugar, and water to a boil and cool. Layer herring with onion slices, pepper, and dill. Pour vinegar mixture over all. Cover and store in refrigerator. This is often served for breakfast.

Yield: 6 servings, 1 quart

Miniature Doughnut Cookies (Jortitog)

1/2 cup sweet butter, softened
1 cup sugar
4 eggs, slightly beaten
3½ cups unbleached all-purpose flour
oil for deep frying

Cream the butter, gradually adding sugar until well blended and fluffy. Mix in the eggs. Add the flour 1/2 cup at a time and mix well. Refrigerate at least 1 hour.

Place a large sheet of waxed paper on a flat surface. Pinch off a piece of dough about 2" by 1/4" and roll between your fingers until it is 5 inches long. Form into a ring and press ends together to form a little doughnut. Set on waxed paper. Repeat with remaining dough.

Heat the oil to 375° or prepare electric deep-fryer according to manufacturer's instructions. Fry a few at a time, so that they do not touch each other, for about 2 minutes, turning once. Drain on paper towels.

Yield: 5 dozen±

4

EASTERN EUROPE

Czech Republic

The cuisine of the Czech Republic has echoes of German tradition influenced by its Slavic neighbors. It's a fairly homey menu, with a lot of sour cream, lemon, vinegar, or citric acid added to impart a tang to dishes that might otherwise be bland. Holiday food, such as roast goose or pork, is served with *knedliky*, sauerkraut, vegetables, and fruit. Poultry and fish, such as trout and carp from freshwater rivers and lakes, are combined with abundant grains and mushrooms. Dessert is sometimes *kolac*, rolls made with a yeast dough and filled with fruit, sweetened poppy seeds, or cheese. *Palačinky* are crepelike pancakes served with fruit preserves or chocolate syrup. Of course, at the moment, the people of Prague are eating around the world in their neighborhoods, too. Cafes serve *burritos*, *spanakopitas*, and California-style pizzas.

Potato Dumplings (Bramborove Knedliky)

2 pounds potatoes
1/2 cup farina
3/4 cup unbleached all-purpose flour
1 teaspoon salt
1/2 teaspoon ground black pepper
2 eggs, slightly beaten

Boil the potatoes until they are fork tender. Meanwhile, set 3 quarts of water to boil in a stockpot. Peel and mash potatoes. Incorporate the farina, flour, salt, and pepper into the potatoes until well blended. Mix in the eggs and form into 6 large round dumplings. Lower them into the boiling water and cook for 20 minutes. Remove and drain.

Yield: 6 servings

Pork with Horseradish (Veprove s Krenem)

2 tablespoons vegetable oil
2 pounds lean pork, cubed
2 medium onions, diced
2 medium carrots, peeled and sliced
salt and pepper to taste
2 teaspoons caraway seeds
1 cup apple cider vinegar mixed with 2 cups water
1/3 cup grated horseradish

Heat the oil in a skillet and brown the pork, onions, and carrots. Add seasoning and vinegar mixture. Cover and simmer for 1½ hours. Stir in horseradish and serve with potato dumplings.

Yields: 6 servings

Poppy-Seed Loaf

6 tablespoons sweet butter, plus additional for greasing pan
1 cup sugar
6 eggs, separated
3 cups all-purpose flour, plus additional for flouring pan
1/2 teaspoon cinnamon
1/4 teaspoon cloves
1 cup poppy seeds, ground
2/3 cup raisins
grated zest of 1 lemon

Preheat oven to 325°.

Butter and flour a loaf pan. Cream the butter, then incorporate the sugar. Beat in egg yolks, then add flour, spices, and poppy seeds. Mix in raisins and lemon zest.

Beat egg whites until soft peaks are formed, but before they are stiff and dry. Fold egg whites into batter and scrape into prepared loaf pan. Bake for 1 hour or until golden brown and a cake tester comes out clean.

Yield: 1 *loaf cake*

Poland

Poland, bordered by the Baltic Sea to the north, the Carpathian Mountains to the south, Russia to the east, and Germany to the west, has an amalgam of western European and Russian culinary tradition. Throughout most of the nineteenth century, the rivers and forests of Poland were divided among Austria, Prussia, and Russia. Polish cooking is primarily home cooking and, as a result, most of the recipes are very flexible. Each family tends to cook things a bit differently, and a little more of this or none of that will usually produce a delicious dish. Polish hams, sausages, and cold cuts are remarkable; many large American cities have markets where they can be purchased.

Cereal grains such as barley, buckwheat, and rye are hearty additions to American diets. Soups of excellent quality are to be found in most Polish restaurants and, when in doubt, are a sure bet. Some of Poland's typical soups include thick soup such as *czarnina*, a duck

From the menu of

Warszawa

1414 Lincoln Boulevard
Santa Monica, CA 90401

Appetizers

Hot dried plums wrapped in lean bacon garnished
with caramelized walnuts

Wine-cured herring with shredded apple and scallion sauce

Ravioli, Polish style, lightly sauteed,
choice of vegetarian or meat

Golden crispy potato pancakes with cinnamon apples
and plums

Regional Polish grilled sausage served
with creamy horseradish sauce

Soups

Fragrant chicken broth with fresh handmade angel hair pasta

Pastas, Etc.

Handmade Pierogi

Polish ravioli—light and delicate pasta shells
with choice of fillings:

White cheese and chives
Potato puree and caramelized onions
Wild mushrooms and shredded cabbage
Chicken breast and herbs, served with sorrel sauce
Braised beef, carrots and onions

Lamb dumplings served in piquant Dijon sauce
(eastern Polish specialty)

Salmon-filled dumplings served with basil sauce

Paper-thin crepes with spinach mousse,
or wild mushroom mousse,
or sauteed beef with champignon filling

Fish

Filet of salmon poached in Chardonnay served with sorrel sauce

Your choice of rainbow trout:

Simmered with leeks, Roma tomatoes, rosemary and dill
Poached in Chardonnay, served with
light creamy lemon dill sauce

From the menu of Warszawa (continued)

Poultry and Meat

*Crispy Long Island duckling infused with herbs and lemon,
roasted with apples*

*Morsels of veal in spicy paprika and fresh tomato sauce
served with homemade egg-drop dumplings
and caramelized onions*

*Steamed cabbage leaves filled with beef, jasmine rice and
sauteed onions baked in tomato and paprika broth*

*Warszawa beef stroganoff with wild mushrooms served over
egg-drop dumplings*

Pork schnitzel served with potato and leek puree

Desserts

*Vanilla crepe filled with lemon cheese served hot
with raspberries*

*Dark mocha chocolate cream layer torte
with light vanilla sauce*

soup; and *krupnik*, made from barley and potatoes; to refreshing savory cold soups like *chlodnik*, made from cucumbers, crayfish, sour cream, and dill; to the sweet, iced cherry or plum soups; they are tasty and quite distinctive. There are many versions of hot and cold *barszcz*, based on beets or beet juice and sometimes cooked with vegetables and sometimes with meat. It is served thick with liver dumplings and cabbage, or as a puree.

Bigos,⚫ or hunter's stew, is virtually the national dish. Filled pasta pockets called *pierogi*⚫ are made in great variety, as are noodles of all kinds. Forest mushrooms are so abundant that they are dried and used to release their woodsy flavor in soups and stews.

Often *zakaski* (assorted hot and cold small dishes), with a nod to modern eating styles, make up the entire meal instead of its introduction. They can include hot and cold savory meat and fish, dumplings, pickles, bread, and garnishes, such as horseradish sauce and varieties of mayonnaise.

Tea and coffee are served everywhere, but vodka distilled from rye with blades of buffalo grass in the bottle is regarded as the national drink.

Warsaw Hunter's Stew (Bigos Warszawski)

Stew base:

2 pounds sauerkraut, drained and rinsed
2 pounds ham on the bone or pork spareribs
8 cups beef or chicken stock
1 ounce dried mushrooms or 1/2 pound fresh white mushrooms, sliced
1½ teaspoons cracked black peppercorns
1 teaspoon cracked allspice berries

Meat-and-cabbage mixture:

3/4 pound bacon, cut in dice
2 large onions, sliced
1½ pounds green cabbage, shredded
1/2 pound Polish smoked sausage, such as kielbasa, sliced
1/2 pound Polish fresh pork and garlic sausage

In a large stockpot, combine the sauerkraut and the ham or spareribs, cover with beef or chicken stock, and bring to a boil. Add mushrooms and seasonings. Boil for 15 minutes. Lower heat, cover pot, and simmer for 1 hour.

In large skillet, over medium heat cook bacon until almost done. Gradually stir in onions and cabbage, lightly coating them with bacon drippings. Cook for 15 minutes, stirring occasionally. Mix in sliced sausages and cook additional 10 minutes.

Remove ham or spareribs from stockpot. Debone and cube the meat. Return the meat to the stockpot, and add the cabbage and sausage mixture. Cook uncovered for 1/2 hour. Serve with large boiled potatoes seasoned with butter and caraway seeds.

Yield: 8 servings

Dried Mushroom Barley Soup (Grzybowy Krupnik)

2 ounces dried mushrooms
1 cup warm water
8 cups soup stock or water
1/2 cup pearl barley
1 large onion, diced
3 Idaho potatoes, cubed
2 large carrots, sliced
2 parsnips, sliced
1/2 pound fresh button mushrooms, sliced, optional
2 tablespoons fresh parsley leaves, minced
1 tablespoon fresh dill, minced
salt and pepper to taste

Brush the dried mushrooms free of grit. Break them into half-inch pieces and soak in 1 cup warm water for 1 hour. Bring stock or water to low boil, add the barley, and boil for 10 minutes. Drain the dried mushrooms, add them with the remaining ingredients, and simmer for 1 hour.

Yield: 8 servings

Tomato Soup (Zupa Pomidorowa)

3 tablespoons sweet butter
5 pounds ripe tomatoes, peeled, seeded, and sliced
6 ounces tomato paste
juice of 1/2 lemon
6 cups vegetable stock
1 tablespoon sugar
salt and pepper to taste
2 tablespoons "instant flour"
1 cup sour cream
2 tablespoons fresh dill, minced

Over medium heat, melt the butter in the bottom of a pan large enough to hold all ingredients. Stir in the sliced tomatoes until quite wilted. Add tomato paste and lemon juice. Stir in vegetable stock, sugar, salt, and pepper. Bring to a low boil, lower heat, and simmer for 10 minutes. Mix together the flour and sour cream. Stir in a cup of the tomato mixture, then add it to the simmering soup. Simmer for another 10 minutes, while stirring. Garnish with dill and serve hot.

Yield: 8 servings

Pierogi

Basic dough:
3 cups unbleached all-purpose flour
2 eggs
3 cups sour cream
3 tablespoons peanut oil
pinch of salt
1/2 cup water

Place flour in large bowl and make a well in the center. Break eggs into the well and add the sour cream, oil, and salt. With wooden spoon or fingertips blend the ingredients together, gradually adding water until the dough is smooth and pliable. Divide the dough in half, keeping one-half covered while the other is being rolled out about 1/8 inch thick on a floured board. Cut into 4-inch circles, and place 4 teaspoons of one of the fillings that follows in the center of each. Fold over and crimp the edges to seal. Cover them until all are ready to cook.

To cook *pierogi,* bring 3 or 4 quarts of water to boil with 1 teaspoon of salt. Gently lower 6 or 7 *pierogi* (as many as will cook without touching) into the boiling water. Boil for 5 to 7 minutes or until they float. Remove from water, drain, and place on platter. When all *pierogi* are cooked, they can either be sautéed with onions and butter and served hot with sour cream, or fried until crisp in peanut oil and served hot with sour cream or applesauce.

Yield: 40 pierogi

Mushroom-meat filling:

2 tablespoons unsalted butter
1 medium onion, minced
1/2 pound ground beef or pork
1 pound fresh mushrooms, chopped
1 egg, lightly beaten
1/4 cup fine bread crumbs
salt and pepper to taste

Melt the butter in a skillet and add the onion. Sauté, then add meat and mushrooms. When the meat is cooked, remove from heat and transfer to a mixing bowl. Stir in slightly beaten egg, bread crumbs, and salt and pepper.

Yield: 4 cups, to fill 40 pierogi

Cheese filling:

2 pounds farmer cheese or
2 pounds cottage cheese mixed with 4 tablespoons softened butter
3 eggs
salt and pepper to taste.

Place all ingredients in food processor or blender and work till smooth but still textured, about 7 seconds.

Yield: 4 cups, to fill 40 pierogi

Hungary

Festivals and celebrations are frequent cause for enormous feasts in Hungary. It is traditional for guests to bring the food for weddings, and elaborate cakes five- and six-feet long are carried in to honor the bride and groom.

One seasoning stands out from among the many flavors and techniques Hungary shares with her neighbors—paprika is the one spice most associated with the cooking of Hungary. The Turks established the use of paprika during their occupation of Hungary in the seventeenth and eighteenth centuries. It is often used in a mixture called *lesco*, which is composed of diced, sautéed green sweet peppers, onions, and tomatoes. *Paprikas*, chicken or beef-braised dishes are seasoned with paprika and thickened with sour cream. Caraway and poppy seeds are also used extensively.

Because Hungary is landlocked, Hungarian fish dishes are made with freshwater fish such as carp, catfish, pike, sturgeon, and trout. *Gulyas*, ✹ virtually the national dish, is named for the cooking pot in which nomadic shepherds cooked soups made from meat and pickled cabbage.

Strudel, known as *retes* in Hungary, is made sweet or savory. Many home bakers use thawed frozen filo dough to make the strudel, because the paper-thin dough, which must be made with a high-gluten flour, takes patience and elbow room. Hungarian wine is exported and is available in stores throughout the United States. *Tokaji*, Tokay in English, is a popular dry or sweet wine that is drunk with meals or snacks. E*gi* Bi*kaver*, Bull's Blood, is available in many areas.

Summer Cucumber Soup

3 tablespoons sweet butter
6 shallots, diced
4 leeks, white part only, sliced
3 tablespoons fresh parsley, minced
4 large cucumbers, peeled, seeded, and diced
4 Idaho potatoes, peeled and diced
8 cups soup stock (vegetable or chicken)
salt and pepper to taste
1 cup yogurt
1 tablespoon paprika for garnish
1 tablespoon fresh dill, minced, for garnish

Heat the butter in a skillet over medium heat and lightly sauté the shallots, leeks, and parsley. Do not let them get dark. Bring the cucumbers and potatoes to a boil in the stock. Lower heat, add salt and pepper, and simmer for 30 minutes. Stir in leek mixture and remove from heat. In a blender or food processor, process the soup to a coarse purée. Return to the soup pot and simmer for 10 minutes. Place in a tureen or covered bowl and refrigerate overnight or until chilled through. Stir in yogurt and garnish with paprika and dill.

Yield: 8 servings

Pickled Salmon (Pácolt Lazac)

4 pounds fresh salmon, in one piece
1 lemon, cut in half and seeded
2 quarts fish stock (water may be substituted)
1/2 teaspoon salt
1 cup white or white wine vinegar
1 large white onion, sliced paper thin
3 tablespoons peppercorns
1/4 cup whole allspice
1 tablespoon mustard seeds
4 bay leaves

Place the salmon in a poacher, filled to the steaming shelf with water into which the lemon halves have been placed. Fish may also be poached in a nonreactive skillet. Poach for 10 minutes for each inch of thickness. Remove the salmon and reserve.

Boil the cooking liquid until it is reduced by half. Strain 1½ cups of liquid into a saucepan and add the vinegar, onion, and spices. Simmer for 15 minutes. Skin and debone the salmon, and cut into 1½ inch slices. Place in ceramic or glass deep dish. Pour pickling liquid over the fish. Cover with lid or plastic wrap and chill overnight. Remove fish from liquid and serve cold with thinly sliced buttered bread.

Yield: 8 *servings*

Red Cabbage with Caraway Seeds (Fuszeres Voroskaposzta Komenymaggal)

3 tablespoons peanut oil
1 medium onion, sliced
1 sweet green pepper, seeded and sliced
3 pounds red cabbage
1/2 cup raisins
1 teaspoon caraway seeds
2 teaspoons sugar
3 tablespoons apple-cider vinegar
1/2 teaspoon salt

Heat the oil in a skillet large enough to hold all the ingredients. Sauté the onion and pepper over medium heat. Shred cabbage as for cole slaw. Add to the skillet and stir in the raisins, caraway seeds, sugar, vinegar, and salt. Lower heat, cover, and simmer for 45 minutes. Stir from time to time, adding up to 1/2 cup water if necessary. Serve hot or cold.

Yield: 8 *servings*

Beef Goulash (Marha Gulyas)

3 tablespoons vegetable oil
2½ pounds boneless beef chuck or round, cut in 1-inch cubes
1 medium onion, diced
4 cloves garlic, minced
2 green sweet peppers, seeded
1½ tablespoons paprika, sweet, hot, or mixed
3 tomatoes, peeled, seeded, and cut into 1-inch pieces
3 tablespoons tomato paste mixed with 1 cup water
1 pound small white onions, peeled
3 pounds potatoes, peeled, and cut into 2-inch pieces
1 teaspoon caraway seeds
salt and pepper to taste

Heat the oil in a skillet with a cover or Dutch oven large enough to hold all the ingredients. Brown the beef on all sides and remove to a platter. Sauté the onion, garlic, and peppers. Return beef to the pot and add the paprika, stirring to distribute evenly. Brown for a few minutes and add the tomatoes, tomato-paste mixture, and small onions. Cover, lower heat, and cook for 1½ hours. Add potatoes and cook for another 30 minutes or until potatoes are tender.

Yield: 6 servings

Russia, Georgia, Ukraine

The seven-million square miles of Russia traverse northern Asia from Finland to the Bering Strait, which separate it from Alaska. Russian food, as you might expect, varies. In St. Petersburg in the northwest, even in the last century boats along the canals brought live fish from the Neva and the Moika: noble red salmon and sturgeon, fresh and salted caviar, barrels of perch, eels, and crawfish, smoked and dried fish, as well as the whole fish that were frozen in blocks of ice and shipped as far as Berlin.

Market stalls, then and now, sell prepared food: *piroghi* and *blini* with *smetana* or *knishi* with *kaimak*, meat pies, and gingerbread. Finnish and Germanic influences are apparent.

In the far north, Mongol culture is present in the cuisine not only in the skewering and grilling of meat, but in the profusion of Asian-style dumplings and noodles. The south shares the subtropic zone with its neighbors. Georgia has dishes that taste surprisingly Middle Eastern. In Ukraine, cooks prepare soups and bake bread that only a native can tell from those of Poland.

In New York, we are lucky to have a great variety of Russian, Ukrainian, and Polish restaurants, from unpretentious counters that sell the best soups in the world to places like Petrossian's with the best caviar and blini, to the landmark Russian Tea Room (recently closed) with its elegant array of Russian Court cuisine. Brighton Beach in Brooklyn has Russian nightclubs that make every meal a party.

Ukrainian Borscht

3 tablespoons vegetable oil
2½ pounds beef chuck, bone in
2 large onions, peeled and sliced
4 garlic cloves, peeled and minced
1 cup small white mushrooms, sliced
1½ pounds cabbage, shredded
2 carrots, scraped and sliced
2 parsnips, scraped and sliced
4 medium beets, scraped and diced
3 tablespoons tomato paste
1 teaspoon sour salt (citric acid)
3 tablespoons sugar
salt and pepper to taste
3 medium tomatoes, peeled, seeded, and diced
2 Idaho potatoes, peeled and diced
2 tablespoons fresh dill, minced
1 cup sour cream, optional, as garnish

In a Dutch oven large enough to hold all ingredients, heat the oil, and brown the beef, onions, garlic, and mushrooms. Add 3 quarts of water, all the vegetables, and seasoning. Bring the borscht to a boil, lower heat, and simmer for 1½ hours. Remove the meat and bones. Dice the beef and return to the soup. Serve hot with a dollop of sour cream.

Yield: 8 servings

From the menu of

Russian Tea Time

77 East Adams Street
Chicago, IL 60604

Soups

Classic Ukrainian Borscht

Soup of beets, cabbage, carrots, onions, potatoes and tomatoes
served with sour cream or yogurt

Salads

Tashkent Carrot Salad

The most elegant culinary creation of our hometown, Tashkent,
the capital of Uzbekistan. Airy-sliced carrots marinated in our
house vinegar and delicately spiced with coriander seeds

Russian "Pink" Salad Vinaigrette—Vinegret

Steamed beets, boiled potato and carrots, chopped onions,
pickles, apples, green peas, sauerkraut, gently mixed with
olive oil and red wine vinegar

Appetizers or Zakuski

Potato Pancakes—Latkes

Hot fresh potato pancakes served with sour cream and
apple sauce

Stuffed Mushrooms, Azerbajiani Style— Gribi Farshirovannie Po Azerbadzhanski

Four baked white mushrooms stuffed with sautéed spinach, onions, garlic and assorted cheese

Georgian Beet Caviar with Walnuts and Prunes

Baked beets with prunes and roasted walnuts, garlic, coarsely chopped and mixed with mayonnaise, and a touch of fresh lemon juice

Legendary Georgian Bean Salad—Lobio

A classic Georgian salad—parboiled kidney beans, chopped onion, fresh cilantro with a touch of lemon juice and vinegar

Chopped Eggplant Orientale—Baklazhanaya Ikra

Chopped eggplant simmered with tomatoes, carrots, pepper and onions, served chilled

Dough Appetizers

Ukrainian Pumpkin Piroshki

Stuffed with pumpkin and onions; served with carrot salad and sour cream

Lamb Uzbek Pastry—Samsa

Puff pastry stuffed with ground lamb and onions, with a touch of cumin. Unlike Pakistani or Indian "samosa," Uzbek samsa is very lightly spiced

Ukrainian Potato Dumplings—Vareniky

Dumplings filled with potatoes and shaped as a half-moon, boiled and then tossed in butter. Served with sour cream and yogurt sauce

From the menu of Russian Tea Time (continued)

Main Course

Kebabs

A skewer of juicy kebabs (lamb or chicken), marinated with coriander, grilled over charcoal

Chicken Kiev—Kotleti Po-Kievski

Chicken breast stuffed with butter, fresh lemon juice, breaded, baked and then deep-fried to a golden brown

Wild Game

Grilled Quail with Dried Cherries— Zharennaya Perepelka S Vishnyami

Marinated and grilled quail with sun-dried cherries served with a pomegranate sauce and traditional garnish

Marinated Venison with Raspberry Sauce, Careme Style— Oleniatina Po-Franzuski S Malinoi

Two venison chops, grilled and served over raspberry and wine sauce, with poached prunes, baked apple and marinated beets

Salmon and Mushroom Kulebiaka (Kulebiaka S Nachinkoi Iz Ryby I Gribov)

Crust:

5 cups "instant" flour
1 teaspoon salt
1¾ cups sweet butter, chilled and cut in cubes
2 eggs, slightly beaten
1 cup iced water
1 egg white, slightly beaten, to brush dough before baking
2 tablespoons sweet butter, melted, to brush dough after baking

Pour the flour and salt into a food processor with a metal blade and pulse for a few seconds. Incorporate the butter, pulsing until the mixture looks like coarse bread crumbs. Add the eggs and pulse until they are incorporated. Add the water and pulse only until blended. Turn out onto a floured board. Shape into a rectangle about 8 inches by 12 inches. Wrap in plastic wrap and refrigerate up to 3 hours.

Mushroom layer:

4 tablespoons sweet butter
2 pounds small button mushrooms, sliced
1/4 cup minced parsley leaves
1 medium onion, peeled and diced
1/2 cup minced green onions
3 eggs, hard cooked and diced
salt and pepper to taste
2 tablespoons flour
1/2 cup sour cream

Heat butter in a skillet and sauté the mushrooms, onion, and green onions. Remove from heat and stir in the hard-cooked eggs, and salt and pepper to taste. Mix together the flour and sour cream and stir into the mushroom mixture. Reserve until the *kulebiaka* is assembled.

Poached salmon layer:

2 pounds salmon filet
3 cups stock or water
1/4 cup fresh lemon juice or wine

Bring the liquid to a boil and poach fish 10 minutes for each inch of thickness. Slice the fish into 1-inch slices and reserve for assembly.

Sautéed salmon layer:

2 tablespoons sweet butter
1 pound salmon filets, cut in slices
1½ cups cooked rice
salt and pepper to taste

Heat butter and sauté the salmon. Stir in the rice until well mixed and reserve until ready to assemble.

Preheat oven to 400°.
   Roll the dough out 13-inches wide by 18-inches long. If there is any excess dough, reserve it. On the 13-inch width make a light score with a dull knife 3½ inches from each end. This will leave a center panel 6-inches wide. Place the rice and sautéed fish mixture along this rectangle. Spread the mushroom mixture over it. Top with a layer of poached salmon. Bring the sides up over the filling to meet in the middle. Brush the dough with the beaten egg white, and crimp the seam together by pinching it with your thumbs. Pierce the length of the *kulebiaka* with a sharp knife to make decorative steam vents. If there is any dough remaining, it can be cut into decorative shapes and attached to the surface of the dough with the egg white. Bake for 30 minutes or until the dough is golden brown.

Yield: 6 servings

5

THE MIDDLE EAST: GREECE, TURKEY, AND ISRAEL

In this region, the site of the Garden of Eden, and the soil of Judaism, Christianity, and Islam, there are blurred and debated culinary borders and the menus sometimes read like Bible verses. Historically, these eastern Mediterranean coastlands and islands have been called the *Levant*, from the French "to rise" first used for the direction in which the sun rises, then as a colloquialism for the East. (In Europe, the Far East was referred to as the *High Levant* until the seventeenth century.)

The extraordinary beauty of the region is overwhelming. It is rich in grain, olives, figs, honey, wild herbs, spices, vegetables, nuts, and fruit. Fish, game, sheep, and goats are abundant. Bread, such as pita, and varieties of sweet pastries have been made in similar fashion for ages. One of the most familiar is *baklava*, made from paper-thin layers of *filo* or *kataifi* dough and chopped nuts, baked in a syrup of honey and rosewater. A similar confection, rolled into lady fingers, is called *Asabe'a*. *Usmalia* is a Middle Eastern cream puff formed with shredded filo dough, filled with cream, bathed in syrup, and topped with pistachios and candied orange blossoms.

From corner falafel stands to roadside kabob vendors, the food of the Middle East is something we are accustomed to throughout the United States. Fine restaurants are in evidence as well. Food ignores politics, and Arab and Israeli from Lebanon, Syria, Israel, and the surrounding areas enjoy the same dishes made with the same ingredients and light touch. At even the smallest establishment, there is a sink near the door so that you may wash your hands before you eat.

Driving along the West Bank of the Jordan with a friend, we stopped in Jericho and bought date palms still on the branch. In markets in Beersheeba and Gaza, warm, spicy small dishes are sold accompanied by olives, pita bread, and small cups of dark, sweet coffee. The foods of parts of Turkey and Greece are almost identical and are equally delicious. At seaside taverns, there are fish grilled minutes after they are caught, as well as small baked pastries, savory and sweet, as pick-me-ups.

Turkey

Turkey is a land bridge between Asia and Eastern Europe. As such, it has been a crossroads for many culinary influences that have traveled in and out of the Middle East. The Ottoman Empire established Istanbul on the site of the Byzantine capital of Constantinople where the Sultanate had as many as 1500 cooks at the Topkapi Palace.

The hospitality of the area is expressed in the *meze*, an array of small dishes. There are one hundred or more recipes for *borek*, a sweet or savory small pie made with a pastry called *yufka*. Though it is a predominately Muslim country, *raki*, an anise-flavored liqueur is popular. A *raki* table is *meze* served with liquor.

In Turkish cuisine, spices, herbs, and seasonings are used not only in preparing food but as lavish garnishes. Olive-oil dishes are offered with fresh parsley, mint, or dill. Since most of these dishes are served at room temperature, the freshness of the herbs enhances the flavors. Black peppercorns, chilies, allspice, cinnamon, cloves, cumin, fennel, fenugreek, and ginger flavor many dishes. Oregano, saffron (among the best in the world), safflower, savory, sweet basil, tarragon, and thyme are used with a free hand.

Yogurt is of excellent quality and not only eaten plain, but made into soups, sauces, and desserts. A wonderful beverage called *airan* is a yogurt shake, similar to the Indian yogurt drink, *lassi*. Butter and buttermilk are used as well. Cheese called *kelek* is incorporated into everything from pilafs to desserts.

From early times in Central Asia, Turkish traditions involved both rapid cooking like kebabs, or long cooking in underground ovens called *tandirs*. Preservation of meat was done by salting and sun-drying, called *pastirma*. Lamb and goat continue to be preferred over beef.

Dolma and *sarma*, wrapped or stuffed vegetables, are cooked in imaginative ways to produce delicious and healthful dishes.

Rye and wheat are the main grains; corn, millet, nuts, and seeds are also used. Soups, pilafs, bulgur, and salads are based on these.

Fresh fruit such as citrus, apricots, cherries, and plums are abundant in season and dried for storage. *Kak*, the name for all dried fruit, is softened and often sweetened with a molasses made from grapes, and turned into a pudding served with nuts and yogurt. By far the most popular desserts are the layered pastries made with buttery *phyllo* dough, filled with ground nuts, and doused with honey or syrup, called *baklava* or *sobiyet*. Sugar has replaced molasses and honey, but pistachios, walnuts, cream, and cheese are still the basic fillings.

For centuries, eating at home was from a copper or brass *sini*, a tray table set 8 or 9 inches over a newly placed tablecloth. People sit cross-legged or kneel at the table, with long narrow napkins across their laps. Spoons and bread were the utensils of choice. Today, even in the countryside, tables and chairs set with cloths and napkins and a full array of flatware are found.

Tradition says that hands must be washed before eating, and in a room with no running water an ornamented pitcher and bowl are set in a corner. Even small restaurants in Turkey have easily available sinks with decorative towels for washing and drying the hands before eating. It is considered rude to leave food on one's plate and, in even moderately religious homes, a form of grace is said, which usually begins, "I start with the name of God." If bread is dropped on the floor, it has to be picked up, kissed, and set aside to feed pets or livestock.

Though there is poverty, as in all countries, Turkey has a tradition of established soup kitchens that serve meals to the needy twice a day.

THE TURKISH KITCHEN

Owned by Ilgar Peker and Sedat Dakan, the Turkish Kitchen is a New York landmark. Mustafa Durdu is the chef in charge. The mood is set in a comfortable dining room with Turkish carpets on the walls and Turkish music playing softly. We start with *kirmizi mercimek çorbasi,* a red lentil soup that is made smooth and creamy with the addition of butter to blend the flavors. Crisp croutons and parsley leaves add texture. *Meze* follows: *Patlican salatasi,* roasted eggplant salad; *humus,* chickpea salad; *yaprak dolmasi,* stuffed grape leaves; *kalamar tava sarmisakli sirkeli salçqa,* fried squid with garlic sauce; *zeytin yagli enginar,* fresh artichoke heart with vegetables; and *cigeri* with *sogan salatasi,* liver cubes with onion salad. *Karides pilaf,* shrimp pilaf, is made with shrimp, sweet peppers, fresh tomatoes, and cheese served with long-grain rice cooked with a little butter. As we talk, Ilgar Peker explains that one of the tests of Turkish cooking is that everything tastes natural and fresh: enhanced by herbs and spices, but cooked in its own juices without sauces or wines. Vegetables and grains are treated with the same attention as fancy cuts of meat and fish. *Icli kofte* is a pan-fried bulgur-wheat shell filled with ground beef, rice, currants, and pine nuts, flavored with allspice and cumin. *Doner kebab* is a spit-roasted lamb dish served with a rice pilaf that is simple and elegant.

Dessert is pastry—hazelnut *baklava* and pistachio *sobiyet,* flaky and light, served slightly warm. Other options are rice or almond pudding.

Turkish coffee ends this meal, as it usually does. In the morning, tea is drunk and is sipped throughout the day, as are soft drinks like *ayron,* a yogurt drink, or spring water like *Pinar Sasal,* a popular brand. *Kavaklidere* is a well-known vintner that produces red and white wines that are available at the Turkish Kitchen. They also make a sweet dessert wine that is very pleasant.

Creamy Red-Lentil Soup
(Kirmizi Mercimek Çorbasi)

Courtesy Chef Yakup Karatas—Turkish Kitchen

1 cup red lentils
1½ cups chopped white onions
4 tablespoons sweet butter
6½ cups chicken, beef, or vegetable stock
2 tablespoons unbleached all-purpose flour
2 egg yolks
1 cup milk

Croutons:

3/4 cup white bread, cut in small cubes
3 tablespoons sweet butter
1/4 cup fresh parsley leaves for garnish

Pick over lentils, wash, drain, and reserve. In a stockpot large enough to hold all the ingredients, sauté the onions in 2 tablespoons of the butter until golden. Add the stock and bring to a boil Add lentils, cover, and simmer for 30 minutes. Purée the lentils in a food mill or processor.

Melt the remaining butter in the pan, add flour, and stir till it is light brown. Stir the flour mixture, as you pour the lentil purée back in the pan. Simmer.

In a small bowl, beat the egg yolks and milk, season with salt to taste. Slowly add 1 cup of soup to egg mixture, then pour the mixture into the soup, stirring continuously. Bring it almost to a boil and serve. Soup will keep but may need to be thinned with water or stock.

Fry bread cubes in butter till they are medium brown.

Serve soup with croutons and garnish with parsley leaves.

Yield: 6 servings

From the menu of

Turkish Kitchen

386 Third Avenue
New York, NY 10016

Appetizers

Pastirmali Sigara Boregi

Pan-fried phyllo scrolls stuffed with aged beef filet mignon

Midye Dolma

Mussels seasoned and stuffed with rice, onions, pine nuts and
currants. Cooked with olive oil and served room temperature

Lahmacun

Thin pie dough topped with spicy lamb filling

Zeytinyagli Fasulye

Green string beans cooked with onion, tomatoes, lemon and
olive oil. Served cold

Patlican Kozleme

Char grilled smoked baby eggplant with homemade garlic sauce

Soslu Patlican

Cubes of eggplant baked with olive oil and garnished with
tomatoes, green peppers, onions and garlic

Piyaz

White kidney bean salad. Garnished with onions, hard-boiled eggs,
parsley and black olives. Served with olive oil and vinegar dressing

Mucver

Pan-fried zucchini pancakes served with yogurt and garlic sauce

Karisik Dolma

Green pepper and tomato, stuffed with rice, currants, pine nuts and herbs. Cooked with olive oil and served room temperature

Haydari

Thick cream of yogurt mixed with walnuts, garlic, and olive oil and garnished with dill

Imam Bayildi

Whole eggplant stuffed with tomatoes, onions and herbs. Cooked with olive oil and served room temperature

Entrées

Tavuklu Hunkar Begendi

Pureed eggplant topped with baked chunks of chicken, marinated in tomato sauce

Tavuk Koftesi

Hand-chopped chicken meat patties, seasoned with Turkish spices and char grilled

Kul Basti

Boneless lamb chops, char grilled and served over a bed of white rice and pan-fried potatoes

Bildircin Izgara

Char grilled quails served with zucchini pancakes and rice

Bonfile sis

Chunks of filet mignon grilled on a skewer with mushrooms, green peppers and onions

Levrek

Whole striped bass, char grilled. Served with romaine salad, topped with onions and lemon oil dressing

Roasted Eggplant Salad (Patlican Salatsi)

Courtesy Turkish Kitchen

1 ¼ pounds eggplant
3 tablespoons fresh lemon juice
3 garlic cloves, peeled and crushed
salt to taste
6 tablespoons olive oil
1/4 cup fresh coriander or parsley leaves for garnish

Roast the eggplant over a grill or gas flame, turning it with tongs until skin is blackened and the eggplant is soft. Cool the eggplant and remove skin. Discard the seeds. Place in a colander, cover with 3 tablespoons of lemon juice, and let drain for 20 minutes.

Press out all the moisture. In small portions, pound the eggplant and garlic in a mortar, or put in a processor and blend. Add oil gradually with remaining lemon juice. Serve on a shallow platter topped with coriander or parsley leaves.

Yield: 1 *pint*

Crisp Fried Squid with Garlic Vinegar Sauce (Kalamar Tava Sarmisakli Sirkeli Salçqa)

Courtesy Turkish Kitchen

Squid:

2 pounds squid, cleaned and sliced
1 teaspoon salt
1 cup unbleached all-purpose flour

Batter:

1/2 cup cornstarch
1/2 cup unbleached all-purpose flour
salt and pepper to taste
2 cups light beer
2 eggs, separated

Safflower oil for deep frying
1½ cups garlic-vinegar sauce❀

Put the squid in a bowl and sprinkle with the salt. For the batter, mix the cornstarch, flour, salt, and pepper. Add the beer and egg yolks and whisk until well blended. In a separate bowl, beat the egg whites into soft peaks and fold into the batter.

Drain the squid and coat with flour. Heat oil in a fryer to 350°, or follow electric fryer instructions. Drop the rings in batter and lift with fingertips or long-tined fork, letting excess batter drip back into bowl. Fry until dark golden brown. Drain on paper towels, and serve immediately with sauce.

Yield: 4 servings

Garlic Vinegar Sauce

Five 1/2-inch slices French bread, crusts removed
1 small head of garlic, peeled
1/4 teaspoon salt
3/4 cup olive oil
1/4 cup red wine vinegar

Soak the bread in water to cover. Squeeze dry and set aside. Pound the garlic cloves in a mortar with salt until thoroughly pureed. Stir in the bread and blend with the garlic. Gradually add olive oil and vinegar. Add salt and additional vinegar to taste. Sauce will keep covered in the refrigerator for several days. Thin with water, if desired.

Yield: 1½ cups

Fresh Artichoke Hearts with Vegetables (Zeytin Yagli Enginar)

Courtesy Turkish Kitchen

4 large artichokes
1 cup fresh lemon juice
2 medium onions, peeled and quartered
4 medium carrots, scraped and sliced 1/2-inch thick
1 cup fresh green peas
1 tablespoon sugar
6 tablespoons olive oil
pinch of salt
1 pound small potatoes, peeled and trimmed to same size
1 tablespoon unbleached all-purpose flour dissolved in 1 cup water
3/4 cup chopped fresh dill

Remove the outer leaves from the artichokes and trim stalks leaving 2-inches of stalk, or as much as possible. With a very sharp knife, pare artichokes down to the heart. Scoop out the chokes and drop artichokes into a bowl of water. Add 1/2 cup lemon juice to the water to prevent discoloration. When the artichokes are ready, place them in a deep sauté pan that will hold them side by side with the vegetables.

Place the onions, carrots, and peas over the artichokes. Add the sugar, olive oil, salt, 2 tablespoons lemon juice, and 2 cups of water. Cover and simmer for 30 minutes. Add the potatoes and cook till they are tender. Mix the flour and water with remaining lemon juice. Pour over vegetables and cook, uncovered, for 5 minutes. Arrange artichokes on a serving platter stem-side up, surrounded by vegetables and a small amount of the liquid. Chill and top with dill before serving.

Yield: 4 servings

Hazelnut *Baklava* (Findikli Baklava)

Courtesy Turkish Kitchen

Pastry:

 1 pound hazelnuts
 1/4 cup sugar
 butter for greasing baking sheet
 1 pound frozen filo pastry, defrosted
 1/2 pound sweet butter, melted

Syrup:

 1¾ cups sugar
 1¼ cups water
 2 teaspoons lemon juice

Preheat oven to 350°.

   Coat a 9- by 13-inch baking sheet with butter. Coarsely grind the hazelnuts and sugar in a processor and set aside. Place the baking sheet on counter, and start by putting a half-sheet of filo on the sheet, letting the other half lay over the side. Butter the pastry lightly and fold the other half of the pastry over it. Brush with melted butter and repeat, until one-third of the pastry is used.

   Spread the nut mixture over the pastry and continue layering and buttering the pastry until it is all used.

   Pour the remaining butter over all, and score into diamond shapes with 1-inch sides. Bake 20 minutes, then cover lightly with parchment paper, and bake for 30 minutes more.

   While the baklava is baking, bring the sugar and water to a boil, simmer syrup for 5 minutes, and stir in the lemon juice. Stir and simmer for 3 minutes. Remove from heat and cool.

   Remove the baklava from the oven and drain any excess butter. Pour the syrup over the baklava and recut the pieces all the way through. Let stand for several hours before serving.

Yield: 30 pieces

Spiced Olives

1/2 pound small black olives
1/2 pound green olives
1 cup olive oil
6 garlic cloves, slightly crushed
1 teaspoon *harissa*
1 lemon, sliced paper thin, skin on, seeds removed
2 tablespoons fresh coriander leaves

Bring the olives to a boil in water to cover, then drain. Place the olives in cold water and bring them to a boil again. Boil the olives 1 minute, and then drain. Make slight incision in the green olives. Mix all the ingredients and store in a covered jar in the refrigerator.

Yield: 1 quart of olives

Harissa

1 ounce hot chili pepper, dried
3 cloves garlic, minced
1/2 cup olive oil.

Place the chili in a bowl and pour hot water over it to cover by 1 inch. Drain, mince, and blend with garlic in mortar and pestle or processor. Add to olive oil and store in covered container.

Yield: 1/2 cup

Bulgur Salad (Taboulah)

2 cups medium bulgur
3/4 cup fine olive oil
3/4 cup fresh lemon juice
1 cup chopped green onions, minced
4 large tomatoes, peeled, seeded, and diced
3 cucumbers, peeled, seeded, and diced
1/2 cup flat-leafed parsley leaves, minced
1/4 cup fresh mint leaves, minced
salt and pepper to taste

Place the bulgur in a bowl large enough to hold all the ingredients. Pour 1 cup of boiling water over bulgur and stir. Let sit while preparing the other ingredients. Stir all ingredients together until light and fluffy. Serve warm or cold.

Yield: 1 quart of salad

Greece

Delphi, with ancient olive trees and swarming honey bees, is evoked in the many Greek restaurants throughout North America. No ancient oracle I've read about predicted that we would be enjoying the food of the gods in our busy cities from coast to coast. Originally, Greek coffee shops popularized a small portion of the cuisine. The best known Greek dishes in this country have been *mezes*, small hot or cold savory dishes that can make up an entire meal. In an age-old tradition, platters of small dishes have been set out at various times of the day, usually to the accompaniment of something to drink, in homes and public places. They may be as simple as little bowls of olives, spicy almonds, or honeyed walnuts. Plato describes a *meze* table with these dishes, and radishes, greens, figs, beans, seeds, cheese, and myrtle.

Some other *mezes* are small baked or fried filo dough pastries filled with spinach, cheese, mushrooms, or chicken and limited only by the chef's imagination. Yogurt- or eggplant-based dips are served, as well as roe and seafood salads. Stuffed grape leaves and stuffed mussels are other favorites. A classic *zoupa* was made of grilled bread, placed in a bowl over which was poured warm red wine and verdant olive oil. Spit-roasting is popular, from *souvlakia* and other tidbits to whole baby lamb. Fish and seafood are served along the endless shore simply broiled or fried and sometimes in stews and layered dishes.

From the menu of

Pegasus

130 South Halsted Street
Chicago, IL 60661

Appetizers

Saganaki "Opa"
Greek kaseri cheese

Tiropitakia
Feta cheese enveloped in thin layers of filo dough

Kalamarakia Yemista
Stuffed squid with spinach, feta cheese and herbs in tomato-wine
sauce

Taramosalata
Red Greek caviar

Tzatziki
Yogurt with grated cucumbers, salt, garlic, and olive oil

Melizanosalata
Eggplant made into a spread

Scordalia
Garlic dip

Traditional Greek Specialties

Spanakotiropita
Spinach cheese pie, savory feta cheese, fresh leaf spinach, eggs, and spices in thin delicate layers of filo dough

Dolmathes
Seasoned ground meat and rice wrapped in grape leaves topped with egg-lemon sauce

Gyros Plate
Served with onion, tzatziki and pita bread

Arni Kokkinisto
Braised lamb served with your choice of cooked vegetables, rice or potato

Arni Psito
Roast leg of lamb, natural au jus served with your choice of cooked vegetables, rice or potato

Greek Pastas—Macaronades

Shrimp Aegean
Imported spaghetti in a delicious aromatic sauce of tomato, herbs, shallots, garlic, fresh basil, feta cheese and large shrimp

Yuvetsaki
Tender morsels of choice beef or lamb, braised with fresh plum tomatoes, olive oil, wine, fresh herbs and imported pasta, baked individually in a casserole crowned with plenty of Myzithra

From the menu of Pegasus (continued)

Makaronada Orphanie

Imported macaroni cooked to order sauteed in butter with
Myzithra cheese

Makaronada Horiatiki

Made to order imported macaroni sauteed in butter with tender
chunks of beef in a rich tomato-herb sauce

Macaronada alla Greca

Imported macaroni sauteed in sizzling butter, topped with our
delicious ground beef in tomato-plum sauce with herbs and plenty
of Myzithra cheese

Macaronada Mediterranean

Imported spaghetti with our special salsa of plum tomatoes, herbs,
shallots, fresh basil and a hint of garlic

Cucumber and Yogurt Dip (Tzatziki)

2 cups plain yogurt
2 large cucumbers
4 cloves garlic, crushed, fibrous parts discarded
1 tablespoon vinegar
2 tablespoons olive oil
1/2 teaspoon cumin
salt and pepper to taste

Line a colander with a double thickness of dampened cheesecloth. Put the yogurt into the colander. Place over a bowl to catch drippings, and refrigerate 4 hours or overnight. Peel, seed, and grate cucumbers. Drain. Mix all ingredients and blend. Place in four bowls and serve cold with warm or toasted pita bread.

Yield: 4 servings

Lemon Soup (Avgolemono)

1½ quarts chicken stock
1 skinless chicken breast, diced
1 medium carrot, diced
2 stalks celery, diced
1 small onion, diced
salt and pepper to taste
2/3 cup orzo
2 eggs, separated
juice of 1 lemon

Bring the chicken stock to a low boil and add the chicken, carrot, celery, and onion. Simmer 8 minutes. Season and add orzo. Boil 6 minutes, or until orzo is tender. Lower heat and keep at a slow simmer. Beat egg whites. Whisk the egg yolks and lemon juice and fold into egg whites. Add 1 cup hot stock to lemon sauce and stir. Add to simmering soup and serve immediately.

Yield: 6 servings

Stuffed Tomatoes (Yemistes Domates Laderes)

6 large tomatoes
1/4 teaspoon salt
1 teaspoon sugar
1 cup olive oil
1 large onion, diced
1/2 cup pine nuts
1/4 cup fresh parsley, chopped
1/4 cup fresh dill, chopped
1/4 cup currants
1 cup rice, uncooked
salt and pepper to taste

Preheat oven to 350°.

Slice off the tops of the tomatoes and set aside. Scoop out the pulp of the tomatoes, discarding as many seeds as possible. Dice pulp and reserve. Sprinkle the tomato shells with salt and sugar.

Heat 1/3 cup olive oil in a skillet and brown the onions and pine nuts. Remove from heat and stir in the parsley, dill, and currants. Add 1/3 cup olive oil and the rice and stir until well mixed. Add 1/3 cup water and tomato pulp. Gently fill the tomatoes and cover with tops. Place in casserole or baking pan with 1/3 cup olive oil and 1/4 cup water. Cover and bake for 30 minutes. Serve at room temperature.

Yield: 6 servings

Beef Stew with Tomatoes and Onions (Stefado)

3 tablespoons sweet butter
2 pounds beef round, cubed
1 medium onion, diced
4 garlic cloves, minced
1/2 cup red wine
1/2 cup red-wine vinegar
2 cups tomatoes, peeled and seeded, fresh or canned
3 tablespoons tomato paste
2 teaspoons sugar
3 cinnamon sticks, slightly crushed
1 teaspoon dried oregano
1 bay leaf, crushed
salt and pepper to taste
3 tablespoons olive oil

3 pounds small, whole, white onions (not pearl), peeled
2 tablespoons fresh parsley leaves, minced
2 teaspoons grated lemon zest

In a stove-top casserole, melt the butter and brown the beef, diced onions, and garlic. Add the wine and stir until the wine is almost entirely absorbed. Add the wine vinegar, tomatoes, and tomato paste. Stir and mix in sugar, cinnamon, oregano, salt, and pepper. Cover and stew over medium heat. Heat the olive oil in a skillet and brown the small onions. When they are well glazed, add to the beef stew. Cover and simmer on low heat for 1 hour, stirring from time to time. Serve hot, garnished with parsley leaves and lemon zest.

Yield: 6 servings

Pocket Bread (Pita)

1 package dry yeast
1/4 teaspoon salt
1/2 teaspoon sugar
1¼ cups warm water
3½ cups unbleached all-purpose flour
2 tablespoons olive oil
olive oil for coating bowl and baking sheets

Place the yeast, salt, sugar, and 1/4 cup warm water in a large mixing bowl. After 5 minutes, beat in the remaining 1 cup water, 1½ cups flour, and 2 tablespoons olive oil. Beat for 5 minutes. Add the remaining flour, incorporating it by hand. Knead for 10 minutes. Place in an oiled bowl, turning once so that surface is coated with oil. Cover and let rise for 1 hour.

Preheat oven to 400°.

Punch down dough and divide into 10 equal pieces. Form each piece into a 6-inch disk with the palms of your hand. Place on greased baking sheets. Cover and let rise again for 30 minutes. Bake for 25 minutes, or until lightly browned and puffed. Serve warm or wrap in aluminum foil, cool, and reheat when needed.

Yield: 10 pieces

Lamb-Eggplant Casserole (Moussaka)

2 medium eggplants, sliced thin
1 tablespoon coarse salt
3 tablespoons olive oil
2 medium onions, diced
2 green peppers, seeded and diced
4 cloves garlic, minced
1½ pounds ground lamb
2 teaspoons sweet paprika
1/2 teaspoon cracked black pepper
1/4 teaspoon salt
1/2 teaspoon cinnamon
3/4 cup plain yogurt
4 egg yolks
1 tablespoon "instant" flour

Preheat oven to 350°.

Place the eggplant slices in a large colander. Salt them and let drain for about 20 minutes.

In a large skillet, heat the olive oil and brown the onions, peppers, and garlic. Add the ground lamb, paprika, pepper, salt, and cinnamon. When the meat is crumbled and cooked, remove it to a bowl and set aside.

Sauté the eggplant slices in the skillet, adding more oil if necessary. When the slices are browned on both sides, remove them and set them aside.

In a flat casserole, alternate layers of the eggplant and the meat mixture. Cover casserole. (You may use aluminum foil.) Bake for 45 minutes. Beat together the yogurt, egg yolks, and flour. Leave oven heat on and remove casserole. Remove the cover and spread the yogurt mixture over all. Return uncovered casserole to the oven and bake for 15 minutes. Serve hot.

Yield: 6 servings

Greece—Glossary

amigthala   almonds

arni   lamb

avgolemono   egg-and-lemon mixture

baklava   flaky pastry filled with chopped nuts and soaked in honey syrup

boureki (or *bourekakia*)   filo puffs with various fillings

dolmades   meat- or rice-filled grape leaves

domate   tomatoes

ellies   olives

feta   salty, white, goat cheese

filo (or *phyllo*)   paper-thin pastry sheets, usually bought frozen, used in both sweet and savory dishes

garides   shrimp

glikaniso   anise, base for *ouzo*

gouvetsi   casserole

kafes   coffee

kalamaria   squid

kasseri   creamy, mild sheep cheese

keftedes   meatballs

keik cake

kota chicken

kourabiedes butter cookies

laderes food cooked in olive oil served cold

ladolemono oil and lemon juice dressing

masticha slightly bitter tree sap, used in some bread and cookies

melitzanosalata eggplant salad

mezedakia (*mezes*) savory appetizers

mosharaki veal

myzithra cheese, served soft or used hard for grating

orzo rice-shaped pasta

ouzo anise flavored liquor

pastitsio layers of macaroni and spicy meat with a creamy topping

pilafi rice cooked with savory ingredients, such as onions, nuts, raisins, and spices

psari fish

retsina white or rosé wine flavored with pine resin

rigani oregano, used widely

skordalia garlic sauce

skortho garlic

spanakopeta spinach in filo puffs

tarama gray-mullet roe

taramasalata fish-roe spread

thiosmos mint

tighanito fried

tiropetes cheese-filled filo puffs

tis skaras broiled food

tzatziki cucumber-yogurt dip

viourti yogurt

vothino beef

voutiro butter

vrasto boiled or poached

yiahni stew

zesto hot

zoumi broth

Israel

Israeli cuisine has incorporated traditional Middle East fare with the dishes that settlers from different regions have brought. Fish is eaten in great quantities, along with the fruit and vegetables of the orchards and farms developed in the last fifty years. The grapes are remarkable, as are the famous oranges and tomatoes that are imported to North America in great quantities.

Only a few Israeli restaurants are kosher. According to kosher law, these restaurants must never serve dairy and meat products together. Separate sets of dishes and cooking equipment, as well as utensils, must be organized. Meat must be from an animal that chews its cud and has a divided hoof. Beef and lamb can be kosher, pork and rabbit cannot. Meat, including chicken, must be slaughtered in a ritual way and often salted before cooking. Only fish with fins and scales may be eaten: No shellfish or eels are permitted. There is a large group of foods that is considered *pareve*, or neutral. Grain, fruit, vegetables, eggs, nuts, and so on may be eaten with either dairy or meat.

Falafel on pita♠ has become a universal favorite.

Fat-Free Pocket Bread (Israeli Pita)

1 package dry yeast
1/2 cup warm water
2 teaspoons salt
2 tablespoons honey
6 cups unbleached all-purpose flour
2 cups warm water
oil for greasing rising bowl

Mix the yeast in 1/2 cup warm water with salt and honey. Let stand 10 minutes. Place 4 cups of flour in a large bowl and beat in the yeast mixture with 2 cups of warm water. Turn out on a floured board and knead for 10 minutes. Oil a large bowl, place the dough in it, and turn so that entire surface is coated with oil. Cover and let rise for 1½ hours.

Preheat oven to 450°.

Punch down the dough and divide it into 12 pieces. Roll each piece into a disk about 5 inches across. Place the disks on 1 or 2 ungreased baking sheets. Cover and let rise for 12 minutes. Bake for 8 to 10 minutes. If they do not puff up, spray them with water and raise the oven temperature to 475°. Serve immediately, or cool and freeze.

Yield: 12 *pieces*

Fried Chick-pea Cakes (Falafel)

1 cup dried chick-peas
1 teaspoon baking soda
1/2 teaspoon salt
1 teaspoon ground cumin
1 teaspoon ground coriander
1 medium onion, sliced
1 clove garlic
2 tablespoons chopped fresh parsley leaves
1 tablespoon lemon juice
1/2 teaspoon chili powder
oil for deep-fat frying

Soak the chick-peas in 6 cups of water for 24 hours. Pulse all ingredients, except for oil, in processor until well ground. This may also be done in a meat grinder, putting the mixture through twice.

Heat oil to 350° in fryer or wok. For electric deep fryer, follow manufacturer's directions. Form the chick-pea batter into about 12 balls, 1½ inch in diameter, and fry. Set on paper towels to drain. Serve on warm pita with shredded lettuce, tomato, tahini,❦ and *zhoug.*❦

Yield: 4 servings

Hot Sauce (Zhoug) (*sometimes called* chugintkus)

1 cup fresh red chilies
8 cloves garlic
1 teaspoon ground cumin
salt and pepper to taste

Grind all ingredients together in mortar and pestle or food processor. Scrape into covered jar and store in refrigerator.

Yield: 1 cup

Spicy Sesame Sauce (Tahini)

1 cup sesame paste
1/4 cup water
1/4 cup fresh lemon juice
2 cloves garlic, minced
salt and pepper to taste

Whisk the sesame paste and water together. Gradually incorporate the other ingredients until smooth. Store in covered container in the refrigerator.

Yield: 1 cup

St. Peter's Fish with Sesame Sauce (Amnun with Tahini)

1/4 cup olive oil
2 medium onions, sliced
4 small *mousht* (4 whole trout or 4 bluefish filets may be substituted)
1/2 cup sesame seed paste (*tahini*) ◐
1 large lemon, juice and grated rind
2 garlic cloves, crushed
salt and pepper to taste

Preheat oven to 350°.
    Heat the oil in a skillet and sauté the onion until it is golden brown. Add the fish in one layer. Sauté for 1 minute, turn, and brown the other side. Place fish side by side in a shallow baking dish. Mix together *tahini*, lemon juice, rind, garlic, salt, and pepper. Pour over fish.

Yield: 4 servings

Gefilte Fish (Dag Memula)

Fish:

2 pounds carp, head, skin, and bones removed and reserved
1/2 pound pike filets
1 large onion, quartered
2 carrots, scraped, and cut in 1-inch pieces
1/2 cup matzo meal flour
1 carrot
1 tablespoon oil
1 tablespoon sugar
salt and pepper to taste
2 eggs, separated

Broth:

2 quarts water
4 carrots, sliced
2 medium onions, sliced
salt and pepper to taste

Slice the fish and, along with the onion and carrots, grind in meat grinder or food processor. Fish may also be chopped with a stainless steel chopper in a wooden chopping bowl. Add the matzo flour, oil, sugar, salt, and pepper. Lightly whisk the egg yolks and add to fish mixture. Beat the egg whites until light and airy but not stiff, and incorporate into the fish mixture. Chill for 1 or 2 hours.

For the broth, place all the ingredients in 2 quarts of water and bring to a boil. Over medium heat, boil gently for 30 minutes.

With wet hands, form chilled fish mixture into 20 egg-shaped pieces. Gently lower them into the broth with a long-handled spoon. When all the fish is in the broth, lower heat so that the liquid is smoothly simmering. Partially cover the pot and simmer for 1½ hours. Remove fish with a slotted spoon. Cover lightly and refrigerate. Strain broth, reserve, and chill. Serve with cold boiled carrots, potato slices, jellied broth, and horseradish.

Yield: 8 servings

Horseradish (Hrein)

1 pound red beets
1/4 pound fresh horseradish root
1/2 cup vinegar
3 tablespoons sugar
1 teaspoon salt

Wash beets and boil them about 12 minutes. They should still be firm. Cool, peel, and grate. Peel and grate horseradish root. Mix with vinegar, sugar, and salt. Refrigerate in a covered glass or ceramic jar.

Yield: 1 pint ±

Chopped Liver (Kahvid Ouf Kahdsuts)

1/2 cup peanut oil
2 large onions, diced
2 pounds calves liver, trimmed, deveined, and cubed
1 pound chicken liver, trimmed, deveined, and cubed
salt and pepper to taste
2 tablespoons rendered chicken fat (optional)
1/4 tablespoon thyme
1/4 cup brandy

Heat the oil in a skillet and sauté the onions and liver. Cook thoroughly, but do not overcook. Drain, and chop liver and onion mixture in a wooden bowl. Season and add chicken fat, if using. Incorporate brandy and adjust seasoning.

Yield: 10 servings

Israel—Glossary

Bevakasha.   Please.

Todah rabah.   Thank you very much.

Lehaiyem.   Cheers.

cholent   meat-and-bean stew

gelida   ice cream

gevina   cheese

kafe   coffee

lehben   yogurt

lehem   bread

marahk   soup

marahk ohf   chicken soup

mayim   water

oogah   cake

orez   rice

payroht   fruit

payroht leeftahn   fruit compote

salat   salad

shahmenet   sour cream

shemin zayut   olive oil

te   tea

temahreem   dates

6

AFRICA

Morocco, Algeria, and Tunisia make up the *Maghreb*, which, though it means "West" in Arabic, is the Northwestern part of Africa. Algeria is mostly taken up with the Sahara Desert, where Bedouin traditions prevail and food is often seasoned and roasted on a spit and served with *kesra*, a flatbread that can be quickly cooked. In other respects, it shares the cuisine of its neighbors. We benefit from many Moroccan imports in North America, and half the fun of a Moroccan restaurant are the weavings and pottery that create a lively setting.

Probably the most famous regional dish is *couscous*, which is made in as many varieties as there are kitchens. Though it can be made many ways, the *couscousière* is the cooking utensil of choice. The base is a graceful round-bellied stockpot, and the upper portion a large steamer with a tight-fitting lid. The stew ingredients are put in liquid in the bottom portion, and the aromatic steam rises to cook the *couscous*, a grain processed from wheat or semolina. Generally served with *harissa* and soft flatbread, Algerian *couscous* tends to be vegetarian with lots of tomatoes; Moroccan couscous is cooked with lamb or poultry in addition to vegetables flavored with saffron. Tunisian tends to be the hottest and includes *brik*, which is a flaky pastry filled with a spicy egg mixture, and *chakchouka*, a dish of spicy cooked tomatoes and peppers topped with poached eggs. *Merguez*, a Tunisian hot sausage, is available in some specialty stores.

From the menu of

Marrakesh

517 South Leithgow Street
Philadelphia, PA 19147

Three Salad Platter

Cooked Eggplants in Tomato Sauce

Cucumbers and Bell Peppers in Mediterranean Seasoning

Oasis Carrots with Coriander

The B'Stella

Layered Pie with Chicken, Assorted Nuts, Almonds, Eggs, Parsley and Onions
Topped with confectioners sugar and traced with cinnamon

First Main Course

Chicken with Lemon and Olive

Rabbit with Prunes

Spicy Chicken in Cumin Sauce

Chicken with Eggs and Parsley Sauce

Second Main Course

Marinated Berber Beef Shish Kebab

Tajine of Lamb with Almonds and Honey

Lamb with Chick Peas and Onions

Third Main Course

Couscous Grand Atlas
Topped with vegetables, chick peas and raisins

The other classic dish is the *tagine*, which is the name of the dish and clay pot it is made in. Salads and sweets are served in abundance, along with both coffee and sweet mint tea.

Morocco

Poulet Pie (Basteeya, Pastilla)

Chicken:

> 3 tablespoons olive oil
> one 3–3½-pound chicken, cut in 8 pieces
> 2 medium onions, diced
> 2 cloves garlic
> 1-inch piece fresh ginger, sliced
> 1 teaspoon turmeric
> 1 teaspoon cracked black pepper
> 1 small dried red chili
> 6 cloves
> 2 pieces stick cinnamon
> 1 tablespoon fresh parsley leaves
> 1 tablespoon fresh coriander leaves
> 1 teaspoon saffron, stirred into 1/4 cup warm water

Almond mixture:

> 3 tablespoons olive oil
> 1½ cups almonds, brown skin removed
> 2 tablespoons sugar
> 1 teaspoon ground cinnamon

Egg mixture:

> 10 large eggs
> 1/3 cup lemon juice
> 1 cup stock from chicken preparation
> 3 tablespoons sweet butter

Pastry:

> 1 pound thawed frozen filo dough at room temperature
> 1 cup melted sweet butter

Preheat oven to 375°. A buttered 12-inch springform pan should be put in the refrigerator while the ingredients are being prepared.

To make the chicken, heat the oil in a skillet and brown the chicken, onion, and garlic. When it is well-browned, add the spices and herbs and stir. Pour the saffron mixture and water over all, lower heat, and cook, covered, for 45 minutes. Remove from the heat and remove the chicken with tongs. Reserve 1 cup of strained liquid. Remove the chicken from its bones and cut in bite-sized pieces.

To prepare the almonds, heat the oil in a skillet. Brown the nuts. Remove and drain on paper towel. Roughly crush and mix with sugar and cinnamon. Reserve.

Mix together the eggs, lemon juice, and chicken stock. Heat the butter in a skillet and scramble the eggs. Some liquid will separate. When eggs are fully cooked, lift out with a slotted spoon and reserve. Discard excess liquid.

To assemble the pie, lay the filo dough on a flat surface next to the buttered springform pan. Brush a sheet of dough with butter and place in pan so that one side of the dough goes up the side of the pan with some overage. Repeat this for 8 sheets of filo, turning the pan so that the overage is all around the edges of the pan. Fill first with the chicken mixture, then the egg mixture. Cover with remaining filo, folding the overage on top of the top layer. Bake 45 minutes.

Yield: 8 servings

Couscousière

Moroccan (Hermoula)

1/2 cup chopped, fresh coriander leaves
1/2 cup chopped, fresh parsley leaves
6 garlic cloves, minced
1 small onion, minced
1 teaspoon paprika
1 teaspoon ground cumin
1/2 teaspoon ground cardamom
1/2 cup dried red chilies, crushed
1/2 teaspoon coarse salt
1/4 teaspoon cracked black peppercorns
2 tablespoons lemon juice
3 tablespoons olive oil

Stir all the ingredients in a bowl. Using either a mortar and pestle or a food processor, coarsely pulverize the mixture. Serve with *basteeya*. May also be used as an accompaniment for lamb dishes.

Yield: 1 pint

West Africa

Throughout the Americas, the influence of African culture is evident, though for a long time it was not identified. Much of American southern cooking gives it more than a nod, with the use of peanuts (called *groundnuts* in most of Africa), and peanut or palm oil for frying, okra, black-eyed peas, sesame, coconuts, yams, bananas, sugar cane, salt meat, and fish. *Gumbo* is an African dialect word for okra, and *benne* is sesame. Cornmeal cooked like grits or fried into hush puppies is from Western Africa. Black pepper, the finest of which comes from Sumatra (once so valuable it was used in trade and made up dowries), has graced French cuisine since the fourteenth century. Varieties of chili peppers abound. Cayenne, of course, originates in Cayenne, French Guiana. In Africa, hundreds of indigenous greens are eaten; here mustard and collard greens, kale, chard, and dandelion have become substitutes. Onions and shallots are frequently combined with nuts and fruit, such as papaya, mango, and even dried dates and raisins. Bluefish and snapper, as well as many varieties of shellfish, are served, as are chicken, lamb, and some beef. A celebration dish called *calaloo*

Stuffed Mango

combines a little of each cooked with okra and greens, and served with corn cakes.

In Western Africa, prevailing techniques are deep frying, boiling, roasting, and some steaming. The countries of Gambia, Ghana, Ivory Coast, Nigeria, Mali, and Senegal are often represented in American West-African restaurants.

Nigeria

Shrimp and Okra Stew (Ila)

1/2 cup peanut oil
2 medium onions, diced
1½ pounds small okra, scrubbed and sliced
1 large plantain, diced
2 small red chilies, crushed
1 pound small shrimp
6 large ripe tomatoes, peeled, seeded, and diced
salt and pepper to taste
juice of 1 lime mixed with 1/2 cup of water

Heat the oil in a skillet large enough to hold all the ingredients. Lightly brown the onion, then add the okra, plantains, and chilies and stir. Add shrimp and stir for a few minutes. Add tomatoes, seasoning, and lime-and-water mixture. Cook on low heat for 25 minutes.

Yield: 8 servings

Chicken (Imoyo)

1/4 cup peanut oil
2 medium onions, diced
one 3½-pound chicken, cut in 8 pieces
3/4 pound small okra, scrubbed, stems removed
4 small red chilies, minced
4 cloves garlic, crushed
4 cups water
5 medium tomatoes, peeled and crushed
3 tablespoons tomato paste
2 tablespoons lime juice

Heat the oil in a heavy skillet large enough to hold all ingredients. Brown onions and chicken. Stir in okra, chilies, and garlic. When well incorporated, add water, bring to a boil, and simmer for 20 minutes. Add tomatoes, tomato paste, and lime juice. Serve with rice and a side dish of yams boiled and mashed with ripe bananas.

Yield: 6 servings

Baked Bananas

6 ripe-but-firm medium bananas in their skins
juice of 2 limes
3 tablespoons brown sugar
1/2 cup heavy cream, warmed slightly
3 tablespoons roasted peanuts, crushed

Preheat oven to 350°.

Place the bananas on an ungreased baking sheet and bake for 15 minutes. Place on platter or individual dishes and remove half of the banana peel lengthwise. Drizzle lime juice over bananas, then sprinkle with brown sugar. Pour heavy cream over the bananas and top with crushed peanuts.

Yield: 6 servings

Peanut Soup

3 tablespoons sweet butter
2 tablespoons flour
6 cups chicken or vegetable stock
1/2 pound roasted, unsalted peanuts, roughly chopped
1 cup creamy peanut butter
1/2 teaspoon cayenne pepper
1 teaspoon salt, or to taste
2 teaspoons cumin
2 cups cooked, diced chicken, optional
1 cup heavy cream
3 tablespoons minced fresh parsley leaves, for garnish

In a heavy-bottomed soup pot, heat the butter and mix in the flour, stirring until the mixture is a light-brown paste, or *roux*. Continue stirring and pour the stock into the pot slowly so that the *roux* is incorporated. Add the peanuts, peanut butter, and seasoning. Mix until peanut butter is dissolved. Simmer for 20 minutes. Add chicken, if desired, and cream. Stir and simmer, without boiling, for 5 minutes. Serve garnished with parsley.

Yield: 8 servings

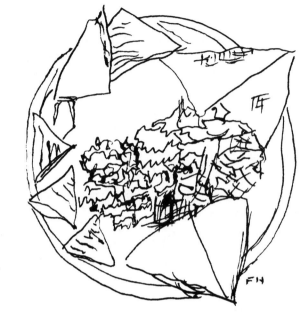

INJERA
DORO WAT

Injera Yeorowat

East Africa

Though there are influences from Egypt and India, the cuisine is based very much on local products and cooking techniques.

Ethiopia

From New York to Seattle, there are authentic Ethiopian restaurants that offer not only meals but the atmosphere and, often, the art of this ancient culture. In Ethiopia, virtually all food is served on *injera*,❀ a large, soft, fermented *teff* flatbread. *Teff* is a flour or paste made from millet. It usually serves as bread, plate, eating utensils, and napkin. When serving two or more the *injera* is often made tray-sized, or several are overlapped and placed on straw mats or woven tables with tops that are really platter-sized shallow baskets, on which the bread is placed. The *injera* is then piled with distinct sections of stewed lamb, vegetables, beans, and salad.

Azefa is a lentil dish cooked with mustard and green peppers, and *yemiser alecha*◉ is a stewed lentil dish seasoned with ginger, garlic, and white pepper. They are milder versions of *yemesir wat* or *shiro wat*, which are, respectively, lentils and chick-peas cooked with *berbere*◉ sauce. Also prepared with *berbere* is *yedoro wat*, chicken cooked slowly with onions, garlic, and ginger. The lamb version of this dish is *yebeg alecha*. *Gomen besega* is beef cooked with garlic, ginger, and greens.

In the official language, Amharic, *berbere* means pure red-chili powder, and this paste is the thumbprint of almost all Ethiopian meals. It accompanies the *wats* that are variations on the national dish.

Tej is a honey wine that has been made since ancient days. Each area that has honey bees ferments this wine. There are also rough beers made from barley, corn, or wheat.

Red-Chili Paste (Berbere)

2 cloves garlic
1 small onion, diced
1/4 cup vinegar
1/2 cup water
1/2 cup paprika
2 tablespoons chili-pepper flakes
1/2 teaspoon cayenne
1 teaspoon salt
1/2 teaspoon ground ginger
1/2 teaspoon ground cloves
1/4 teaspoon ground cinnamon
1/4 teaspoon ground allspice

Blend the garlic, onion, vinegar, and water in blender or processor. To be more authentic, it may be rubbed to a paste in a mortar and pestle. In a small skillet, stir all the dry spices together over medium heat until they are aromatic. Cool, then add to the mixture in blender and incorporate. Return to pan and heat, stirring continuously until mixture thickens. Place in covered container and refrigerate.

Yield: 1+ cup

Ethiopian Millet Bread (Injera)

---

2 cups millet flour (available in many natural-food shops)
1 package instant dry yeast
1 cup warm water
2 to 3 cups water

Mix 1/2 cup millet flour with the yeast and stir into 1 cup of warm water. Let stand for 15 minutes. Mix in the rest of the millet flour and 2 cups water. Mixture should resemble pancake batter. Add up to 1 additional cup water. Heat a heavy, ungreased griddle and brown breads on both sides. They will rise as they cook.

Yield: 8 breads

Ethiopian Lentil Stew (Yemiser Alecha)

---

4 teaspoons sweet butter
2 large onions, diced
1 clove garlic, minced
1½-inch piece fresh ginger, minced
3 cups split lentils
1/2 teaspoon ground cayenne pepper
1 teaspoon salt
6 hard-cooked eggs

Heat butter in a heavy pan large enough to hold all the ingredients. Brown onions slowly. Add garlic and ginger and cook until translucent. Stir in lentils, cayenne, and salt. Add water to cover by 2 inches. Bring to boil, lower heat, cover, and simmer for 1½ hours. Serve with hard-cooked eggs and millet bread.

Yield: 6 servings

7

INDIA

Indian maps of ancient cosmology depict the earth as an island surrounded by seven seas in concentric circles. Each sea provides nourishment. The innermost is made of salt and, proceeding outward, are seas of sugar, wine, *ghee*, milk, curds, and water. Heaven and earth are depicted laden with honey for strength and wealth.

In India, two-hundred languages and one-thousand dialects are spoken by a population second in size only to that of China. The cuisine has been influenced historically by the Chinese, with whom India traded wheat for rice since the days of the silk route, and by others throughout its history. The Greeks, on the heels of Alexander the Great, established an Indo-Greek culture in India that lasted for centuries. The thirteenth-century Turkish conqueror Tamerlane's descendants brought Turkish sweets. Bananas, peanuts, and okra were brought from Africa. In 1498, the Portuguese explorer Vasco da Gama reached Calcutta and introduced the chilies that he had found in earlier travels. The Dutch and British followed, but they took more culinary culture back to their own countries than they brought to India. The Sanskrit for cook is *supakara*, maker of soup. *Supa* and the English word *soup* are both rooted in the Indo-European *seu*.

Traditional food preferences and taboos in India are tied to religion, though many strictures are not rigid. With the exception of the interdiction against alcohol, there is great variety. Muslims may not eat pork, for example. Jains disavow most food and will not even eat root vegetables because as they are being pulled up, insects might die. For the most part, Hindus eat no beef.

In the North, the cuisine is clearly influenced by the Persian table and, in Moghul cookery, one finds chicken or lamb and raisins with rice, or potatoes cooked with ginger. Delhi, the capital, is founded on the ruins of seven ancient cities, and old traditions mingle with the new. In Agra, the home of the Taj Mahal, one finds both country fare and court cuisine. The local *sharbat*, a chilled drink of mango, melon, and pomegranate with a squeeze of lime, is the precursor of American sherbets.

In the state of Punjab, the predominantly Sikh city of Amritsar is home to the Golden Temple, whose setting is described as a "pool of nectar." Sikh cooking features corn and wheat, cooked in *ghee*,◉ and often sugar is added. Many breads are made from wheat, corn, and millet. There are Indian restaurants throughout the United States named "Golden Temple."

In the South, the city of Varanasi on the banks of the Ganges, formerly called Benares, attracts thousands of visitors daily because it is one of the holiest of Hindu cities. Shiva is said to reside there, but it is also home to Annapurna, the Goddess of food, to whom homage and sacrifices are made. Sarnath, the city where Buddha preached his first sermon, is nearby. Southern Indian cooking consists primarily of vegetables, lentils, rice, and breads such as multilayered *parathas*, fluffy *naans*, or pancakes made from chick-pea flour. Sauces tend to be very thin and spicy. Some food is steamed. There is little wheat (noodles are made from rice flour), and sesame and coconut are the main cooking oils. From the southern port of Mangalore come recipes for delicious simple shrimp curries with coconut.

When you read an Indian restaurant menu, you will notice that many dishes from the state of Madras feature grains and pulses. In Goa and Kerala, fish predominate. Most menus offer a dish like *machi malabar*, a rich fish curry, that I once saw subtitled "thousand-year-old fish dish." It is often made with Kari leaves and coconut milk. Goa curry is much like a fish-and-seafood soup.

Bombay, the capital of the state of Maharashta, called the "Gateway to India," is a region of several islands with a history of diversity. As in many enormous cities, there is a sizable indigenous population, but Bombay is also home to millions of people from all regions.

The subtly flavored, creamy dishes of the Punjab reflect the royal cuisine, while the hot spicy dishes of the south reflect the flavors of many hot climates. From simple tandoori-oven-cooked food to elaborate fifty-dish buffets, you can follow the dictates of your own taste in Indian cuisine. Tea is virtually the national drink in India, though home-grown coffee is served with milk and sugar for breakfast, along with *dosai* (pancakes), served with lentils or potatoes and condiments.

It is the custom in Indian restaurants to present food either on large or small *thalis*—metal trays on which bread and rice are served,

Indian Buffet

along with *katoris*, small bowls filled with savory dishes. Chutneys, varied sweet-and-sour side dishes that may be either cooked or fresh, are served with most meals. Fruit chutneys made from mangoes, peaches, tamarind, or other fruit are often cooked with sugar and hot chilies. Fresh mint and coriander are often used in uncooked chutneys. Cucumber, mint, mustard seed, coconut, cashew, bananas, or even minced, dried fruit are stirred into yogurt to make the cooling refreshers called *raitas*. Pickles are made from lemon, gooseberry, mango, and even turnips.

The breads that accompany Indian food vary from *naan*, which resembles a pocketless pita, to *chapatis*, sometimes called *rotis*, thin circles of dough, cooked on the side of a tandoori oven or on an ungreased griddle. *Pooris* are whole-wheat disks that balloon when fried. *Parathas* are made of many thin layers of dough spread with *ghee*, then cooked in *ghee* or butter. Breads are usually served warm and plain, but they can be ordered stuffed with potatoes, onions, or other seasoned vegetables.

Regional Specialties

Bangladesh, formerly the state of Bengal, is now an independent country. It has always had a few distinctive dishes. One is *macher kalihya*, fish cooked with vegetables and yogurt, then simmered with fried onions and *paneer*. *Ambal* is a vegetable stew flavored with tamarind and sweet spices. *Rasgulla* appears on many Indian menus and is made from cheese and nuts simmered with rose water and sweet spices.

In Nepal, though most people are Hindus, they are not vegetarian. Regional dishes include *khuras ko anda*, scrambled eggs with hot chilies, fresh chopped coriander, and other spices.

With few exceptions, there are no four-star Indian restaurants—not because there are no great chefs and dishes, but because culturally food is so much a part of the community that most restaurants strive to be inclusive as opposed to "exclusive." In India, meals are eaten with forks and spoons and the table is set accordingly. If one forgoes utensils, food can be eaten or passed only with the right hand.

In Indian cuisine, one finds the great symphonies of spice. As all Western music is orchestrated from eight notes in endless variety, so it is with the composition of Indian dishes. Arranged and rearranged, the fresh, roasted, and ground spices are the elements in meals that range from grand opera to simple folk tunes. Nowhere else is this rich array used in so many home kitchens. The real secret of the extraordinary perfume of Indian food lies in the fact that the spices are left whole and freshly roasted or toasted and ground before using. The only spice in the West given a freshness statement is the ubiquitous black peppercorn.

DAWAT

I talked with Autar Walia, co-owner of the Dawat Restaurant in New York. The restaurant has been open in New York City for 10 years and in White Plains for a few years less. For 8 years they have received awards naming them the best Indian restaurant in the USA. This is not surprising, considering that Madhur Jaffrey, author of many books on the food and cooking of India, is their food consultant. Mr. Walia gives more than a nod to the fact that, by and large, the best Indian food, in India, is cooked and eaten at home. Dawat offers not only a tremendous variety of dishes but the cordiality of a pleasant home.

Most Indian cooking is generous. Humble breads served with spicy potatoes and aromatic tamarind paste are as delicious as shrimp in coconut milk. Teas flavored with *garam masala*◉ and cool *lassi,*◉ yogurt drinks that may be either sweet or savory, are as refreshing as far more complicated beverages.

Curry

Curry differs widely throughout India and the rest of Asia. By and large, the ubiquitous curry powder that can be bought premixed will give you just a quick hint of what it might be like to have a real curry. The word *curry* seems to be an approximation of the Tamil word *kari,* which means sauce. It can be flavored with some or many of the spices that made India a destination for the voyagers we read about in history books. Aniseed, allspice, cardamom, mace, nutmeg, cinnamon, coriander, cloves, cumin, black pepper, mustard, chili, turmeric, fenugreek, ginger, and poppy seed can all be made into curry powders according to your taste. Here are some combinations that would be called *masalas* in most parts of India. When these mixtures are added to water, vinegar, yogurt, or coconut milk, they are called *wet masalas*.

Curry Powder

2 tablespoons coriander seeds
1 tablespoon ginger powder
1 tablespoon cumin
1 teaspoon turmeric
1 tablespoon mustard seeds
1 tablespoon fenugreek
1 tablespoon black peppercorns
3 3-inch sticks cinnamon

Grind all ingredients in a mortar and pestle or crush with a rolling pin. Mix and store in a glass jar that can be closed tightly. A conventional spice grinder can be used. (I grind spices in an electric coffee grinder that is used only for that purpose.)

Yield: 2/3 cup

Garam Masala

1/2 cup whole cardamom pods
3 3-inch cinnamon sticks
1/4 cup whole cloves
1/4 cup coriander seeds
1/4 cup cumin seeds
1/4 cup whole black peppercorns

Remove cardamom seeds from pods. Grind all spices together and store in a clean, airtight container. This can be made into a wet sauce by the addition of sautéed onions, garlic, and yogurt. A lovely iced tea can be made by adding a tablespoon of *garam masala* to a quart of hot Darjeeling or mint tea. Strain and continue according to your favorite method.

Yield: 2 cups

Ghee is the preferred cooking oil of most of India, because it has a longer shelf life. It is easy to make at home.

Easy Ghee

2 pounds sweet butter, cut in chunks

Place butter in a heavy 4-quart saucepan over low heat, and stir until melted. Increase heat and bring to a boil (do not leave unattended). When it is covered with foam, lower heat as much as possible and simmer gently for 45 minutes to an hour.

Line a strainer with 3 layers of dampened cheesecloth and careful strain *ghee*. It should be perfectly clear. If it isn't, strain it again. Pour *ghee* into a clean crock or glass jar and refrigerate. It will keep for up to 3 months.

Yield: 3 cups

Rice

Rice is the blank canvas of most Indian food. It is often spread out on one's plate and one chooses from an array of side dishes placing one sort of curry on one spot and a different curry on a free area and so on, so that the distinctive flavors enhance each other and are echoed by the rice.

Any rice may be used in Indian cooking, but Basmati rice is preferred. It is most often simply boiled and served plain, but it can be cooked with lentils and called *khichiri*❀ (*kedgeree*) or with spices, raisins, and nuts and fried in *ghee* to make a *pilau*. With the addition of meat and/or vegetables it is called *biryani*. Turned into soup and combined with coconut milk and aromatic spices, it is called "mulegootunne" or the *mulligatawny*.❀

For plain white rice, a common way to cook it is to soak the rice in a proportion of 1 cup of rice to 2 cups of water and let it soak for 1 hour in a heavy pan with a cover. Bring the rice to a boil, lower the heat, and simmer till all the water is absorbed and all grains are separate. The smaller the amount of rice you are cooking, the more you can expect to have to add some water before this process is complete.

Easy Coconut Milk

1 cup boiling water
2 cups fresh or packaged grated unsweetened coconut

Pour the water over the coconut in a deep bowl, and let stand for 30 minutes. Drain through cheesecloth-lined strainer. Lift cheesecloth and squeeze coconut to extract all the flavor.

Yield: About 1 cup

Khichiri

3 tablespoons *ghee* or vegetable oil
2 medium onions, minced
1/2 teaspoon cardamom
1/4 teaspoon cloves
1/2 teaspoon cumin
1/2 teaspoon cinnamon
1 cup rice
1 cup soaked *dhal* (split lentils)

Heat the *ghee* or oil in a heavy saucepan and add onions and spices. Stir until the onions are transparent. Add the rice and stir until it is almost transparent. Add 2½ cups of water and the *dhal*. Bring to a boil and cook for about 45 minutes or until both rice and lentils are cooked to taste.

Yield: 4 servings

Mulligatawny

4 tablespoons *ghee* or vegetable oil
1 teaspoon cumin
1 teaspoon turmeric
1/2 teaspoon fenugreek
1/4 teaspoon cloves
1/4 teaspoon cayenne
2 medium onions, minced
4 garlic cloves, minced
1 cup soaked *dhal* (dried split lentils), whole lentils may be substituted
but they should be soaked first
4 kari or bay leaves
5 cups chicken stock
1 tablespoon tamarind paste
1 cup coconut milk (or canned unsweetened coconut cream)
freshly chopped coriander for garnish, optional
1 lemon, sliced paper thin, seeds removed, for garnish, optional

Heat the *ghee* or oil in a saucepan, stir in spices, and stir until aromatic.
Add the onions and garlic, stir until transparent. Add the *dhal*, kari
leaves, and chicken stock. Simmer for 30 to 40 minutes until the *dhal* is
quite tender. Remove leaves, stir in tamarind paste until dissolved.
Add coconut milk and heat through. Serve with freshly chopped coriander and lemon slices, if desired.

Yield: 6 servings

Yogurt

In the West, we are accustomed to sweetened yogurt. You may be surprised at how delicious it can be either as a savory drink, *lassi*, used in
curry sauces before or after cooking, or in spicy side dishes.

Plain Basmati Rice

2 tablespoons *ghee*
1½ cups Basmati rice
2¾ cups water
salt and pepper to taste

Heat *ghee* in a saucepan and stir in rice. Stir rice about one minute. Add water, salt and pepper and bring to a boil. Cover and lower heat to simmer for up to 20 minutes, until tender.

Yield: 3 cups

Microwave Basmati Rice

1 cup Basmati rice
2¼ cups of water

Wash the rice and rinse several times. Place in 2-quart dish suitable for a microwave oven and add water. Cover with plastic wrap. Pierce wrap 2 or 3 times to release a bit of steam. Microwave at 100% for 5 minutes and 50% for 18 minutes. Remove from oven and let sit for 5 minutes. Uncover, fluff and serve.

Yield: 3 cups

Saffron Coconut Rice

3/4 cup coconut milk
3/4 teaspoon saffron threads
3 tablespoons *ghee* or vegetable oil
8 cloves, crushed, or 1/4 teaspoon ground cloves
10 cardamom seeds, crushed, or 1 teaspoon ground cardamom
10 black peppercorns, crushed, or 1/2 teaspoon cracked black pepper
1 2-inch piece cinnamon, ground, or 3/4 teaspoon ground cinnamon
salt to taste
1 large onion, diced
2 cups Basmati rice

Warm coconut milk and add saffron, stir, remove from heat, and set aside. In a skillet that has a cover, heat *ghee* or oil and stir in spices till aromatic. Add onion and stir until golden. Stir in rice and stir until it is almost transparent. Add coconut milk and cook till it is absorbed. Add stock or water (about 1½ to 2 cups), stir, and cover. Cook over low flame until liquid is absorbed.

Yield: 4 cups

Chutneys, Pickles, Raitas and Bhurtas

I was lucky enough to learn something of Indian cooking from a neighbor in Spain, a painter from the Punjab, who missed home cooking. I still make at least two large batches of chutney a year to share with friends and family. Vast assortments of chutneys and other relishes are used as accompaniments to most dishes on the Indian subcontinent. Generally speaking, they are sweet and spicy, usually containing fruit, raisins, and sugar. Pickles have an acid base. Raitas are yogurt-based side dishes. Bhurtas are savory side dishes, usually vegetable, with potatoes or eggplants as a base.

Papaya Chutney

3 firm papayas, peeled and cut into chunks
3 medium-large onions, sliced paper thin, diced
2 whole lemons, sliced paper thin, seeds removed, diced
3/4 cup raisins
1/4 cup minced fresh ginger root (about 2 ounces)
2 cups sugar
1 tablespoon mustard powder
2 tablespoons crushed red pepper
cider vinegar to cover (up to 2 cups)

Place all ingredients in nonreactive saucepan and slowly bring to a boil while stirring continuously. Lower heat and simmer about 1/2 hour until mixture thickens and gets syrupy, stirring occasionally. Place in clean, covered jars and refrigerate. This will keep at least 6 weeks.

Yield: 1 *quart*

Lime Pickles

6 limes
1/4 cup salt
1 tablespoon *ghee* or vegetable oil
3 dried hot red chili peppers
2 teaspoons fenugreek
1 teaspoons mustard seed
1 teaspoon asafetida
1 teaspoon turmeric
1 cup apple cider vinegar
2 cups sugar

Slice limes lengthwise into sixths without cutting through and severing the base. Remove seeds and place in a container that will hold them all. Sprinkle with salt, cover tightly, and place in a cool place, or refrigerate for 2 days, turning them occasionally.

In a heavy saucepan, heat oil, and brown chili peppers, fenugreek, and mustard seed until aromatic. Add asafetida and stir until blended. Remove from heat and grind spices together until powdered. Slice limes into 1-inch pieces and place in pan with lime liquid, vinegar, sugar, and spice blend. Bring to a boil, lower heat, and simmer till liquid is thickened. Cool and place in covered bowls or jars and refrigerate.

Yield: 1½ pints

Cucumber-Yogurt Sauce (Raita)

16 ounces plain yogurt (low-fat may be used)
1 cucumber, peeled, seeded, and diced
1 teaspoon cumin
1 tablespoon fresh coriander leaves
salt and pepper to taste
1 small, fresh, green chili pepper, minced, optional

Mix ingredients until well blended. Serve immediately or refrigerate up to 2 days.

Yield: 4 cups

Potato Bhurta

(B*hurtas* are savory vegetable dishes.)

4 baking potatoes
1 medium onion, minced
2 cloves of garlic, crushed
1 green chili, minced
6 fresh mint leaves, minced
1 teaspoon mustard oil (*ghee* or vegetable oil may be substituted)
juice of 1 medium lime
salt and pepper to taste

Boil the potatoes and mash them. In a small bowl, mix together the onion, garlic, chili, mint, and oil. Whisk in the lime juice, and then beat the onion mixture into the potatoes. Add salt and pepper to taste.

Yield: 6 servings

Eggplant Bhurta

---

2 large eggplant
1 medium onion, minced
1 green chili pepper, minced
juice of 1 medium lemon
2 tablespoons olive oil

Preheat oven to 375°.

Bake the eggplant until they are soft, about 45 minutes. Peel the eggplant and mash until creamy. Blend the other ingredients in a bowl, whisk them together, and beat the mixture into the eggplant.

Yield: 6 servings

Tomato Bhurta

6 large, ripe tomatoes, peeled and seeded
1/4 teaspoon crushed red chili pepper
1/2 teaspoon powdered ginger
1 large onion, chopped
1 lemon with peel, sliced paper thin, and chopped
1 lime with peel, sliced paper thin, and chopped
12 fresh mint leaves or 2 teaspoons crushed dried mint

Mix all ingredients and serve room temperature or chilled.

Yield: 6 servings

Gosht Biryani

1/2 cup *ghee* or vegetable oil
2 large onions, chopped
1 pound lean lamb, cubed
1 1-inch piece fresh ginger, minced
1 cup yogurt
1 teaspoon salt
1/2 teaspoon cardamom
1/4 teaspoon cloves
1/2 teaspoon black pepper
1 teaspoon cinnamon
4 cups cooked saffron coconut rice❀ or plain Basmati rice❀

Heat the *ghee* or oil in a heavy skillet and sauté the onions until transparent. Add the lamb and brown lightly. Mix in the yogurt and spices. Cook over low heat until the meat is tender and the sauce is thick. Layer half the rice on a serving dish and spread the lamb mixture over it. Top with remaining rice and serve.

Yield: 6 servings

American-Style Tandoori Chicken

2 broiling chickens, split in half
1 tablespoon coarse salt
juice of 2 lemons
1 1/2-inch piece fresh ginger, minced
1 tablespoon *garam masala*◉
6 garlic cloves, crushed
1½ cups plain yogurt (low-fat may be used)
1/4 teaspoon cayenne
2 tablespoons yellow food color mixed with 1 tablespoon red color,
optional

Remove the skin from the chicken and discard. Rub the salt on the chicken, then pour the lemon juice over the chicken, using your hand to rub it in. Set aside for 20 minutes.

In a food processor, blend all other ingredients into a smooth paste. Rub the mixture on the chicken halves, covering both top and bottom. Place chicken in single layer on a baking sheet(s) lined with aluminum foil, and place in refrigerator 4–5 hours or overnight.

Preheat oven to 500°. Roast the chicken for 20 minutes. Reduce heat to 350° and cook another 30 minutes or until done.

Yield: 6 servings

Koftah Curry

1 pound ground beef
2 medium potatoes, boiled, peeled, and mashed
2 green chilies, finely minced
1 teaspoon curry powder
1/4 teaspoon salt
1 egg, slightly beaten
4 tablespoons *ghee* or vegetable oil
6 cloves garlic
1 large onion, chopped
2 tablespoons curry powder
4 medium tomatoes, chopped
2/3 cup coconut milk

Thoroughly mix the ground beef, potatoes, and chilies with the curry, salt, and egg. Form into balls the size of apricots. Heat oil in a skillet large enough to hold the meat in one layer. Fry the meatballs, turning them until they are golden brown, about 10 minutes. Add the garlic, onion, and curry powder and cook for 5 minutes. Add the tomatoes, stir until well-blended, and add coconut milk. Simmer for 20 minutes.

Yield: 6 servings

Samosas

2 cups all-purpose unbleached flour
1/2 teaspoon salt
3 tablespoons *ghee*
1/2 to 3/4 cup water
extra flour for rolling
oil for deep-frying
potato or meat filling

Mix the flour and salt in a bowl and knead the *ghee* into the mixture. Add enough water to make a soft dough (if necessary, add a few more tablespoons water). Knead for 10 minutes. Cover and set aside. (May be refrigerated up to 24 hours. Remove from refrigerator while you make the filling.) Divide into 18 to 24 pieces. Roll each piece on a board or waxed paper dusted with flour. Place 1 heaping tablespoon of filling on each piece. Fold over into half-circles and crimp the edges. Fry 1–2 minutes per side, until golden. Drain and serve, or keep warm in 200° oven.

Yield: 18 to 24 samosas

Potato Filling

2 tablespoons *ghee* or vegetable oil
1/2 teaspoon mustard seeds
1 teaspoon fennel seeds
1/2 teaspoon cumin seeds
1/2-inch piece fresh ginger, minced
1/2 cup chopped onion
2 cups mashed potatoes
1/2 cup cooked, fresh, green peas (frozen may be used)
salt and pepper to taste
1 tablespoon minced fresh coriander leaves
1/4 teaspoon cayenne pepper, optional

Heat the *ghee* in a skillet and add the seeds, stirring until they start to pop and become aromatic. Add the ginger and onions, stirring until onion is transparent. Add potatoes and peas and mix thoroughly. Add salt, pepper, coriander, and cayenne, if desired.

Yield: filling for 24 samosas

Minced-Meat Curry Filling

2 tablespoons *ghee* or vegetable oil
1 onion, chopped
2 cloves garlic, crushed
1/2 pound lean ground beef
1/2 teaspoon ground ginger
1/4 teaspoon crushed red pepper
1 teaspoon curry powder
juice of half a lemon

Heat the *ghee* in a skillet. Add the onion and garlic, brown. Add the ground beef and scramble with a spatula so that it breaks up into mince. Add the ginger, pepper, and curry. Stir until cooked through. Remove from heat and add lemon juice.

Yield: filling for 12 samosas

Cabbage Side Dish

---

4 tablespoons *ghee* or vegetable oil
1 tablespoon black mustard seeds
1/2 teaspoon turmeric
1 tablespoon ground coriander
1 teaspoon salt
1 medium cabbage, quartered and cut into 1-inch slices
juice of 1 lemon

Heat the *ghee* in a skillet large enough to hold the cabbage. Add mustard seeds and stir until they pop and sputter. Add all other ingredients and stir until the cabbage is cooked.

Yield: 8 servings

Shrimp Curry

---

3 tablespoons *ghee* or 1/3 cup vegetable oil
1 pound shrimp, peeled and deveined
1 1/2-inch piece fresh ginger, minced
1 medium-large onion, diced
4 cloves garlic, sliced
1/2 teaspoon crushed red pepper
1 teaspoon cumin
1 tablespoon curry powder blend
4 medium tomatoes
1 lime, cut in 6 wedges

Heat the *ghee* or oil in a skillet and lightly sauté shrimp. Remove shrimp and set aside. Add ginger, onion, garlic, and spices and stir till onions are transparent. Add tomatoes and cook for 10 minutes. Return the shrimp to the skillet and cook for about 5 minutes more. Serve with rice. Garnish with lime.

Yield: 6 servings

BOMBAY PALACE

Prem Nath Motiram has been the executive chef of the Bombay Palace restaurants for many years. He comes from a family of chefs, and is faithful to authentic taste and presentation. During my visit to his kitchen, we talked about the many feasts, fasts, and festivals on the Indian calendar that mark the New Year, usually in late October. Generally Tuesday is a national fast day in India, and no meat or fish is eaten. Celebrations are observed with huge feasts, featuring at least one centerpiece rice dish such as a *biryani* and twenty or thirty others, with desserts of carrot *halva*, *gulab jamun*❀ (rose-flavored fritters with sugar syrup), and *rasomalai* (sweet fried dumplings with pistachio-rosewater sauce). *Kulfi*,❀ a pistachio ice cream, is a special treat. Various teas, soft drinks, and *lassi*❀ (flavored yogurt drinks) are served as beverages.

Pistachio Ice Cream (Kulfi)

Courtesy Executive Chef Prem Nath Motiram, Bombay Palace

2 quarts milk
1 pint heavy cream
1½ cups sugar
1 teaspoon vanilla
1 cup finely ground pistachios
1/2 cup coarsely ground pistachios

Pour the milk and cream into a heavy saucepan and bring to a boil. Lower the heat and, stirring constantly with a wooden spoon, simmer 45 minutes until liquid is reduced by about half. Add the sugar and vanilla and simmer 15 minutes more. Remove from the heat and stir in 1 cup of finely ground pistachios. Pour into ice-cube trays or a plastic container and freeze at least 4 hours. The mixture may also be made in any ice-cream maker, following the manufacturer's directions. Serve topped with coarsely ground pistachios.

Yield: 6 servings

From the menu of

Bombay Palace Restaurant

30 West 52nd Street
New York, NY 10019

(Hot-Cold Appetizers)

Aloo Papri
A tangy combination of chick peas, potatoes and onions tossed in tamarind sauce sprinkled with black Indian salt, served cold

Chicken Pakoras
Juicy chicken fritters with tangy sauce

Vegetable Pakoras
Savory vegetable fritters with a choice of potatoes or cauliflower

Vegetable Samosas
Flaky pastry parcels of lightly spiced peas and potatoes

Tandoori Namoone

Prawns Tandoori
Prawns marinated in a yogurt mixture with ginger and garlic and grilled over charcoal

Noorani Kebab

Boneless chicken marinated in yogurt, fresh garlic and
ground spices, carefully broiled in the tandoor

Chicken Tikka

Tender boneless chicken dipped in Tandoori marinade and
broiled in a clay oven

Tandoori Chicken

Spring chicken marinated overnight in our marinade of yogurt and
freshly ground spice and grilled over charcoal

Seekh Kebab

Juicy lamb-mince rolls with spice and herbs,
grilled over a charcoal flame

Roti (Indian Bread)

Naan

A popular light bread baked to your order in the clay oven

Palace Naan

Naan stuffed with chopped chicken, onions and herbs

Alu-Paratha

A flaky stuffed brown bread baked in the Tandoor

Roti

Leavened whole wheat bread

From the menu of Bombay Palace Restaurant (continued)

Chicken Specialties

Chicken Tikka Masala
Diced tandoori chicken cooked in our exotic cream and tomato
sauce

Chicken Vindaloo
The famous red Goan curry chicken

Saag Chicken
Boneless chicken pieces cooked with chopped spinach and
freshly ground spice

Lamb/Beef Specialties

Karai Gosht
Chunks of lamb/beef cooked with ginger, tomatoes and hot spice
in a deep iron pan

Sali Boti
Tender lamb cubes stewed with spice and dry apricots garnished
with fine straw potatoes

Gosht Patiala
Tender boneless lamb pieces cooked with ground onion, ginger,
garlic and garam masala

Long Grain Rice Specialties

Shahjehani Biryani

Tender lamb or chicken, marinated in yogurt and garam masala
and steam-baked with rice, served with raita

Shrimp Biryani

Served with raita

Navratana Biryani

Basmati rice cooked with garden vegetables, spice and yogurt

Vegetarian Specialties

Paneer Mutter Makhani

Home-made cottage cheese cooked in a rich sauce with cashew
nuts, and garden peas

Vegetable Jalfrazi

Fresh vegetables sauteed with mild spice and coriander

Daal Maharani

Creamed lentils with aromatic spice

Saag Paneer

Fresh green spinach cooked lightly with home-made cottage
cheese and delicately spiced

Rose-Flavored Fritters in Sugar Syrup (Gulab Jamun)

Courtesy Executive Chef Prem Nath Motiram, Bombay Palace

Sugar syrup:

    2 pounds granulated sugar
    2 quarts plus 1 pint water
    2 tablespoons rose water (available at specialty stores)

Dough:

    3 cups powdered milk
    1 cup unbleached all-purpose flour
    3 tablespoons baking powder
    2½ cups heavy cream
    4 cups oil for deep frying

To make the syrup, bring the sugar and water to boil in a heavy sauce-pan over high heat. Lower to medium heat and simmer for about 20 minutes until the mixture is thick. Lower heat to the lowest setting possible and add rose water. Keep warm.

For the dough, mix the powdered milk, flour, baking powder, and cream to make a stiff batter. Heat oil until it gets a slight haze over it (do not let it smoke), form the dough into golf-ball-sized round fritters, and fry a few at a time for about 5 minutes, turning them with a slotted spoon until they are a rich brown all over. Drain on paper towels and continue until all the batter is used.

Place fritters in a deep bowl and pour warm syrup over them. Let stand for several hours or overnight. They will keep a week in the refrigerator.

Yield: 25 small fritters

Yogurt Drink (Lassi)

Courtesy Executive Chef Prem Nath Motiram, Bombay Palace

Sweet:

1 pint fresh yogurt
1 quart iced water
4 ounces sugar
1 tablespoon rose water (optional)

Whisk or shake all ingredients. Serve immediately.

Salted:

1 pint fresh yogurt
1 quart iced water
1/2 teaspoon salt

Whisk or shake all ingredients. Serve immediately.

Yield: 6 servings

India—Glossary

aloo   potato

aviyal   vegetable curry

baingan   eggplant

barfi   fudgelike textured sweets flavored with rose water, coconut, or pistachio

bhuna   sautéed dishes

bhurta   mashed, spicy, roasted vegetables

biryani   rice, usually saffron-flavored, cooked with raisins, nuts, and meat or fish

bondas   small vegetable fritters

chapati   soft pancakelike bread fried on a griddle

chat   salted tidbits or snacks

chutney   hot-and-spicy, sweet, thick, fruit conserve or savory condiment *dhal*   generic name for dried beans, lentils, or peas, whole or split

chana dhal   dried chick-peas

masur dhal   split orange lentils, most commonly used when the menu refers to *dhal* with no further description

do pyaza   cooked with onions

dosai   rice-flour pancakes served plain with chutney, or filled with savory mashed potatoes and peas and rolled

gosht   meat (usually lamb)

idli   steamed bread made from lentil and rice flour

jalebi   dessert cruller dipped in sugar syrup

jhinga   large shrimp

kababs   skewered cubes of chicken, meat, or seafood and vegetables or fruit

karhai   Indian wok

katoris   small metal bowls

keema   chopped meat

khir   cream-of-rice dessert

kofta   meatballs

korma   braised dishes in heavy curry sauce with yogurt

lassi   sweet or savory yogurt drink

machi   fish

masala   ground seasoning

matar   fresh green peas

matar paneer   stewed, fresh, green peas with yogurt-cheese cubes

methi   fenugreek

murg   chicken

naan   white-flour flatbread, usually baked on the side wall of a tandoor urn-shaped clay oven

paan   assorted seeds and spices, often chewed after a meal instead of an after-dinner mint

pakora   deep-fried savory appetizers

paneer   cheese prepared from yogurt, often cooked with vegetables

panipuri   tamarind-filled puri

pappadum   a spicy crisp flatbread made from lentil flour

paratha   chewy flatbread, sometimes filled with spiced potato or cauliflower

pulau or pilau   rice cooked with spices and meat, poultry, or seafood
raita   yogurt mixed with mint or other herbs and spices
roshgulla   cheese balls cooked in rosewater syrup
roti   layered bread baked in a tandoor oven; also generic for *bread*
sag or *shag*   spinach
sag paneer   spinach stewed with yogurt-cheese cubes
samosa   fried turnover filled with spiced meat or potatoes
tandoor   deep clay oven used for grilling food and bread
thali   metal tray on which *katoris* filled with food are arranged
vindaloo   vinegar-based, highly spiced curry

8

SOUTHEAST ASIA

Indonesia

Indonesia is one of the largest countries in the world. This equatorial archipelago is several-thousand miles long and inhabited by almost 150 million people. Part of this group, the fabulous Moluccas or "Spice Islands," has been known since 400 B.C.E. for nutmeg and cloves, which have been an essential part of world and culinary history. Settlers came to Indonesia from China and India; Buddhists and Hindus have lived among Moslems from the Arab countries, and the Dutch, Portuguese, and British have also had an impact.

Rice is the major staple, usually served fragrant with aromatic spices. Hot chilies, peanuts, coconut, and coconut milk are used, along with various fish and shrimp pastes that add depth to many dishes. Curries, vinegar, sugar, tamarind paste, and a soy-sauce-based *ketjap* (with no tomatoes) are common condiments. Fish and shellfish are abundant, as is poultry. Vegetables and fruit, both indigenous and those imported by sailors from all over the world, grow luxuriously. Fruit is the most frequently served dessert—sweets are usually eaten as snacks. Tea, coffee, and cocoa are drunk, as are coconut and fruit-based punches. There are very few alcoholic beverages served, because a majority of the country is Muslim. Beer is usually the choice of those who are permitted to drink it.

Until very recently the most popular "Indonesian" meal that could be found outside Indonesia was the *rijsttafel* or "rice table," where often one-hundred dishes are set out to impress guests with the host's affluence and service staff. *Rijsttafel* is a Dutch word and is a formal way of presenting what in Indonesia is done more casually. Happily this colonial style, which offends many, is being replaced in regional restaurants by dishes and combinations of dishes served as they are traditionally eaten.

Nasi goreng, a fried-rice dish, is quite popular as is *bahmi goreng*, the same dish made using noodles. Rice is sometimes festively served in the form of a tall cone, flavored and colored with turmeric and saffron. *Sambals*, small spicy dishes flavored with hot chilies, citrus juice, and onions, often accompany it. *Satays*◆ are usually skewered meat or poultry in a spicy sauce including coconut milk, chilies, and ground peanuts.

White Rice

2 cups extra-long-grain rice
5 cups boiling water

To prepare rice Indonesian style, with each grain separate and fluffy, do the following: In a colander, rinse the rice thoroughly and drain. Stir the rice into the boiling water, stirring continuously. Bring back to a boil. Stop stirring. Cover pan and lower heat. Cook for 20 minutes. Remove from heat but do not remove cover. Let stand for 5 minutes. Fluff rice with a fork before transferring it to a warm serving dish.

Yield: 6 servings

Chicken in Coconut Milk (Opor Ayam)

1 tablespoon coriander seeds
12 peppercorns
1 teaspoon cumin seeds
3 cloves
10 macadamia nuts (20 raw peanuts may be substituted)
4 tablespoons peanut oil
1 medium onion, minced
4 garlic cloves, minced
1-inch piece fresh ginger root, minced
1/2 teaspoon turmeric
1 teaspoon galingale powder (optional)
1 3-pound chicken, cut in 8 pieces
4 stalks lemon grass
3 bay leaves
2 cups coconut milk

In a mortar and pestle or spice grinder, crush the coriander, pepper-corns, cumin, cloves, and nuts. In a wok or skillet large enough to hold all the ingredients, heat the peanut oil. Stir in the crushed spices with the minced onion, garlic, and ginger, and stir into a paste. Add the turmeric and galingale powder. Thoroughly brown the chicken in the mixture, turning so that each piece is evenly coated with the seasoned mixture. Add the lemon grass and bay leaves. Cook about 20 minutes over medium heat. Stir in the coconut milk, and cover. Cook for 45 min-utes over medium-low heat, or until chicken is fully cooked and fork-tender. Remove lemon grass and bay leaves, and serve on warm platter.

Yield: 4 servings

Indonesian Vegetables (Gado Gado)

1 cup green beans
1 cup cauliflower florets
1/2 cup green peas
1/2 cup bean sprouts
2 cups bok choy, shredded
1 cup cooked potatoes, cubed
2 hard-cooked eggs, cubed
1 cucumber, peeled, seeded, and sliced
1 small bunch of watercress

Bring a pot of salted water to a boil and cook the green beans, cauliflower, and peas until they are cooked but still firm. Lift from water with a slotted spoon and drain. Drop bok choy and bean sprouts into boiling water for 3 minutes and drain.

Arrange the cooked and raw vegetables attractively on a platter and top with *satay* sauce❦.

Yield: 8 servings

Spicy Peanut Sauce (Satay)

1/4 cup peanut oil
3/4 cup raw peanuts
2 cloves garlic, minced
1/2 cup fresh red or green chili pepper, minced
1/4 cup fresh lemon juice
1/2 cup coconut cream
1/4 cup soy sauce
1 teaspoon Indonesian fish sauce, optional

Heat the oil in a wok or skillet and stir-fry the peanuts and garlic until pale brown. Drain and place fried peanuts and garlic in a blender or processor with the remaining ingredients and blend until smooth. If mixture seems too thick for your liking, add more coconut cream. This can be served with vegetables, grilled meat, or poultry.

Yield: 2 cups

Eggplant Sambal (Sambalan Terong)

3 medium eggplants of the same size and shape
1 tablespoon coarse salt
1 cup shallots, minced
1/2 cup medium hot chilies, seeded, minced
1/2 cup peanut oil
1 tablespoon tamarind paste, mixed with 1/4 cup warm water

Cut the eggplants in half, leaving decorative stem if possible. Sprinkle cut sides with salt, and place cut-side down on paper towels over cake racks. Let drain for 30 minutes. Rinse and pat dry. Work together the shallots and chilies to make a paste.

Heat the oil in a wok or skillet and cook the eggplant on all sides until soft but still holding together. Remove the eggplant from the wok and stir in chili paste until it is dark and aromatic, about 5 minutes. Add tamarind mixture and stir. Return the eggplant halves to the wok and turn until they are coated with the sambal mixture. Serve hot.

Yield: 6 servings

Indonesia—Glossary

ajam   chicken

asem   tamarind

asin   salted

atjar   pickles

babi pangang   roast pork

bebek   duck

boemboe   spice-and-herb blends

djahe   ginger

gado gado   mixed vegetable dish

goela djawa   brown sugar

goreng   fried

ikan   fish

ketjap benteng   soy-sauce paste

klapper   shredded, dried coconut

kroepoek   crackers made from tapioca flour and shrimp

laos   galangale powder (a form of southeast Asian ginger)

lombok   hot red-chilies

lumpia   spring rolls

nasi   rice

nasi goreng   fried rice

nasi rames   dish of rice served with various small portions of savory tidbits or condiments on it

oedang   shrimp

padi   rice, as it grows in the field

petis   shrimp paste

pisang   banana

pisang goreng   fried banana

sayur   soupy spicy vegetable-based dish

sambal   small dish seasoned with hot chili peppers

santen   coconut milk

satay   dish served with spicy ground peanut sauce, or just the sauce

sereh   lemon grass

tjampoer   mixed

Thailand

Bordering this ancient kingdom, once called Siam by Westerners, are Burma, Cambodia, and Malaysia. As part of the "Golden Triangle," Thai culture and cuisine have been influenced not only by its neighbors, but by Chinese, Japanese, and Portuguese cuisines. It is one of the most uniquely seasoned and lowest-fat cuisines of the region. There are vegetables and fruit in abundance.

Dishes are often cooked quite simply, with one or two rules. Traditionally, most dishes contain something sweet, sour, salty, and piquant. The individual dishes are also planned so they are pleasing to the eye. Food is cooked for the minimal amount of time required; it is not unusual for a dish to combine cooked and raw vegetables, as well as hot and cold components. Rice is served with almost every meal, and *kin khao*, "eat rice," is said as a greeting in Thai homes. As is also true in many parts of China, even though a meal may include noodles, rice is still served. Fish, shellfish, poultry, pork, and beef are all eaten, often served grilled on a bed of fresh salad, in a very modern manner.

Yunk namtok is grilled beef, thinly sliced, served over watercress or other greens, and topped with fresh mint, parsley, or coriander leaves. Garlic, ginger, lemon grass, and various hot chilies are used with a free hand, as is *nam pla*, a pungent fish sauce. Basil, referred to as *holy basil* or *gaprow* on menus, and fresh coriander (cilantro) are popular herbs. Curries are used and range in intensity from hot to mild, and in texture from dry to soupy with coconut milk and cream.

Pad thai, Thai noodles, is virtually a national dish and is served by street vendors as well as fine restaurants. These seasoned, stir-fried rice noodles can be served with bits and pieces of everything from shrimp to tofu, bean sprouts, peanuts, dried and fresh fish, and various vegetables. My favorite is made with tofu, chicken, and eggplant, topped with mint, chilies, and fresh coriander.

Other satisfying dishes are soups and *jooke*, a rice porridge similar to congee. A soup many restaurants serve is *tom yum*, a seafood soup with shrimp and mushrooms, aromatic with lemon grass. Traditionally, all dishes are served at the same time. In Thai restaurants in this country, by and large the choice is yours. Dessert is most frequently fruit and an occasional sweet jelly. Beverages are fruit punches, iced tea, and sweetened iced coffee. Beer is the alcohol of choice.

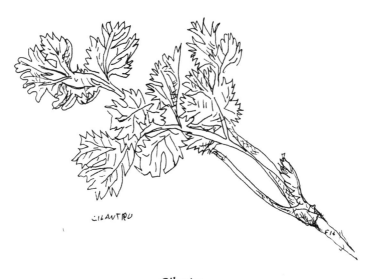

Cilantro

From the menu of

Siam House

829 Simonton Street
Key West, FL 33040

Appetizers

Spring Roll

Authentic Thai egg roll—spring roll skin stuffed with chicken, fresh cabbage, celery, and carrot, served with plum sauce

Keaw Tod—Fried Wonton

Well-seasoned ground pork in a blanket of wonton skin, served with plum sauce

Mee Krob—Sweet Crispy Noodle

Crisp fried vermicelli mixed well with sweet tamarind sauce garnished with shrimp, bean sprout and spring onion

Nam Sod—Spicy Lemon Pork

Well-cooked ground pork mixed with ginger, peanut, spring onion, and flavored with spicy lemon dressing

Neau Nam Tok—Spicy Lemon Steak

Grilled tenderloin beef mixed well with rice powder, onion, and flavored with spicy lemon dressing

Yam Neau—Thai Beef Salad

Grilled tenderloin beef, cucumber, tomato, onion and green salad flavored with spicy lemon dressing

Traditional Thai Curry Dishes

Gaeng Dang—Red Curry

Your choice of beef, pork or chicken cooked with our unique Thai
red curry paste, bamboo shoots and coconut milk

Gaeng Panang—Thick Brown Curry

Beef cooked in panang curry and coconut milk

Gaeng Masamun—Sweet Brown Curry

Your choice of beef or chicken, stewed in masamun curry with
onion and potato, served with cucumber salad

Gaeng Kiew Wan—Green Curry

Your choice of beef or chicken cooked in green curry and
coconut milk

Stir-fried Dishes

Pad Khing

Choice of meat sauteed with shredded garlic, scallion,
black mushrooms with ginger sauce

Pad Prig Sod

Choice of meat sauteed with onion, sweet pepper and scallions,
in traditional Thai sauce

From the menu of Siam House (continued)

Entrees

Crispy Fish

Crispy whole red snapper with side order of fish sauce, tamarind, garlic and hot peppers

Basil Fish

Whole red snapper steamed in hot and sour broth spiced with lemon grass, kaffir lime leaves and sweet basil leaves

Pla Jien—Ginger Fish

Deep fried whole red snapper topped with pork, ginger, black mushrooms and scallion

Rice and Noodles

Pad Thai

Authentic Thai soft noodles, sauteed with shrimp, pork and chicken with special sauce, garnished with bean sprouts and scallion

Sautéed Squid with Mint

1/2 cup peanut oil
1 medium onion, diced
4 garlic cloves, minced
1 red or green sweet pepper, seeded and diced
1½ pounds squid, cleaned and sliced
1 tablespoon oyster sauce
1 tablespoon Thai fish sauce (*nam pla*)
1 tablespoon black-bean paste
1/2 teaspoon cracked black peppercorns
2 medium tomatoes, peeled, seeded, and diced
2 tablespoons fresh lemon or lime juice
6 green onions, sliced
8 sprigs fresh mint, leaves only

Heat the oil in a skillet and sauté the onion, garlic, and sweet pepper until wilted and slightly browned. Add the calamari and cook for 3 minutes, while stirring. Add the oyster sauce, fish sauce, black-bean paste, and black pepper. Stir until well mixed. Add the tomatoes and lemon juice. Stir and cook for 3 minutes more. Serve on platter or individual plates topped with green onions and mint.

Yield: 6 servings

Cold Minced Beef Salad (Laab)

2 tablespoons uncooked white rice
4 small dried chilies, split in half, seeds removed
3 tablespoons peanut oil
1½ pounds lean beef, minced or coarsely ground
4 cloves garlic, minced
3 stalks lemon grass, minced
juice of 2 limes
2 tablespoons Thai fish sauce (*nam pla*)
4 green onions, sliced thin
4 sprigs fresh mint, chopped
1/4 cup fresh coriander (cilantro) leaves, chopped
24 lettuce leaves
2 cucumbers, peeled, seeded, and sliced
6 sprigs fresh mint
6 sprigs fresh cilantro

In a dry skillet, roast the rice and chilies until the rice is medium brown. Remove from the heat and grind into coarse meal in a blender or food processor. Heat the oil in the skillet and brown the meat and garlic, stirring until the meat is just cooked. Remove from the pan and drain on paper towels. Place the meat in a bowl and mix in the rice-and-pepper until the mixture is grainy. Add the lemon grass, lime juice, fish sauce, chopped green onions, mint, and coriander. Mix thoroughly. On a large platter or on individual plates, place a layer of lettuce leaves. Top with the meat mixture and garnish with the cucumber and sprigs of mint and coriander.

Yield: 6 servings

Coconut Chicken Soup (Tom Kha Kai)

4 cups coconut milk
2 cups chicken broth
2 stalks lemon grass, minced
1 1/2-inch piece fresh ginger, minced
4 tablespoons fish sauce (*nam pla*)
2 tablespoons brown sugar
juice of 1 lime
1 pound chicken breast, minced
2 cups white mushrooms, sliced

Variation:

3 tablespoons curry paste
2/3 cup heavy cream

In a nonreactive stockpot, bring the coconut milk, chicken broth, lemon grass, ginger, and fish sauce to a boil, then lower heat and simmer for 1 hour. Strain out the solids and return the soup to the pot with the sugar, lime juice, chicken, and mushrooms. Bring to a boil. Lower heat and simmer for 45 minutes.

To make curried soup, stir in the curry paste when the chicken is added, and stir the cream in just before the soup is removed from the heat.

Yield: 6 servings

The Philippines

The independence of the Philippines was established on July 4, 1946. Though the original inhabitants were Malay and Polynesian, for centuries various groups have settled there and influenced the culture and the cuisine. From The Netherlands, Java, China, Portugal, Spain, and America, explorers and adventurers came. The Arabs stayed long enough to impart Islam; the Spanish, Catholicism. Though the official language is Pilipino, English is spoken by a majority of people. This island group, about the size of Great Britain, is only a couple of hundred miles from the coast of China.

Asian cooking techniques combined with those of the Spanish have created a recognizable but unique cuisine. Abundant coastal waters provide fish and shellfish, as do the lakes and streams. Rice, coconut, corn, sugar cane, bananas, yams, manioc, and citrus fruit dominate the crops. Hot spices are used, but the signature flavor is a somewhat tart overtone evoked by the tamarind, lemon, or vinegar used with most dishes—even sweet ones. Food is often roasted, stewed, or grilled and when it is sautéed or fried it is in olive oil.

A favorite dish is nicknamed *turo-turo*, which means "point-point." As a main course each diner is given a bowl of rice and then they point to the topping they want served on it. For dessert, sweet rice is served with a variety of fruit and sweet-bean toppings. Paella has become a

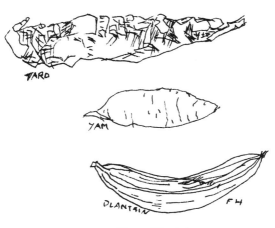

Taro, Yam, Plantain

regional dish; pork is substituted for the chicken used in Spain, but saffron is used with a generous hand to flavor the shellfish, sausage, and local clawless lobster.

Lumpia are bought from street vendors, to be eaten as appetizers or snacks. They are soft, thin spring rolls made of rice flour and wrapped around fillings of well-cooked shrimp or pork and uncooked greens, seasoned dried tofu, beans, or assorted vegetables. They are eaten plain or with a variety of dipping sauces.

Noodles are made in many widths and served in diverse sauces, often in a spicy sauce with beef. Chinese *shao mai* are very popular, and these little open-topped dumplings are usually filled with a combination of ground pork and shrimp.

Fish is served, as it is everywhere, as fresh as possible, cooked quickly: sautéed, fried, roasted, or steamed on their own or wrapped in banana leaves. *Kilawin* is a popular dish made by marinating fish cubes in lime juice, with tomatoes, onions, spices, and medium-to-hot chilies.

Adobo is a barbecue dish, usually made with chicken or pork marinated in a soy-sauce-ginger base, which always has a sour element such as tamarind or vinegar. *Bagoong*, a shrimp or fish paste, or *patis*, a liquid fish sauce, is used to give the food a deep flavor. Coconut and coconut milk are used a great deal, as well. *Sawsawan pinakhet* is an eggplant-based vegetable stew that offers a sampling of the marketplace. *Porchero* or *cuchido* is a garlicky stew that combines chicken and beef with vegetables in a savory sauce.

Desserts are often light flans made with touches of corn or coconut. Some simple cakes and sorbets are made from fruit in season, such as banana, citrus, coconut, or mango.

Talking and eating with Romy Dorotan, the owner and chef of Cendrillon on Mercer Street in New York's Soho, is a lesson in a successful culinary synthesis.

The weekend brunch features tasty *lumpia* and *suman*, which are variously filled sticky rice dumplings steamed in banana leaves. *Bibingka* are rice pancakes made with sweetened coconut milk, eggs, bacon, and cheese spread on banana leaves and baked. In addition to traditional beverages, the restaurant offers an infusion of dried fruit and berries made at your table in a French press.

Lunch and dinner are similar, although portion size and the number of dishes vary. *Sinigang na isda*, a fish soup, is a lovely lunch dish,

Wonton

as is the steamed tofu with mushroom and tomato broth. There is a savory dish of bean-thread noodles and grilled squid that looks deceptively simple, but the layers of flavors are sophisticated. There is the fish-of-the-day cooked with tamarind and hot chilies, or the *Dinaing* N*a*, a chicken dish cooked with lemon grass, basil, and coconut—traditional flavors cooked with a modern, light touch. The *adobo* is redolent of garlic, vinegar, *patis* (fish sauce), bay leaves, and spicy bird's eye pepper.

The sorbets offered are avocado, *calamansi* (a limelike fruit), or guava; the ice creams are yam or coconut, any of which may be served with a slice of yam and berry tart. The ginger lemon grass flan with ginger-caramel sauce is an original.

Vietnam

The Mekong is a river that originates in Tibet, forming a delta in southern Vietnam that is the basis for vast rice farming. There are many varieties of rice grown. One of the most unusual is black rice, which is just gaining popularity in this country. It is often used for sweet or sweet-and-sour dishes.

From the menu of

Nam Phuong

19–21 Sixth Avenue
New York, NY 10013

Appetizers

Nem Nuong
Grilled minced pork on a skewer with rice paper

Bo Nuong Lui
Grilled beef with sesame seasoning

Chao Tom
Grilled minced shrimp on sugar cane

Banh Cuon Cha Lua
Steamed rice crepe with slices of ground pork sausage

Soups

Soup Mang Cua
Crabmeat with asparagus soup

Canh Chua Ca
Hot and sour fish soup

Rice Dishes

Com Tom, Bo, Ga Xao Gung Hanh
Sautéed shrimp, beef or chicken with ginger and scallion

Com Tom, Bo, Ga Sao Sate
Sautéed shrimp, beef or chicken with sate sauce

Frogs

Ech Xao Lan
Frog with curry in casserole

Ech Xao Sa Ot
Frog sautéed with lemon grass and green pepper

Crabs

Cua Rang Muoi
Pepper-salted fried crab

Cua Xao Gung Hanh
Crab sautéed with ginger and scallion

Pork

Heo Xao Chua Ngot
Sweet and sour pork (sautéed)

Heo Xao Bong Cai
Pork sautéed with broccoli

Squid

Muc Xao Dau Que Ca-Ri
Squid curry with string beans and chili sauce

Beef

Bo Xao Sate
Beef sautéed with sate sauce

Bo Xao Gung Hanh
Beef sautéed with ginger and scallion

Noodles are eaten everywhere, and *pho* is the national dish. The word means "individual bowl." In Vietnam, food stalls and restaurants make versions of *pho* and, in the United States, it is often part of a restaurant's name. P*ho bo* is beef-based. The broth is flavored with basil, chilies, cinnamon, ginger, and mint, with rice-stick noodles, bean sprouts, and slices of beef often filling half the bowl. There are accompaniments on the table, but fresh lime is a clear favorite. There are, however, limitless variations. A soup popular in Saigon is *mee quang*, made with a basic broth filled with rice noodles, shredded pork and chicken, cucumbers, lettuce, fresh herbs, and fish sauce, topped with spicy peanuts. *Cha gio*◉ are spring rolls filled with cellophane noodles, fresh greens, mushrooms, shrimp, mint, and basil, wrapped in *banh trang*, an almost-transparent rice-paper wrapper. They are served with a *nuoc cham*, a piquant sweet-and-sour dipping sauce made from *nuoc nam*, minced hot chilies, jaggery or sugar, and lime juice. Sometimes ginger and garlic are added; it is often thickened with shredded carrots. Another popular restaurant dish is *chao tom* or shrimp-paste-covered sugar cane, which is grilled and served with a spicy peanut dipping sauce called *nuoc leo.*◉ Whole fish, usually steamed, sometimes fried, is served with ginger and green onions, and often with rice or cellophane noodles. At Vietnamese grocery stores, it is often possible to buy delicious sandwiches made with *cha luo*, a sausage made from pork and shrimp or seasoned beef or chicken, served with fresh greens, including coriander and mint, and topped with any one of a number of prepared sauces.

Nuoc mam◉ is the strong fermented fish sauce of Vietnam, and is similar to the Thai *nam pla*. It is used as frequently as salt is in other cuisines. *Mam nem* is an anchovy sauce similar to European anchovy paste. The hot sauces are *tuong ot* or *nuoc cham*. Chilies, garlic, and ginger are often enhanced with tamarind or lime juice. Basil, coriander, lemon grass, mint, and parsley are favorite fresh herbs. Anise, cloves, cumin, white pepper, and varieties of mixed spices are used with a light touch.

During T*et*, the New Year Festival, choice delicacies are served everywhere. Some are costly treats, others are traditional favorites like glutinous rice cakes stuffed with spicy meat and steamed in banana leaves. Others are sweetened with fruit and coconut. Green and black teas are the most common beverages, but flower and herb teas are drunk as well. Beer and rice wine are the alcoholic drinks available. Cane, coconut, and fruit juice are sold as snacks. One of the most popular drinks served in this country is a Vietnamese iced coffee, which is made with espresso and condensed milk.

Vietnamese Fish Sauce (Nuoc Nam *Sauce*)

---

2 dried hot chilies, about 1½-inches long
2 garlic cloves, sliced
1-inch piece fresh ginger root
2 teaspoons sugar
juice of 1 lime
3 tablespoons Vietnamese fish paste (*nuoc mam*)

Seed and devein the chilies. Crush them with the garlic and ginger in a mortar and pestle or grinder. Add the sugar and lime juice. Incorporate the fish paste until well blended. Add up to 2 tablespoons of water to thin, if necessary. The sauce will keep several weeks in the refrigerator if it is stored in a nonreactive, covered jar.

Yield: 1/2 cup±

Spicy Peanut Sauce (Nuoc Leo)

---

1 cup raw peanuts
1 cup chicken or vegetable stock, plus 1/2 cup
2 tablespoons peanut oil
3 cloves garlic, minced
1–2 teaspoons crushed red pepper, to taste
3/4 cup hoisin sauce (Chinese bean paste)
3 tablespoons brown sugar

Roast the peanuts in a 350° oven for 7 minutes. (You may use pre-roasted, unsalted peanuts.) In a food processor, blend the peanuts and 1 cup of stock until it is the consistency of chunky peanut butter.

Heat the oil in a heavy skillet that can hold all the ingredients. Add garlic and red pepper and stir till aromatic. Stir in the hoisin sauce and brown sugar. Add the peanut mixture and up to 1/2 cup additional stock to make a creamy sauce. Serve hot or at room temperature. Sauce may be stored in the refrigerator or frozen. It may be necessary to add some water so that it is brought back to a creamy consistency.

Yield: 3 cups

Beef Stew (Thit Bo Kho)

2 tablespoons peanut oil
2 pounds beef chuck, in 2-inch cubes
2 stalks lemon grass, outer stalks discarded and center part crushed
1-inch piece fresh ginger, not minced
4 shallots, minced
salt and pepper to taste
6 cups water
2 tablespoons fish sauce (*nuoc mam*)
2 3-inch pieces of cinnamon
2 tablespoons tomato paste

In a small Dutch oven or stove-top casserole, heat the oil and brown the beef with the lemon grass, ginger, and shallots. Stir until well-browned, then add the salt and pepper. Pour in water with fish sauce and cinnamon. Stir, cover, and simmer for 2 hours.

Yield: about 6 servings

Spring Rolls (Cha Gio)

1 4-ounce package cellophane noodles
3 tablespoons peanut oil
1 medium onion, chopped
5 green onions, chopped
1/2 pound ground pork, optional
1/2 pound fresh shelled shrimp, chopped
1/2 teaspoon crushed red pepper
1 teaspoon sugar
3 carrots, shredded
1/2 cup fresh mint leaves, chopped
1/2 cup fresh coriander (cilantro) leaves, chopped
1 package Vietnamese rice-paper spring-roll wrappers (*banh trang*)
1 tablespoon brown sugar dissolved in 1 cup warm water
5 spring onions, each lengthwise section separated into one long strip
nuoc nam sauce☙
fresh mint sprigs for garnish
fresh cilantro sprigs for garnish

Soak the cellophane noodles for 15 minutes in lukewarm water. Drain and cut them into 2-inch sections.

Heat the oil in a wok or skillet, add both kinds of onions, and lightly brown. Stir in the pork, if using, until it is cooked. Add the shrimp, pepper, and sugar, and cook for 4 minutes.

Soften wrappers by brushing them with the sugar water. Place the cooked filling topped with shredded carrot, mint, and coriander leaves, in a rectangle in the center of the wrapper and roll by folding the sides in and then rolling from top to bottom. Use the single long strips to wrap the roll in a decorative fashion. The rolls may be served at this point with the *nuoc nam* sauce and herbs. If you like, the rolls can also be fried and served hot.

Yield: 12±

Banana Cake

2 pounds very ripe bananas
1/2 cup heavy cream
1¼ cups coconut milk
1/4 cup shredded coconut
1 cup "instant" flour
1/2 cup sugar

Preheat oven to 350°. Butter and flour a 9-inch cake pan.

Mash the bananas thoroughly, incorporating the cream. Add the coconut milk and coconut and beat well. Add the flour and sugar and beat only until incorporated. Pour into the prepared pan and bake for 50 minutes. Serve warm or cold.

Yield: 1 9-inch cake

9

EAST ASIA

China

The oldest continuous cuisine in the world is from China. The nicety of chopsticks is described in written records three-thousand-years old. In such an ancient tradition, there has been plenty of time for keen observation of the nutritional and healthful benefits of various foods, as well as the development of a literature of both fact and fiction about the remarkable attributes of some foods. Chicken is not only a barnyard favorite, easy to raise and delicious to eat, "a hero of cuisine," but a sacred bird used for prophecy and divination. The goose and duck represent fidelity and joy; the fish, prosperity, wealth, and regeneration. The perseverance of a carp will be given to the person who eats it. Eating smooth, gelatinous jellyfish or the bumpy, sticky, sea cucumber will moisturize the skin and reduce signs of aging. Oranges and tangerines will give you energy and keep sweetness in life.

In my travels through China, I was continually impressed by the attention paid to food and the respect given its preparation. This quality is becoming more and more apparent in the Chinese food stalls and restaurants of North America, as people from all parts of China are becoming food entrepreneurs.

So many delicious ingredients from the Chinese kitchen have turned out to be very valuable for maintaining health and well-being. Ginger, garlic, tofu, and green tea have been the most well reported. Shark's fin or bird's-nest soup is as good a tonic as chicken soup—many say better.

Yin and yang is taken into consideration in classic dishes to harmonize the body's need for balance so that our organs, including the brain, function well. Qi, which in its simplest translation means *energy*, is also maintained by good diet.

For the most part, the food that we think of as exotic in Chinese cuisine is also considered exotic in China. Some are regarded as prized delicacies, and appear at banquets and special occasions. Some feast delicacies like shark's fin soup and bird's-nest soup have long been regarded as so beneficial that high prices do not stop people from enjoying them as a treat.

Vegetarian dishes are abundant. In addition to the straightforward ones made with vegetables or tofu served with rice or noodles, there are rather elaborate ones. Duck, pork, sausage, beef, and chicken have all been copied in a dazzling display of fakery.

There are also wine spreads or *chiu hsi*, as they are called, when desserts such as eight-treasure rice pudding are eaten. Western-style desserts are not part of usual Chinese meals. In fact, it is considered healthier to eat sweets before a meal, with soup being served at the end. Sliced oranges are frequently offered to end a meal. Sweet red-bean soup or puddings made from chestnut, yam, or taro are presented to those who want to have a little something more. A modern dessert is a kind of almond gelatin topped with fresh or canned fruit salad.

Even though moderation is the key, Americans are usually surprised at the number of dishes to be found at a single meal. An ordinary dinner out for eight people will consist of four cold dishes and four hot dishes, soup, and rice. A banquet would consist of four cold dishes and eight or ten hot ones, as well as two showpieces such as a whole fish and a roasted duck. Soup, rice, pastries, and fruit would also be served, though most diners might only taste a few bites from each dish. Serving fewer courses would mean the event was not an important celebration. Everyone has his or her own place setting, but dishes are served in large platters and bowls to be shared. There are serving spoons and serving chopsticks for each platter. It is incorrect to help oneself with one's own chopsticks except in the most relaxed company, and, even then, once your chopsticks have touched the food, it is polite to put the food on your plate. Often on the center of the table is a large lazy susan, so that it is easy to serve yourself from the array.

When you are finished eating, the chopsticks are placed parallel over your rice bowl or on chopstick rests. Spoons are set for soup and to assist in serving, but you will rarely see a knife at a Chinese table because the work has been done in the kitchen. Instead of the large dinner plates used in the West, luncheon-sized plates are used and changed frequently throughout the meal. Soup and rice bowls tend to be the same size, and the standard tea cup with no handles is only a bit smaller. Soy sauce and vinegar are provided at the table—one easy way to tell the difference, if they are served in a glass or an open ceramic pitcher, is that soy sauce leaves a film on the inside walls of the container and vinegar does not. The plain rice that accompanies a meal is usually left unseasoned so that it can enhance the rich flavors of the other dishes.

Attractively designed platters of food often serve as centerpieces instead of flowers, since form and color are rated as important as are aroma and taste. Everything on the serving plate is edible; there is nothing there that is meant solely for decoration, no matter how artificial it may look. Food is often the center of conversation as well.

Tea is served throughout the meal, and sometimes special teas with dried fruit and nuts are served at dessert. Wine will sometimes accompany a meal, and beer is becoming more popular. In this country Shaoxing wine and Tsing Tao beer are the most widely available.

Food is cooked in various shapes so that there will be not only visual variety, but because it will absorb the flavors of the sauces and condiments differently. Garlic, ginger, coriander, star anise, Sichuan pepper (*fagara*), cinnamon, cloves, chili paste, sesame paste, and sesame oil are used as seasonings. Various kinds of soy sauces, oyster sauce, black bean, and hoisin sauces, as well as various rice wines and vinegars, are used both in the kitchen and on the table. Food is served seconds after it is cooked, and fragrance is regarded as an important element.

Cantonese cooking is greatly underestimated, since it was the first of the regions to establish restaurants in the United States and to adapt Chinese cuisine to American tastes and ingredients. Cantonese food is often steamed or roasted and is not very oily. Just a little oil is put into the wok to sear the ingredients, then the cooking is finished either by adding a sauce and sautéing the dish or adding water or stock and steaming it. Dumplings and soups are popular. In Hong Kong, there are remarkable restaurants with Cantonese chefs and, by and large, when an American restaurant announces itself to be "Hong Kong Style," it serves good-quality Cantonese cooking.

In the North, where wheat is farmed in abundance, noodles, dumplings, and bread are diet mainstays, with rice a close second. Mandarin cuisine, centered in Beijing, is famous in the West for Peking duck. This imperial court cuisine uses fine rice wine, soy sauce, garlic, and ginger to flavor its sophisticated dishes. Beijing has been an international city for so long that the incorporation of many Asian cuisines has resulted in a vast menu. The fare of the region is greatly influenced by Manchurian and Muslim cuisines, and aromatic lamb dishes are served. Mongolian hot pots cook using boiling water instead of oil and are served in many Chinese restaurants. There are clay-pot casseroles and dramatic sizzling platters for the cold winter months.

Sichuan (Szechuan) restaurants serve food from modern China's largest province. Piquant and spicy dishes using onions and garlic, star anise, ginger, chilies, and peppercorns are abundant. Chicken and pork are used a great deal, as are sautéed vegetables—sometimes the meat is smoked or barbecued. Wrapped dishes include bean-flour-paste noodles, pancakes, and lotus leaves. Sichuan chefs strive for an overall complex flavor. Chili peppers are not indigenous, though they would seem to be. Only a few hundred years ago, they were imported from the Mediterranean. Adjacent Hunan province is responsible for even more fiery dishes than Sichuan. There are many "House of Hunan" and similar restaurants throughout the United States.

Shanghai, the country's largest port, is in the northeast, and in the fall the local crabs and their roe are so popular that visitors travel long distances to taste them. Currently, Shanghai cooking is dominated by stir frying, using small quantities of meat or poultry and large amounts of fresh produce seasoned with sesame oil and soy sauce. The right wok *hay* (aroma) is the sign of a good cook. Often food is steamed and accompanied by preserved or pickled vegetables, depending on the season. Popular Shanghai dishes sometimes use a lot of sugar and rice wine for a sweet-and-sour flavor to accompany the long-cooked meat or chicken.

Sawaddi cuisine is vegetarian and designed for certain Buddhists and others who abstain from animal, fish, or egg protein. For twenty-five-hundred years, vegetarianism has been touted by many. To this day, some of the best vegetarian meals are cooked in temple kitchens by monks or nuns who combine tradition with some modern methods.

Nutrition and health have played an important part in the general preparation of vegetables, although it is still rare to see them served raw. Vegetables are usually well cleaned, trimmed, and steamed or stir-fried quickly to retain their vitamins and minerals. Often they are cooked with ginger and/or garlic, which are known to have many healthful properties. Bok choy, Chinese cabbage, has many forms, as does kale, which is often not like American kale but looks more like flowering broccoli. Yard-long or snake beans are quite similar in taste to green beans. There is squash of all varieties, as well as root vegetables and melons that are used extensively on their own or blended with other ingredients. In some regions, corn and the familiar tiny baby corn is prepared and mixed with carrots and pea pods. Fragile pea shoots are steamed in season and are a vegetable delicacy.

A dish that is just gaining popularity in the United States is congee, often ordered as *jook*, rice cooked into a gruel-like consistency and served with savory bite-sized morsels. Served quite commonly for breakfast, it is also a late-night snack and a good lunch choice. It is almost always served with deep-fried *kuai*, long, thin crullers that are cubed onto the *jook*, much like croutons. The dish is then topped with a combination that may include nuts, roasted chicken, pork or beef, fresh fish or shellfish, smoked eel or abalone, green onions, and freshly minced coriander.

Small snacks are everywhere and are available in hundreds of combinations. Simple tidbits like peanuts, watermelon, pumpkin or lotus seeds, preserved plums and dates, and bean-and-nut cakes are often served with tea. But it is *dim sum*, from the endless steamed and baked round buns to the wonderfully surprising soup-filled dumplings, that we know best in the West. *Cha siu bao* are the famous roast-pork-filled steamed buns. If you prefer them baked, ask for *guk cha siu bao*. *Shao mai* are open-topped steamed shrimp or pork pastries. *Har gau* is another wontonlike dumpling, in which shrimp show through the paper-thin

From the menu of

Great Shanghai

27 Division Street
New York, NY 10002

Cold Appetizers

Chicken with Wine Sauce

Cooked Ham

Spiced Beef

Smoked Fish with Bone

Sliced Jellyfish

Boneless Duck Feet

Spiced Tientsin Cabbage

Hot Appetizers

Spring Rolls

Fried Dumplings

Steamed Dumplings

House Specialties

Braised Shark's Fin with Chicken Meat

Steamed Crab with Wine Sauce

Crispy Chicken Skin Mandarin Style

Braised Whole Yellow Croaker

Braised Shredded Filet of Eels

Braised Sea Cucumber with Shrimp Roe

Braised Pig Tendon with Sea Cucumber

Stewed Pork with Salted Dried Mustard Cabbage

Seafood

Braised Carp's Tail

Fried Sliced Prawns with Chili Sauce

Shrimp with Lobster Sauce

Vegetables

Sauteed Chinese Cabbage with Black Mushrooms

Sauteed Crispy String Beans with Minced Pork

translucency of the rice-flour wrapper. N*or mai gai* are lotus-leaf packages of glutinous rice, sausage, chicken, beef or pork, and mushrooms. Everyone is intrigued by the lotus-leaf-wrapped and tied *ho yip fan*, filled with fried rice. If you can find them, *siu loon baos* are savory soup-filled buns that are delicious and have to be eaten delicately so they don't drip. By and large, the most popular form of *dim sum* from Beijing are *kuo-tiehs*, pot stickers, which are juicy and meaty dumplings, pan-steamed then fried on the bottom so that the bottom of the dough is crunchy and chewy and the top is soft. They are served with *chunkiang* vinegar or scallion-oil dips, but you can dip them as you choose. Another favorite, *woo kok*, are fried taro puffs, which are like a round french fried potato.

Some tidbits are sweet, like *nor mai chi*, coconut cakes; *dahn sarn*, sweet sticky cake with almonds; and *jien dui*, fried sesame-crusted balls of dough filled with sweet red-bean paste.

Tea is, of course, the drink of China. Drunk from morning until night, it is served with meals and in teahouses. Mild green and semi-red teas are most often served with meals. Tea should be purchased in small amounts, especially green tea, which does not store as well as more highly fermented teas. It is best bought fresh and loose, then stored in an airtight tea caddy. The word *caddy* is derived from *catty*, an approximation of a Chinese measure of weight the equivalent of 1.33 pounds.

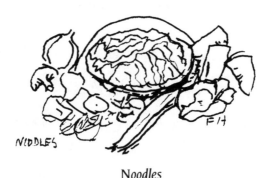

Noodles

Sichuan Cold Sesame Noodles

Sauce:

3 tablespoons Chinese sesame paste
2 tablespoons oil from sesame-paste jar
3 tablespoons honey
4 tablespoons bottled Chinese sesame oil
4 tablespoons soy sauce
2 teaspoons hot chili oil
1/4 cup hot water

Noodles:

8 ounces Chinese rice noodles
2 tablespoons Chinese bottled sesame oil
1/2 cup cucumber, finely julienned
1/2 cup carrot, finely julienned
1/2 cup green onion, finely julienned
3 cakes dried tofu, cubed
1/4 pound small cooked shrimp
2 tablespoons minced, fresh coriander (cilantro) leaves, as garnish

In a medium bowl, mix together the sesame paste and the oil from the jar, gradually stirring in the honey. Add the bottled sesame oil, soy sauce, and hot chili oil. Add the hot water and stir to blend the ingredients.

Follow package directions for the noodles, then rinse under cold water. Drain the noodles thoroughly and place in serving bowl large enough to hold all the ingredients. Stir with sesame oil so that the noodles are coated and will not stick together. Add cucumber, carrot, and green onion julienne and stir. Mix in the tofu and shrimp. Add half the sauce and toss as you would a salad. Garnish with minced coriander leaves, and pass the additional sauce separately.

Yield: 8 servings

Five-Flavor Cold Roast Beef

1½ cups soy sauce
2 cups water
1 cup Chinese rice wine
1 tablespoon sugar
4 garlic cloves, crushed, fibrous part removed
2-inch piece of fresh ginger root, grated
3 tablespoons Chinese five-spice powder
2 pounds top round roast
3 tablespoons chopped fresh coriander leaves
3 tablespoons green onions, chopped

In a pot large enough to hold the roast, bring the soy sauce and water to a low boil. Add the rice wine, sugar, garlic, ginger, and five-spice powder. Mix well and simmer. Add the roast and bring liquid back to a boil. Cover pot and turn heat down to low. Simmer for 2 hours. Cool and refrigerate for several hours or overnight. Slice and serve garnished with coriander and green onions.

Yield: 8 servings

Hot-and-Sour Soup

Meat:

1/2 pound lean pork shoulder sliced and julienned
2 tablespoons soy sauce
1 teaspoon hot chili-infused sesame oil
1 tablespoon cornstarch
3 tablespoons peanut or safflower oil

Soup:

  2 quarts water
  1/2 cup minced green onions
  1 tablespoon sugar
  1/2 teaspoon salt
  1 cup fresh bamboo shoots, julienned
  1 ounce Chinese dried wood-ear fungus, soaked and drained
  2 tablespoons cornstarch dissolved in 2 tablespoons cold water
  3 cakes medium-firm tofu, diced
  3 eggs, lightly beaten

Sour infusion:

  4 tablespoons chunkiang vinegar
  2 tablespoons soy sauce
  1 tablespoon hot chili-infused sesame oil, or to taste
  1 teaspoon ground Sichuan peppercorns (*fagara*)

To prepare the pork, mix together the soy sauce, sesame oil, and cornstarch. Using chopsticks or your hands, coat the pork with the mixture. Set aside while you prepare other ingredients.

In a wok or heavy-bottomed pan large enough to hold all the ingredients, heat peanut or safflower oil and brown the pork, stirring to make sure it is well cooked. Add the water, green onions, sugar, salt, bamboo shoots, and wood-ear fungus. Bring to a boil and simmer for 20 minutes. Add the cornstarch dissolved in cold water, and stir until the texture thickens. Add the tofu. Drop the lightly beaten egg into the soup from a fork, so that it separates into threads. Stir the vinegar, soy sauce, oil, and ground peppercorns together. Place the sour infusion into a serving bowl or tureen. Stir. Pour the hot soup over it and serve immediately.

Yield: 8 servings

Chicken with Chili and Orange Peel

Marinade:

>   2 tablespoons soy sauce
>   4 tablespoons Chinese rice wine
>   1/2 teaspoon finely ground Sichuan pepper (*fagara*)
>   1 teaspoon sugar
>   1/4 teaspoon salt
>   1/2 teaspoon hot chili-infused sesame oil
>   1 tablespoon cornstarch
>
>   1½ pounds boneless chicken breasts
>
>   3 tablespoons peanut or safflower oil
>   1-inch piece fresh ginger root, shredded
>   10 green onions, cut in 2-inch pieces
>   1 dried chili, split and seeded, minced
>   1 ounce Chinese preserved orange or tangerine peel, soaked for 30
>   minutes, drained, and sliced
>   3 tablespoons Chinese rice wine
>   3 tablespoons light soy sauce
>   1/4 cup chicken stock or water

Mix the marinade ingredients together in a shallow bowl. Cut the chicken into slices, then into 1-inch by 3-inch pieces. With chopsticks or your fingers, coat the chicken with the marinade and set aside, covered, in the refrigerator for 1 hour.

Heat the oil in a wok or skillet and add the ginger, green onions, chili, and orange peel. Stir and, when it is aromatic, add the chicken. Stir-fry for 4 or 5 minutes. (Test chicken by cutting into it and seeing if it is cooked through.) Add rice wine, soy sauce, and chicken stock or water. Serve immediately.

Yield: 8 servings

Green Beans with Garlic

1½ pounds Chinese yard-long beans or American string beans
3 tablespoons peanut or safflower oil
2 heads garlic, cloves separated and peeled
2 cups stock or water

Trim the beans and cut into 4-inch lengths if necessary. In a wok or skillet large enough to hold all the beans, heat the oil. Add the garlic and stir-fry until the garlic is lightly browned on all sides. Add the broth or water and cover. Over a medium flame, simmer the garlic for 10 minutes. Remove the cover, bring contents to a boil, and add the green beans. Cook for 5 to 7 minutes, stirring occasionally. Serve immediately or refrigerate and serve cold.

Yield: 8 servings

Steamed Whole Fish

Fish is frequently served whole, with the head pointed toward the guest of honor.

1 3-pound red snapper, cleaned and scaled
3 tablespoons Shaoxing rice wine
3 tablespoons soy sauce
2 teaspoons oyster sauce
4 cups water
2 tablespoons ginger root, minced
6 green onions, minced
1/8 pound Yunan ham (prosciutto may be substituted)
2 fresh bamboo shoots, prepared and julienned
2 tablespoons Chinese sesame oil
1 tablespoon cornstarch dissolved in
2 tablespoons cold water

Wash and dry the fish inside and out. Score the fish in several places. Mix together the rice wine, soy sauce, and oyster sauce. Place fish on heatproof plate that will fit in wok. Pour mixture over both sides of fish and let marinate while the other ingredients are being prepared.

Place the water in a wok with a steaming rack large enough to hold the plate. Cover and bring to a gentle boil, making sure that the water does not go over the rack. Place the ginger, green onions, ham, and bamboo shoots on the fish plate. Sprinkle with sesame oil. Place the plate on the steaming rack and cover with the wok lid. Steam for 20 minutes. Carefully remove the hot plate with the fish and set aside. Pour off all but 3/4 cup of steaming liquid, reserving any vegetables that may have fallen in. Stir in the cornstarch dissolved in cold water, and stir until a smooth sauce is formed. Pour over the fish and serve immediately.

Yield: about 6 servings

China—Glossary

Pinyin is the English-alphabet-based transliteration used throughout China. It is the most helpful form for English speakers who want to express themselves in Chinese, and hope to understand a few words and phrases. Instead of International Phonetics, the equivalent in "sound it out" English is supplied in brackets.

Polite Expressions

Ni Shir-le fan le mai-yo? [nee shir-luh fahnluh may-oh]   Have you eaten yet? (used similarly to: Hi, how are you?)

Qing [ching].   Please.

Xie Xie [sheeyeh sheeyeh].   Thank you.

Bu ke qi [boo kuh chee].   You're welcome.

Dui bu qi [dooee boo kuhchee].   Excuse me (I'm sorry).

Wo keyi yao yi ge caidan ma? [whoa guhyee yaow eeguh tsaye dahn]. May I have a menu?

Qing ni jieshao jiyang nimende hao cai ba [ching nee jeeayshao jeeahng neemenduh how tsaye bah].   Please recommend some good dishes.

Nimen yo mei yo . . .? [neemen yo may yo]   Do you have . . .?

Mei yo [may yo].   There isn't or aren't any! (as an answer)

Qing ni gei wo . . . [ching nee gay whoa].   Please bring me . . .

Gei wo [gay whoa].   I want.

Gan bei [gone bay] (dry cup).   Cheers!

Youyi [you yee].   Friendship! (A toast)

Nin manman chi! [nin mahnmahn chee]   Good appetite!

Shi-fen gan xie [shrfahn gan sheeyeh].   Thank you very much.

Zai jian [dzai j'ohn].   Goodbye.

Ni hao [nee how].   Hello, good morning, good afternoon, good evening.

Wan an [won ahn].   Good night.

Food Places and Phrases

fanguar [fahngwahr]   restaurant

fanting [fahnding]   dining room

chaguan [chahgwan]   teahouse

chufang [choofahng]   kitchen

zao-fan [dzow-fahn]   breakfast

chi [chee]   to eat

fan [fahn]   a meal

chifan [chee fahn]   to eat a meal

hè [hay]   to drink

wu-fan [woo fahn]   lunch

wan-fan [wahn fahn]   dinner

yum cha [ium chah]   tea and snacks (eat tea)

caidan [tsaye dahn]   menu

gei qian [gay cheeahn]   to pay

duo yi dian . . . [dwoh yee deeahn]   more . . .

shao yi dian . . . [shaow yee deeahn]   less . . .

yi diandian [yee deeahn deeahn]   a little bit

goule [gooleh]   enough

hen hao chi [hen how chee]   tastes very good

hao ji le [how jhee lee]   very good

bu hao chi [boo how chee]   terrible food

mama huhu [mama hoohoo]   so-so (literally horse-horse tiger-tiger)

Place Setting

kuaizi [kwyzuh] chopsticks
chizi [cheezuh] spoon
chazi [chazuh] fork
daozi [dowzuh] knife
panzi [p'ahnzuh] plate
beizi [bayzuh] cup
bolibei [bwoh lee bay] glass
canjin [tsahn jeen] napkin

Food

dim sum [dim sum] Cantonese, "dot the heart" (small snacks)
tien hsin [teeyen shin] Mandarin, "touch the heart" (small snacks)
bai fan [buy fun] plain white rice
mian [meeahn] noodles
shucai [shoo tsaye] vegetables
dan [dahn] egg
ji [jhee] chicken
huo ji [who ow jhee] turkey
ya [eeyah] duck
e [ee] goose
yu [you] fish
yu chi [you chee] shark's fin
yan wo [eeyahn whoa] bird's nest
xia [shee yah] shrimp
pang xie [pohng shee yeh] crab
long xia [lahng sheeyah] lobster
niurou [nyooroo] beef
zhurou [dzuroo] pork
xiaoyang [sheeyah owyahng] lamb
tang [tohng] soup
shuiguo [shweegwo] fruit

Methods

zhu [dzu] boiling

kuai ch'ao kwai [kwai chaow kwai] stir-frying

kao [cow] roasting

pao [pow] very fast frying

tan shu de [dan shoed'] poaching

men [mun] long, slow cooking

tun [tun] as though in the top of a double boiler

zheng [dzung] steaming

Beverages

cha [chah] tea

lu cha [loo chah] green tea

kuang shui [kwang shwee] mineral water

pijiu [pee jee oo] beer

qingdao [ching dow] Tsingtao beer

hong putaojiu [hahng boo dow jee oo] red-grape wine

gan bai putaojiu [gone buy boo dow jee oo] white-grape wine

shaoxing [shaowshing] rice wine

bailandi [buyandee] brandy or cognac

Korea

The 1988 Olympics in Seoul brought Korean food to the attention of a large public for the first time. Up until then, there were few Korean restaurants even in big American cities. Korean restaurateurs would often have a double menu to attract diners: Japanese or Chinese food would be featured in addition to Korean, because they reasoned that those cuisines were more familiar to the community. Now one finds good Korean restaurants everywhere.

Historians trace the origins of Korea to Tangan, the first ruler of the former Korean peninsula kingdom of *Chosen*, who led the country for a thousand years. Seoul has been the capital since 1394, and the heart of the city is located on the site of the old capital. It has a population of 11 million and is growing rapidly. Along the Hangang river new buildings are rising amidst the old, and the remains of old fortifications poke through modern areas.

There is a *kimchi* museum in Seoul that traces this national dish to ancient times. Most Korean meals will have one or more dishes accompanied by *kimchi*. It is made in a hundred ways: by adding ground red chilies and salt to whole, shredded, or diced cabbage, which is fermented alone or with white turnips, radishes, cucumbers, and other vegetables, often with the addition of garlic for additional punch. *Kimjang* is the name for the autumn *kimchi* making. Every family makes large amounts that are stored buried in the ground, with the opening of the jars sealed but accessible. It is often served as an accompaniment, but chefs will sometimes incorporate it into dishes, such as the popular *do kimchi juck*, which is a crisp, large pancake filled with well-cooked pork, scallions, and *kimchi*.

In addition to the popular barbecues, a dish found on most Korean restaurant menus is *bulgogi*, in which marinated beef slices brushed with a spicy soy mixture and lots of sesame seeds are grilled over charcoal, either at a central cooker or on individual braziers set at the table. A variation of this is *san juk*, in which beef chunks similarly marinated are skewered with mushrooms and vegetables. Another meat and vegetable dish is *sinsullo*, which is a combination of meat, vegetables, and broth simmered in a tabletop Mongolian fire-pot.

Sul long tang, a soupy noodle dish filled with thinly sliced brisket and rice, is a frequent menu item. A fancier version of this is *abok jeng-ban*, which features slices of pancake instead of rice, to which slices of sweet peppers and Asian pear are added. *Bibinbap* is a popular rice dish served with anywhere from three to eight savory selections of beef, vegetables, fish, or beans and frequently served topped with a fried egg. This dish, as well as so many others, is served with *kimchi* and hot sauce.

During the period known as *Sambok*, the hottest days of the summer, it was long believed that *samgai tang*, a long-cooked chicken dish, is an energy restorer. A whole chicken is stuffed with sticky rice flavored with shallots, garlic, chestnuts, and dates and then simmered. The broth is often flavored with ginseng. Fruit is served not only as dessert but also made into relishes and preserves. *Hwach'ae* are the traditional fruit drinks served with dessert. On special days, *ttok*, rice cakes, and *han-gwa*, rice-flour honey cakes, are served.

Tabang tashil, teahouses, serve not only standard green and black teas but varieties of ginseng, ginger, citron, barley, or walnut tea. The etiquette of drinking tea is called *Tado*, "The Way of Tea."

The alcoholic drink of choice after beer is *suju* or *yakju*, which is distilled from sweet potatoes or yams and drunk throughout the meal by those who like it. It is vaguely similar to vodka and is often made into a cocktail with ginseng extract. The best rice wine is known as *tongdong-ju*.

Nju are the *dim sum* of Korea. These appetizers are served occasionally at the start of a meal but more frequently as a meal to be eaten with tea or drinks as a snack or light lunch or dinner.

A meal served for a group is often composed of several large dishes, and as many as twenty small ones with various accompaniments. Chopsticks, forks, and spoons are used for serving, never the hands. In Korea it is not customary to talk too much during meals and, in many areas, diners still eat alone at small individual tables. After eating is when there is a social time for talking, singing, and playing games, although in the United States this habit is changing rapidly.

The use of medicinal plants is called *hanyak*, and is unique in that it emphasizes the use of flowers more than other systems do, though standbys such as garlic and ginger infuse many dishes.

Korean Buffet

Broiled Beef Ribs (Soekalbiqui)

4 pounds beef ribs
1/2 cup rice wine
1/3 cup sugar
1 head garlic
1/4 cup soy sauce
4 tablespoons sesame salt
1 cup minced green onions
1/3 cup sesame oil
6 green onions, cut into long strips
3 medium onions, sliced paper thin
1/3 cup pine nuts
1 head of strong lettuce, such as romaine or iceberg, separated into leaves

With a very sharp knife, score the ribs. Mix together the rice wine and sugar and pour over the ribs. Peel and crush the garlic, remove the fibrous parts, and mix with the soy sauce, sesame salt, minced green onions, and sesame oil. Rub on the ribs and let stand in a deep bowl for 1 to 2 hours.

   Place ribs on hot grill or under hot broiler, turning them several times until they are thoroughly cooked. Serve topped with green and sliced onions and sprinkle with pine nuts.

Yield: 6 servings

Cold Buckwheat Noodles (Naengmyon)

12 ounces Korean buckwheat noodles, boiled and rinsed in cold water
2 cups beef stock
8 ounces minute steak, cooked and shredded
1½ cups *kimchi*, drained
1 cucumber, peeled, seeded, and julienned, mixed with 2 teaspoons sugar
1 tablespoon vinegar
1 pear, peeled, seeded, and julienned
2 hard-cooked eggs
1 bunch mustard greens or watercress
1/4 pound radishes, scrubbed and sliced

Sauce:

1/2 cup beef stock
2 tablespoons crushed red pepper
2 tablespoons minced green onions
2 garlic cloves, crushed, fibers removed

Mix the noodles with the beef stock. Stir in the beef and *kimchi*. Soak the cucumber in sugar and vinegar.

Place noodle mixture on a serving platter large enough to hold all the ingredients. Arrange the cucumbers, pears, and eggs on top of the noodles. Surround platter with mustard leaves or watercress. Garnish with sliced red radishes. Mix stock, red pepper, green onions, and garlic cloves. Pour over all or serve on the side, since it is quite hot.

Yield: 6 servings

Korea—Glossary

Polite Expressions

Yoboseyo. Hello.
Annyonghaseyo. Good morning, good afternoon, good evening.
Ch'o-um poepgessoyo? How do you do?
Mannaso pangaweyo. Glad to meet you.
Annyonghi gaseyo. Good-bye.
Ye. Yes.
Aniyo. No.
Kamsa hamnida. Thank you.
Ch'onmaneyo. You're welcome.
Shile hamnida. Excuse me.
Mian hamnida. I'm sorry.
Menu chom poyo-chuseyo? May I have a menu, please?
Chogotkwa katun kosul chuseyo. Give me the same as that one.
Mashi issoyo. This is delicious.

Food Phrases

anju appetizers and small dishes
bindaeduk mung-bean pancakes filled with savories

bulgogi   marinated strips of beef, charcoal broiled

dwiji-gwbe   sliced barbecued pork

gochujang   hot chili paste

gulchupan   pancakes served with 9 side dishes

jajaengmein   buckwheat noodles with meat

kalbi   marinated short ribs, charcoal broiled

kalbitang   soup with beef ribs

kingjung chongol   fish, meat, and vegetables cooked in broth

maeuntang   spicy fish soup with vegetables

mandu   steamed or fried dumplings

manduguk   soup with meat dumplings

naengmein   cold noodles with vegetables, eggs, and beef

ojingu gwbe   marinated grilled squid

pibinpap   rice with vegetables and egg

pindaedok   vegetable pancake

poricha   barley tea

saengson chigye   vegetable-and-fish stew

sinsollo   casserole with meat, fish, vegetables, eggs, pine nuts, and ginkgo nuts

takgoki   barbecued chicken

Japan

There are a surprising number of distinct cuisines in Japan, and from raw to cooked, from homey to elaborate, what they share is an attitude. The flavors range from a single accent of ginger to an array that surprises with its sophistication. All food must offer taste, texture, and appearance. The mouthfeel of a morsel is as important as its nutritional component. The eye and the palate are treated equally well. Boiled noodle dishes, crisp tempura, and sushi are the most popular items in Japanese restaurants in North America. Appetizers are often eaten in Japanese restaurants starting with simple miso soup. Pickled vegetables, *oshinko*, are usually on the table and there is a tradition of serving a small tidbit of the chef's specialty.

At Zutto in New York's Tribeca, Charlie Huh, the owner, who has run this neighborhood favorite for fourteen years, talked with me on a busy Saturday night. This smallish, informal space has an unstudied elegance which was actually very carefully planned. Charlie Huh realized that what this high-profile restaurant neighborhood needed was a place where people could come as they are and find dependably good Japanese food. Chef Yukio Kikuchi has led the kitchen since Zutto opened. *Zutto* means "forever" in Japanese and, in the restaurant business, fourteen years is pretty close.

When the restaurant opened sushi was not unknown in New York, but it tended to be presented in elaborate ways. Chef Kikuchi saw to it that the small sushi bar had the classics like yellowtail, *toro*, and *uni*, but also accommodated to local tastes. Special sushi rolls included special combinations, like tuna and papaya, or salmon with jalapeño. When asked how he would reassure people uneasy about raw fish, he said that in fourteen years he had never had one incident and that that was true of virtually all good sushi bars. Quality and freshness are essential, and "a restaurateur would have to be an idiot to take any risks in food safety."

The rest of the menu is an eclectic Japanese mixture that follows the seasons. Vegetable and mushroom dishes are always on the menu as are noodles. The noodles are sometimes served cold, as in a dish of *soba*, buckwheat noodles flavored with bits of tempura in a slightly sweet-and-sour sauce made with soy sauce, ginger, and sweetened vinegar. *Una don*, which is very popular, is smoked eel, marinated, broiled, basted, and served with rice.

Charlie Huh says that by and large his customers seem to be in great shape. There is very little fat and not much cholesterol in Japanese cooking. To introduce a table of four to the cuisine, he says he might recommend *shumai*, *negamaki* (beef rolled around spring onions and grilled), *miso* soup, a salad, and salmon teriyaki, or an east-west dish of lobster teriyaki in creamy mustard sauce. As long as they are in season, the chef favors soft-shell crabs and broiled *shiitake* mushrooms. Hijiki is a dish of assorted seaweeds cooked in sake. There is also a specialty of *ankimo*, which is steamed monkfish liver served in lemon sauce. For the sushi, he recommends *toro* (tuna belly), salmon, and Belon oysters. Though the Japanese are not really big on desserts, the *yukan* (red bean jelly) is typical. Green-tea ice cream and ginger ice cream, invented in the United States, have become popular even in Japan.

Tribeca has become a mecca for upscale theme restaurants, and there was some concern that Zutto would be overshadowed. Very wisely, though aware of the competition, Charlie Huh decided not to

From the menu of

Zutto

77 Hudson Street
New York, NY 10013

Appetizers

Cori Cori
Lightly fried broccoli with mushrooms and garlic

Oshitashi
Boiled watercress or asparagus with dried shaved bonito

Tempura
Deep-fried shrimp and vegetables

Kaki Furai
Breaded deep-fried oysters

Seafood

Karara
Broiled lobster with a creamy mustard sauce

Dondokodon
Tuna steak wrapped with soba noodles and deep fried with
special soy sauce

Una Don
Broiled eel on a bed of rice

Meat

Sukiyaki

Sliced prime beef and oriental vegetables, tofu and glass noodles
in a special broth

Negimaki

Tender beef sliced and wrapped around cheese and scallions

Tonkatsu

Tender pork with cheese, breaded and deep fried

Sushi

Maguro (tuna)

Suzuki (striped bass)

Hamachi (yellowtail)

Unagi (fresh water eel)

Katsuo (bonito)

Saba (mackerel)

Uni (sea urchin)

Ikura (salmon roe)

Mirugai (giant clam)

Tamago (egg omelet)

compete overtly but maintain the style and quality that the neighborhood had grown accustomed to—and it worked. Keeping the *Hakko* or
Bento lunch at reasonable prices has kept people coming in during the
day. At night it is frequently crowded with a crowd as varied as the
dishes on the menu. They all seem at home.

Sushi may be eaten with chopsticks or your hands, but it is considered rude to use a fork. Don't soak it in soy sauce, but lightly dip the
fish into it. Generally, the soy sauce is seasoned with a bit of wasabi
(Japanese horseradish) and *gari* or *shoga,* pickled ginger. Various seaweeds are used to wrap the sushi, or are served separately in a mixed
salad, or steamed in sake or water, and topped with sesame seeds.

Tempura

Tempura is a relative newcomer to Japanese cooking. It is an adap-
tation of the way Portuguese sailors fried their food 400 years ago,
when they began trade with Japan. Street vendors started cooking and
serving it along the docks of Tokyo Bay, using fresh fish and some vegetables. It is still usually made with these ingredients. The vegetables
are usually sliced paper thin, and the batter is left quite lumpy, so that
there are air pockets in the crisp coating after it is fried. The batter cannot sit too long, or it will take on the texture of a dumpling. Usually,
vegetable or peanut oil is used for three-quarters of the oil, with one-
quarter sesame oil making up the volume. The oil is heated to 350° in
a large wok or deep-fryer. Rice flour or, sometimes, yam flour is used
instead of regular wheat flour. Fry in small batches so that the oil
stays hot.

Tempura

---

1 pound medium shrimp
1/2 pound squid, cleaned and sliced into strips
1 medium sweet potato
1 section of lotus root (approximately the size of the sweet potato)
1 large onion
6 large mushrooms
3 small Japanese eggplants

Batter:

1½ cups rice flour or 1 cup of unbleached all-purpose flour mixed with 1/2 cup cornstarch
1 egg, beaten
1 cup of ice cold water (add up to another 1/2 cup if batter seems too thick)
1 tablespoon sake
pinch of salt

Dipping sauce:

2 cups *dashi* (a commercial Japanese stock made from kelp and dried bonito)
1 tablespoon soy sauce
1 tablespoon sugar
1/2 cup finely grated daikon
1 teaspoon freshly grated ginger root
3 green onions, finely minced

Peel the shrimp, leaving the tails on. Butterfly and flatten them. Rinse and dry squid. Scrub the sweet potato and lotus root. Slice them as for chips, 1/4-inch thick. Peel onion, slice into 3/4-inch-thick slices, and separate into rings. Trim stems from mushrooms and cut caps in half. Slice the eggplant, salt the slices, and place in a colander. Let them stand for 20 minutes. Rinse, drain, and dry them.

Bring the oil to 350°. Mix the batter, stopping when it is still a bit lumpy. Mix the dipping sauce ingredients and set aside. Dip shrimp, squid, and vegetables in batter, fry, and drain them. Vegetables take about 2 to 3 minutes. Fish should take no longer than it takes to brown the batter. Serve immediately.

Yield: 6 servings

Daikon

Daikon has become available in many supermarkets in the United States even though only a few years ago most people in this country didn't know what it was. Daikon, or "great root," is a large, mild radish. It is often served raw, peeled and shredded, alongside pickled ginger and wasabi with sushi and sashimi. It is also mixed with other ingredients to make sauces. Fresh daikon with tight, smooth skins taste somewhat like a cross between a small, red, French radish and a turnip. In the East, daikon is regarded as an aid to digestion, as well as a crisp, zesty accompaniment.

For a simple daikon salad, combine half a daikon, shredded, with two shredded carrots and a bit of grated ginger. Douse with three tablespoons of rice vinegar mixed with four teaspoons of sugar, one-half teaspoon of wasabi powder mixed to a paste with a tablespoon of water, and one tablespoon of soy sauce.

A simple way to use them cooked is to braise them like turnips, in a little butter and oil along with some mushrooms and garlic.

Mushrooms

Braised Daikon with Shiitake Mushrooms

3 tablespoons cooking oil
1 large daikon, peeled and cut into 1-inch slices, then into half rounds
8 garlic cloves, peeled and sliced
1/2 pound dried shiitake mushrooms, soaked in water to cover for
2 hours
salt and pepper to taste

Place the oil in a skillet over medium heat. Add the daikon and garlic and sauté, turning the daikon occasionally, for 15 minutes. Drain the mushrooms and reserve the soaking water. Add the mushrooms to the pan and stir for a few minutes. Add 1½ cups of the mushroom water and the salt and pepper. Simmer for 5 minutes.

Yield: about 4 side-dish servings

Sushi Rice

1 cup sushi rice (Cal-Rose is a popular brand)
1½ to 2 cups water
3 tablespoons sushi vinegar (a slightly sweetened Japanese rice vinegar)

Rinse the rice in a colander until the water runs clear. Put rice and water in a pot with a tight-fitting lid. If you are using an electric rice-cooker follow the manufacturer's instructions. In the pot, bring the rice to a fast boil. Boil for 1 minute. Lower heat and simmer for 15 to 20 minutes. Remove rice immediately to a bowl and stir in the vinegar.

Yield: 2 cups

Pickled Ginger (Shoga)

1/2 pound fresh ginger root
1/3 cup Japanese rice vinegar
2 tablespoons sugar
1/3 cup sake

Pare the ginger root and blanch for 1 minute in boiling water. Slice almost paper thin. In a small saucepan, combine the vinegar, sugar, and sake. Bring to a boil. Stir until the sugar is dissolved. Remove from heat. Add the ginger, stir, and pour into a sterilized jar. Cover and refrigerate for at least 4 days before using. It will keep in the refrigerator for a few weeks.

Yield: 1 cup pickled ginger

California Roll

You can use plastic wrap to make sushi rolls, but a *sushimaki*, which looks like a miniature split-bamboo place mat, makes it much easier.

8 sheets *nori* (seaweed squares available at Asian and some large supermarkets)
1½ cups prepared sushi rice*
1 ripe Haas avocado
1 large cucumber
8 ounces cooked crabmeat
wasabi (Japanese horseradish, which can come prepared in tubes or in small cans of powder to which water is added. Follow package directions.)
shoga (pickled ginger)*
soy sauce

Place 1 sheet of *nori* on the sushi roller or on a square of plastic wrap. Spread a layer of sushi rice about 1/3-inch thick over the *nori*, leaving about a 1-inch strip uncovered along one edge. Peel and slice the avocado, and place 1/8 of it on top of the rice. Place an ounce of crabmeat alongside it. Peel and seed the cucumber, and cut it into strips. Place 1/8 of the cucumber on top of the rice. Dampen the *nori* edge slightly with rice vinegar or water and begin rolling from the covered end. Using the bamboo mat as a roller, slowly make the roll, gently lifting and rolling the mat as you proceed. Seal it along the dampened edge. Repeat 8 times. Cut on an angle into three or four pieces. Serve with little dishes of soy sauce, *wasabi*, and *shoga*.

Yield: 4 servings

Broiled Salmon (Sake no Miso Yaki)

4 8-ounce salmon steaks
1/4 cup white soybean paste (*shiromiso*)
1 teaspoon sugar
2 tablespoons low-sodium soy sauce
2 tablespoons sake
2 green onions, thinly sliced

Place salmon under broiler for 5 minutes per side. Meanwhile, mix soybean paste, sugar, soy sauce, and sake. Baste salmon steaks with the mixture and broil another 2 minutes per side. Serve immediately, garnished with the sliced green onions.

Yield: 4 servings

Swordfish Teriyaki

4 8-ounce swordfish steaks
1/3 cup low-sodium soy sauce
1/4 cup mirin (sweet rice cooking wine)
1 tablespoon toasted sesame seeds

Marinate the swordfish steaks for 30 minutes in a mixture of the soy sauce and Mirin. Remove from marinade and broil 5 minutes per side, basting with the marinade. Serve immediately with sprinkling of toasted sesame seeds.

Yield: 4 servings

Fox Noodles (Kitsune Udon)

1 cup *dashi* (Japanese soup stock available at most Asian markets)
2 tablespoons sugar
1/4 cup low-sodium soy sauce
6 pieces packaged fried bean curd (*aburage*, available at most Asian markets)
1-pound package dried udon noodles

Broth:

    4 cups *dashi*
    3 tablespoons low-sodium soy sauce
    2 tablespoons mirin
    2 tablespoons sake

In a saucepan, bring 1 cup *dashi*, sugar, and soy sauce to a boil. Add the bean curd and boil until the liquid is almost gone. Remove from heat and cut bean curd into pieces. Reserve. Boil udon for 12 minutes (or according to package directions) and drain. Rinse under cold water. Divide noodles into 6 bowls and add the bean curd. Bring broth ingredients to a boil and pour over noodles in individual bowls. Serve immediately.

Yield: 6 servings

Miso Soup

    4 cups *dashi*
    4 tablespoons good-quality white miso paste
    1/4 cup *wakame* (dried seaweed), crumbled
    1 cup soft tofu, diced
    1 green onion, thinly sliced

Boil *dashi* and miso paste. Force through a sieve or strainer and reheat. Add seaweed and tofu. Serve garnished with green-onion slices.

Yield: 4 to 6 servings

Cold Tofu Salad

    1 12-ounce package of silken tofu, cubed
    2 teaspoons grated fresh ginger root
    2 tablespoons low-sodium soy sauce
    1 tablespoon honey
    1 tablespoon toasted sesame seeds
    1 teaspoon chili-pepper flakes, optional

Divide tofu into 4 bowls. Mix all other ingredients and pour over individual portions.

Yield: 4 servings

Japan—Glossary

agemono   deep-fried food

amakuchi   sweet sauce

asari   clams

bento   boxed meal

buta   pork

chazuke   soupy mixture of rice and green tea

chi   shrimp

chirasi-zushi   raw fish and vegetables over rice

donburi   rice-based dishes

ebi   shrimp

gari   ginger in vinegar

ginnan   gingko nuts

gohan   rice

gyu   beef

hojicha   brown tea

hotate   scallops

ika   squid

ikura don   salmon-roe sushi

korokke   breaded, deep-fried vegetable or meat croquettes

kyabetsu   cabbage

maguro   tuna

miso shiro   miso soup

mushimono   steamed and baked food

nabemono   quickly cooked stews

negimayaki   green-onion-filled beef rolls

nigirusushi   finger-shaped sushi with wasabi between rice and fish

nimono   simmered food

nori   seaweed or pressed algae

ocha   green tea

okonomiyaki   savory pancakes

oshinko   pickles

sake   salmon

sake   rice wine usually served warm, but becoming more and more popular served ice cold in square balsa-wood cups

sashimi   plain, sliced, raw fish

shabu-shabu   thinly sliced beef cooked quickly in broth

shiitake   Japanese mushrooms

shiso leaves   mintlike garnish

shoga   pickled ginger

shoyu   soy sauce

sukiyaki   thin-sliced beef and vegetables

sunomo or *aemono*   vinegared food and salads

tare   sweet soy-based sauce

tempura   small slices of food, usually fish or vegetables, fried in a light batter

tofu   bean curd

tonkatsu   fried pork chops

toro   tuna belly

tsukemono   pickles

udon suki   fish stew with udon noodles

ume   Japanese plums

unagi   eel

unaju   soy-cooked eel with *sansho* pepper

uni   sea-urchin roe

wasabi   Japanese horseradish, in paste or powder form

yakimono   broiled and pan-fried food

yakitori   barbecued chicken in various forms, marinated, and sometimes skewered

yasai   vegetables

yosenabe   fish and seafood stews

zensai   hors d'oeuvres

DIRECTORY OF
FOOD PURVEYORS

Latin America and the Caribbean

Amazonas Food
10817 Sherman Way
Sun Valley, CA 91352
818-784-2324

Americana Groceries
6128 Columbia Pike
Falls Church, VA 22040
703-671-9625

Burns Farms (Huitlacoche)
16158 Hillside
Montverde, FL 34756
407-469-4490

Caribbean Market
1724 Eastern Avenue
Baltimore, MD 21231
410-276-3690

Carniceria el Paisa
4510 Greenpoint Avenue
Sunnyside, NY 11104
718-784-0430

Compare Food
120 North Main Street
Freeport, NY 11520
516-546-8033

El Mercado Food Mart
3767 North Southport
Chicago, IL 60613
312-477-5020

El Mundo Supermarket
42-16 Junction Boulevard
Corona, NY 11368
718-898-4466

International Market
1901 Fleet Street
Baltimore, MD 21208
410-675-0714

Las Americas
16461 West Dixie Highway
North Miami Beach, FL 33160
305-947-1840

Las Americas
785 Rockville Pike
Rockville, MD 20847
301-424-9550

Mundo Latino
83 Broadway
Passaic, NJ 07055
201-773-8608

Peruvian Import Company
PO Box 469
Mahwah, NJ 07430
201-773-6705, fax 201-458-1996

Two Brothers
312 Harrison Avenue
Harrison, NJ 07029
201-483-0099

West Indies Imports
5318 Park Heights Avenue
Baltimore, MD 21215
410-664-1818

Zion Market
543 Zion Street
Hartford, CT 06106
203-951-1245

Europe

Italy

DiPasquale's Gourmet Italian
  Marketplace
3700 Gough Street
Baltimore, MD 21224
410-276-6787

Mastellone's Deli and Wine
  Shop
7212 Hartford Road
Baltimore, MD 21220
410-444-5433

The Pennsylvania Macaroni
  Company
2000-2016 Penn Avenue
Pittsburgh, PA 15222
412-471-8330

Todaro Brothers
555 Second Avenue
New York, NY 10016
212-532-0633

France

D'Artagnan
399-419 St. Paul Avenue
Jersey City, NJ 07306
1-800-Dartagnan

Made in France
2748 Clearwater Street
Los Angeles, CA 90039
213-663-6027

1301 6 Street—F
San Francisco, CA 94107
415-487-9698

Maison Glace
111 East 58 Street
New York, NY 10022
212-755-3316

Nancy's Specialty Market
PO Box 530
Newmarket, NH 03857
800-688-2433

Germany

Kubys
3121 Ross Avenue
Dallas, TX 75204
214-821-3183

Schaller & Weber
1654 Second Avenue
New York, NY 10028
212-879-3047

Paul Shafer Meat Products
4411 Kenwood Avenue
Baltimore, MD 21206
410-661-5252

Great Britain

Specialty Foods of Ireland
494 Saw Mill River Road
Yonkers, NY 10701
1-888-894-7474

Myers of Keswick
634 Hudson Street
New York, NY 10014
212-691-4194

Stewart's of Kearny
338 Kearny Avenue
Kearny, NJ 07032
201-991-1436

Spain

Harris & Harris
P.O. Box 1589
Williamsburg, VA 23188
757-220-1878

The Spanish Table
1427 Western Avenue
Seattle, WA 98101
205-682-2827

Viva España
3664 Weber Street
Sarasota, FL 34232
941-924-8703

Scandinavia

Ikea Baltimore
White Marsh Mall
8352 Honeygo Boulevard
Baltimore, MD 21236
410-931-5400

Ikea Elizabeth
1000 Center Drive
Elizabeth, NJ 07202
908-289-4488

Ikea Houston
7810 Katy Freeway at Antoine
Houston, TX 77024
716-688-7867

Ikea Philadelphia
Plymouth Meeting Mall
498 W. Germantown Pike
Plymouth Meeting, PA 19462
610-834-1520

Ikea Pittsburgh
Robinson Towne Centre
2001 Park Manor Boulevard
Pittsburgh, PA 15205
412-747-0747

Polarica
73 Hudson Street
New York, NY 10013
212-406-0400

Eastern Europe

Caviarteria
502 Park Avenue
New York, NY 10022
212-759-7410

The East Village Meat Market
139 Second Avenue
New York, NY 10003
212-228-5590

Hungarian Pastry Shop
1030 Amsterdam Avenue
New York, NY
212-866-4230

Old World Delicatessen and
   Bakery
91 Liberty Parkway #18
Baltimore, MD 21222
410-655-5157

Ostrowski's
524 South Washington Street
Baltimore, MD 21231
410-327-8935

Paprika Weiss
1546 Second Avenue
New York, NY 10028
212-288-6117

The Middle East: Greece, Turkey, and Israel

Athena International
77 Legion Parkway
Brockton, MA 02401
508-588-9731

Athens Grocery
324 South Halsted Street
Chicago, IL 60606
312-332-6737

Athens Pastry and Frozen Food
13600 Snow Road
Cleveland, OH 44142
215-676-8500

Atlantic Food Market
7810 Harford Road
Baltimore, MD 21234
410-668-9722

Austin Gourmet
3700 Thompson Street
Austin, TX 78702
512-926-1717

C & K Importing Co.
2771 W Pico Boulevard
Los Angeles, CA 90006-3997
213-737-2970

Continental Pastries
4549 University Way NE
Seattle, WA 9815
206-632-4700

Droubi's Bakery & Deli
7333 Hlllcroft
Houston, TX 77081
713-988-5897

Greek American Foods
223 Valencia Street
San Francisco, CA 94103
415-864-0978

Greek Deli and Grocery
1740 E Burnside
Portland, OR 97214
503-232-0274

Mazzawi & Sons Inc.
2486 SW 17th Avenue
Miami, FL 33145
305-856-0366

Parthenon Imported Foods
514 South Oldham Street
Baltimore, MD 21224
410-675-0036

Sahadi Imports
187 Atlantic Avenue
Brooklyn, NY 11201
718-624-4550

Titan Food Imports
23-52 48th Street
Astoria, NY 11102
718-626-7771

World Wide Foods
1907 Greenville Avenue
Dallas, TX 75206
214-824-8860

India

Bombay Bazaar
1524 West Pratt Street
Baltimore, MD 21223
410-233-6303

House of Spices Inc.
127-40 Willets Point Boulevard
Flushing, NY 11368-1506
718-507-4900, fax 718-507-4683

Kalustyan Orient Export
123 Lexington Avenue
New York, NY 10016
212-685-3451

Shyam Foods
1724 Woodlawn Drive
Baltimore, MD 21207
410-265-5119

Asia

Anzen Import
736 NE Martin Luther King
    Boulevard
Portland, OR 97232
503-233-5111

Asahi Imports Inc.
Austin, TX
512-453-1850

Fuji Mart
1212 East Putnam Avenue
Old Greenwich, CT 06870
203-698-2107

Hanahreum Supermarket
78-14 Roosevelt Avenue
Jackson Heights, NY 11372
212-478-1982

Hanahreum Supermarket
25 West 32 Street
New York, NY 10001
212-695-3283

Hong Kong Supermarket
120 East Broadway
New York, NY 10002
212-967-3388

Japan Food Express
Las Vegas, NV 89101
702-737-0881

Kam Man Food Products
200 Canal Street
New York, NY 10013
212-571-0330

Katagiri & Co. Inc.
224 East 59 Street
New York, NY 10022
212-838-5453

Koyama Shoten
5857 Sawmill
Columbus, OH 43017
614-761-8118

Nancy's Specialty Market
PO Box 530
Newmarket, NH 03857
800-688-2433

Pearl River China Resource
   Products
277 Canal Street
New York, NY 10013
212-219-8107

Sam Bok Grocery
127 West 43 Street
New York, NY 10036
212-582-4730

Super Koyama
1790 Sutter Street
San Francisco, CA 94115
415-921-6529

Takashimaya
693 Fifth Avenue
New York, NY 10022
212-350-0100

Uwajimaya
P.O. Box 3003
Seattle, WA 98114
206-624-6248

Vietnam House
191 Farmington Avenue
Hartford, CT 06105
203-524-0010

Vietnam Imports
922 West Broad Street
Route 7
Falls Church, VA 22046
703-534-9441

Yaohan Plaza
595 River Road
Edgewater, NJ 07020
201-941-9113

Yoshinoya, Inc.
36 Prospect Street
Cambridge, MA 02139
617-491-8221

International

Balducci's
424 Avenue of the Americas
New York, NY 10014
212-260-0400
1-800-Balduccis

Bean & Deluca
560 Broadway
New York, NY 10013
212-225-6800

EAT Gourmet Foods
1064 Madison Avenue
New York, NY 10021
212-772-0022

Frieda's
4465 Corporate Center Drive
Los Alamitos, CA 90720
1-800-421-9477

Gourmet Garage
453 Broome Street
New York, NY 10013
212-941-5850

Superfresh
1020 West 41 Street
Baltimore, MD 21211
410-243-0001

Zabar's
2245 Broadway
New York, NY 10024
212-787-2000

INDEX